Roy Sieve

This book signed by

Roy Sievers

To Joe,
Thanks for your help.
Stay well + Many Blessings,
Paul Scimonelli

Roy Sievers

"The Sweetest Right Handed Swing" in 1950s Baseball

Paul Scimonelli

Foreword by Bob Wolff

McFarland & Company, Inc., Publishers
Jefferson, North Carolina

Library of Congress Cataloguing-in-Publication Data

Names: Scimonelli, Paul, 1949– author.
Title: Roy Sievers : "The Sweetest Right Handed Swing" in 1950s baseball / Paul Scimonelli ; foreword by Bob Wolff.
Description: Jefferson, North Carolina : McFarland & Company, Inc., Publishers, 2018 | Includes bibliographical references and index.
Identifiers: LCCN 2017049792 | ISBN 9781476668697 (softcover : acid free paper) ♾
Subjects: LCSH: Sievers, Roy, 1926–2017. | Baseball players—United States—Biography.
Classification: LCC GV865.S385 A3 2018 | DDC 796.357092 [B] —dc23
LC record available at https://lccn.loc.gov/2017049792

British Library cataloguing data are available

ISBN (print) 978-1-4766-6869-7
ISBN (ebook) 978-1-4766-3024-3

Front cover: Roy Sievers, Washington Senators first baseman and leftfielder (National Baseball Hall of Fame Library, Cooperstown, New York)

Printed in the United States of America

McFarland & Company, Inc., Publishers
Box 611, Jefferson, North Carolina 28640
www.mcfarlandpub.com

Acknowledgments

I would sincerely like to thank Roy Sievers for his patience and generosity with the many interviews I asked of him. He showed me why he was my hero and the hero to thousands of people "of a certain age" who loved, respected, and sat in awe of his baseball talents.

My thanks also to the following:

To William Sievers, Roy's older and very proud brother.

To Roy's children Shawn and Robin, thank you for your candor and your wonderful memories of growing up with a legend who was just "Dad."

To all the legendary ballplayers I had the great fortune to interview on Roy's behalf: Brooks Robinson, Boog Powell, Herb Plews, Albie Pearson, Russ Kemmerer, Frank Howard, Dick Hyde, Bobby Shantz, Frank Thomas, Ned Garver, J. W. Porter, Jim Bunning, Joe Garagiola, Sam Mele, Juan Marichal, and Don Larsen.

To those who knew Roy in their various capacities during his career: Bob Wolff, Maury Povich, Charlie Brotman, Phil Wood, Mark Stang, Steve Terman, Phil Hockberg, Allan Feinberg, Vince Bagli, Ed Carr, Jr. and Bill James.

To the wonderful people in all of the archives and libraries who gave of their time and talents unselfishly to help me with the facts: Cassidy Lent (Reference Librarian, National Baseball Hall of Fame), Marjorie Kehoe (Johns Hopkins University Archives), Linda Carson (Johns Hopkins Medical Archives), Anne Turkos (University of Maryland Archives).

To Brooks Robinson, Nicky Warner, Rachel Weitz and all the people at the Major League Baseball Players Alumni Association.

To Dr. Robert Sataloff for his continued friendship and support.

To my editor, Deborah Kennedy, for your tireless and meticulous work on the manuscript, and from saving me from the perils of Spellcheck. You are a prose pro.

To my children Anthony, Marc, and Natalie for their continued encouragement.

To my wife Virginia, who held my armor while I tilted at all the windmills.

And lastly, my deepest and most sincere thanks to all of you for reminding me that nothing is created in a vacuum.

Table of Contents

Acknowledgments v
Preface 1
Foreword by Bob Wolff 7
Introduction 11

1. Meet Me in St. Louis, Louis 15
2. "A pair of spikes, and they were too big!" 24
3. "I thought, hell, this is easy!" 31
4. The Sophomore Jinx 37
5. Bad Breaks and Small Wonders 48
6. Big Bat and Short Fences 61
7. "The sweetest right-handed swing in baseball" 73
8. The World Is His Oyster 94
9. The Times, They Are A-Changin' 119
10. The Best Is Yet to Come 142
11. Coming Home 159

Epilogue 176
Appendix: Achievements, Awards and Highlights 183
Chapter Notes 187
Bibliography 197
Index 199

"There is a special fascination and poignancy in the careers of almost-famous baseball players. This is particularly so of those who played with under-appreciated excellence for badly run teams in small markets. This fine appreciation of Roy Sievers does justice not only to him but to countless others who, like him, have not been given their due."

—George F. Will

"They didn't come any better than Roy. Just an even tempered guy and a terrific ballplayer. I was just honored to have played with him and I appreciated his abilities. He took good care of himself; he wasn't a carouser."

—Herb Plews, Washington Senators 1956–1959

"Roy Sievers was a pro's pro. He epitomizes what professional baseball is"

—Frank Howard, 1960 Rookie of the Year,
Washington Senators 1965–1971

"Roy Sievers was a full baseball player in every sense of the word."

—Bob Wolff, Senators Radio Broadcaster 1947–1960

"Roy was just wonderful. He had a great attitude, full of enthusiasm and on top of that he was a wonderful ballplayer. When you were on the St. Louis Browns and you got an addition like [Roy] you were really tickled!"

—Ned Garver, St. Louis Browns, 1948–1952

"Roy Sievers was a man of integrity. He was a tremendous talent as a player and a hitter, and a great example for younger players. He was respectful to everyone."

—Albie Pearson, 1958 Rookie of the Year,
Washington Senators 1958–59

"He was one of toughest hitters I ever had to get out and I don't know why. I threw him every pitch I had and he hit every one of them. He just seemed to know what I was going to throw to him all the time."

—Bobby Shantz, 1952 NL MVP,
New York Yankees 1957–1960

"Roy Sievers was my first baseball autograph. He was our hero. Wearing a major league uniform was the equivalent of wearing the Superman costume like George Reeve wore in the TV series. It had that kind of aura to it."

—Phil Wood, author, historian,
Washington Nationals broadcaster

"Roy Sievers was a great ballplayer, solid, down to earth. He doesn't get the recognition he deserves from the Hall of Fame."

—Frank Thomas, 3 time All Star,
Pittsburg Pirates, Philadelphia Phillies

"Roy was the classiest! Going back to my bat boy days, if I think about it, between Roy Sievers and Mickey Vernon, I had about 14 years of the classiest first baseman I ever knew."

—Maury Povich, television talk show personality,
former Senators bat boy and assistant to Bob Wolff

"There never has been any real reason for anyone to go out and see the Senators play ball, except for the hitting heroics of Roy Sievers, Harmon Killebrew, or Frank Howard."

—AP and BBWAA Hall of Fame writer Joe Falls

Preface

Many people have asked me, "why would you write a book about Roy Sievers? He's not Mantle, Mays, Aaron, Williams, DiMaggio, or Berra." And I would always say, exactly! He's not *like* those vaunted superstars. In fact, he's almost the total antithesis of them. Which made writing this book all the more important.

I first met Roy Sievers on Picture Day at Griffith Stadium in 1959. In those days, you could actually walk onto the field and stand next to your heroes like they were your next door neighbors. For a rotund, uncoordinated, ten-year-old neophyte Little League catcher, these six-foot-plus behemoths might as well have been Zeus, Ares, Jupiter, or Mars: gods, superheroes, able to leap tall buildings and all that. The impression was indelible and everlasting.

Flash forward to adulthood. I became, briefly, an events coordinator for the Leukemia and Lymphoma Society of America in the Washington, D.C., chapter during the mid–1990s. This was the heyday of the sports memorabilia craze, and I was one of the craziest. I sold the chapter president, David Timko, on how wonderful it would be for the Society to host sports-related events and auctions to raise money for the cause, and off I went, developing and coordinating sports cards shows, silent auctions, and live autograph signings. The first person I thought of was Roy Sievers. I found his phone number, called him up, and it was like we had known each other for years. He was kind, humble, considerate, and more than happy to help our cause. It was the essence of the man to which I was drawn.

Over the years, Roy became my go-to guy. He was always happy to leave his native St. Louis to fly to the East Coast to do autograph shows. Eventually the old body, sacrificed to the Gods of Baseball, became too worn out to travel—but the spirit was always willing.

In talking to the man, my hero, my idol, I realized there was more to him than just the lofty notions of a ten-year-old. Here was a baseball player who had fought tremendous adversity to go on to lead a decrepit baseball

Roy Sievers, Washington Senators all-time home run leader, kneeling in front of the dugout at old Griffith Stadium (National Baseball Hall of Fame Library, Cooperstown, New York).

franchise into some semblance of propriety, all the while remaining kind, humble, and considerate. It was the character, the essence of the man which prompted the writing of this book.

So, upon my retirement from teaching music at the Landon School in Bethesda, Maryland, the first thing I decided to do was to write this book.

Cursory research showed that aside from small vignettes and chronological playing-day biographies, there was nothing of any depth written about Roy.

Easy enough. I just picked up the phone, called Roy, and asked him if I could write his life story. He acquiesced without equivocation.

My next call went out to the A. Bartlett Giamatti Research Center at the National Baseball Hall of Fame in Cooperstown, New York. Director Jim Gates and reference librarian Cassidy Lent were most kind and generous with their guidance of my project. The Hall provided me with a wealth of material with which to start my journey. Several other research sessions led to even greater memories.

After that, I called Roy to arrange a few days of interviews. Once again, Roy's hospitality was remarkable, made all the more poignant by the stories told to me by his daughter Shawn, his son Rob, and his brother Bill. Here was where I began to learn about the person, the father, the mentor rather than the hero.

From there the journey snowballed. I contacted many of Roy's teammates from the Browns, Senators, White Sox, and Phillies, and had the immense joy of listening not only to their stories of the great rivalries, situations, and incidents, but also to their feelings about Roy, which *always* attested to his character and humility.

Here is where I learned the difference between theory and practice. Many of you, I'm sure, have read a book or seen a movie and said, "I could do better than that!" It is not until you have taken upon you the mantle of responsibility to produce a document that you realize what a Herculean task it truly is.

Stories led to articles led to books led to bibliographies led to greater research. Ancestry.com and Newspapers.com took a chunk out of my wallet, not to mention myriad other research sites. SABR researchers were a godsend, as was their website. Books, periodicals, YouTube videos, and endless other leads gave me a wealth of information about Roy's playing career. Countless archivists and librarians all over the country kindly went out of their way to answer questions, help me follow leads, and dig into old manuscripts and clippings to find the truth about a story, situation, or rumor.

Screwing my courage to the sticking point, I called authors of other baseball books and was pleasantly surprised with their level of interest in my project and their kindness in answering questions and guiding me with research. Orioles Hall of Fame third baseman Brooks Robinson, President of the Major League Baseball Players Alumni Association, and his staff were immensely kind to me in helping me contact players.

However, all was not peaches and ice cream.

In June of 2015, I had to have emergency surgery to remove a cancerous kidney. Talk about taking the wind out of your sails! Part of my "therapy" was to get out of bed and research and write until the pain in my side told me to stop. Luckily, I got stronger every week just having that impetus to spur me on.

Some of the players I hoped to speak with refused my letters. One player, who shall remain nameless, said, "Yeah, Roy was a great player, but I don't want to talk to you!" Some players were terse and obfuscatory. But for the most part, everyone with whom I spoke was effusive with their praise.

But it was two stories in particular that affirmed my writing about Roy Sievers, the person.

In June of 2016, I attended the St. Louis Browns Fan Club reunion dinner, ostensibly to hawk pre-orders for the book. While I was sitting at my table, a middle-aged man who introduced himself only as Jim came up in a state of great excitement and asked to fill out a pre-order form. Without any warning, he began to tell me his story:

After his managing days were over in the early '70s, Roy went to work for Yellow Freight systems in rural St. Louis. Jim used to work on the shipping platform, where Roy was his boss. One day, Jim came up to Roy and said, "I'm thinkin' about goin' back to school, getting a degree or somethin.' What do you think?" Without hesitation, Roy said, "Jim, go to school, get a good education and get outta here. This is no life to make a livin.' Use your brain, you'll be better off."

Jim told me it was the best advice he ever received. He went back to school and became a high school teacher. He told me that talk with Roy changed his life.

Later, at the luncheon, I sat next to 87-year-old William "Skip" Bergman, a retired doctor. Upon learning that I was writing Roy's biography, Skip, with tears welling in his eyes, proceeded to tell me of his high school days in the late 1940s, when he would go out to Sportsman's Park to see Roy play with the Browns. Skip further reminisced as to how he got to talk with Roy at several of the Brownie reunions in the 1990s, always remarking how kind, gentle, and sincere Roy was to his "young" fan.

"He was my hero," Skip said. "Still is."

So why Roy instead of DiMaggio, Williams, Mantle, Berra, Mays, or Aaron? It would seem that the higher one goes on the popularity scales, the more one is surrounded by controversy. DiMaggio's intense drive for perfection and lack of self-confidence made him reticent and, at times, recalcitrant. By reverse token, Williams' braggadocio and truculence made him cannon fodder for the Boston press. Mays and Aaron, who had grown up in the Jim

Crow South and felt the sting of that bigotry even into the 1970s, were by nature cautious and reserved off-field. Mantle tried so hard to be "America's hero" but could be nasty when he drank.

In his heyday with the mid–1950s Senators, Roy would spend countless hours after every ball game signing autographs for fans. DiMaggio in his later seasons would, by contrast, spend endless hours in the locker room with reporters and teammates, trying to wait out the autograph hounds.

Controversy just never seemed to stick on Roy. Sure, he admitted he would have a cocktail or two, but never to his detriment. St. Louis Browns pitching ace Ned Garver remarked poignantly, "Roy wasn't a carouser; he took care of himself."

For everyone with whom I spoke, when I would mention that I was writing the biography of Roy Sievers, their eyes would grow big with memories and they would say things like, "Roy Sievers! He was my favorite player growing up!" Or "Roy was my first baseball autograph." Or "The first game my dad ever took me to, in Griffith Stadium, Roy hit a homer!" And for that brief moment when they were speaking with me, they would no longer be William or Robert or Wendell; they would be Billy, Bobby, or Skip. They were kids again.

It was these kinds of statements that ultimately led me to write this book. As a musician, I hear things differently. I listen for the nuance of the spoken word. And in all these statements, I always heard a cadence of nostalgia mixed with reverence. However, in all these statements, there also lay an unsung longing: "My dad took me to the stadium," "my first autograph at the ball park," "he was so nice and kind to all the kids."

Baseball was that unspoken bond between father and son. What father really knew how to talk to a fourth-grader? But for that day at the ball park, for a few hours, your distant, distracted father became your "dad." As Woody Allen so eloquently put it, "80 percent of life is just showing up." Your dad took the time to pack you and maybe a friend into the car and travel to your hometown stadium, root for your hero to hit a homer, maybe keep score together. It was during that time that we transferred our hero worship from player to father. Both were larger than life.

It is in these testaments to Roy's kindness and humility, in the stories and remarks made by all who played with or coached him during his career, and in the four years it took to finish this project, that I see why Roy Sievers the man was so admired by all, and why that story had to be told.

Foreword

By Bob Wolff

Roy Sievers emerged as one of baseball's premier sluggers despite all the obstacles he surmounted in his career.

His initial obstacle was deciding what pro team to sign with. A versatile baseball and basketball player in high school, his power as a home run hitter caught the scouts' eyes. Roy checked out the rosters of the interested clubs and realized his best chance to get quick action in the majors would be to sign with a weaker team with less money to spend but a quicker chance to play at the highest level.

The Washington Senators and St. Louis Browns were losing teams with slender payrolls eager to sign players with potential. Roy chose his home town team, the St. Louis Browns, but soon realized this was a shaky organization. He did make it to the majors, however, before the Browns traded him to the last-place Senators.

It didn't take long before he starred in the Senators outfield. His short baseball stroke enabled him to smash a baseball with such force it was like a knockout blow by heavyweight champion Joe Louis. Louis left his opponent lying in the ring, while Sievers would send a line drive into the Washington bleachers.

The left field line was 407 feet away and then a small wall to get over in front of the bleachers. On the right side, there was even a greater challenge: a towering right field wall that protected walkers on the sidewalk and the moving transportation from any fly balls that came over the fence. I never saw that happen, but I watched many two-base hits smash into the wall.

Roy and I often wondered what his total number of homers would have been if he had played in Boston's Fenway Park instead of Griffith Stadium. One of Roy's closest friends, Pete Runnels, personally showed what a change in ballparks could mean. Runnels, a lefty hitter, routinely hit line drives to deep left field in Griffith Stadium for long outs when he played in Washington.

But when Pete was finally traded to Boston, he won two batting titles with his left field liners banging off the Green Monster, beating out Ted Williams twice for the league title. Roy Sievers never complained that he didn't have that same opportunity, but just think of the slugging records he could have set in a different ballpark.

When I reminiscence about these lineups at Griffith Stadium, I also think of the long bus travels made enjoyable by the music of the "Singing Senators" and the acclaim for Roy Sievers, Jim Lemon, Truman Clevenger, Russ Kemmerer, and Albie Pearson, who could have been a professional crooner with his romantic voice. Howie Devron was our accordion player and a singer. He owned a popular band in Washington, loved sports, and was a great addition to our baseball group. We introduced him as playing "first bass." An earlier group of singers, before our nationally acclaimed ensemble, included Milt Bolling, Bob Usher, Jim Lemon, Roy Sievers, and myself.

As you may know, the Senators had a large contingent of Cuban ballplayers. Joe Cambria, friend and scout for Calvin Griffith ("The Old Fox," as he was called), had many ties in the pre–Revolution Cuban community and sent a steady stream of Cuban talent to the big club. A lot of those players, due to their limited English-speaking skills, pretty much kept to themselves. One day, while we were singing on the team's bus, pitcher Frank Shea said to me: "We're missing out on some terrific singers. Those guys sitting in the back [the Cuban guys] are great singers, too." We asked them to come up and join us. That suggestion not only integrated our musical ranks, it made for a greater baseball team.

I doubt that today I could put together a group of Singing Senators who performed for the fun of it. It would involve discussions with the network carrying the show, the players' agents, the team's General Manager, the players' manager regarding rehearsal time, the team's PR man, and all those others who share an involvement in the project.

Most of the fans in the early days got to the ballparks by trolley. The only food available was the hotdogs. Nowadays the new ballparks are entertainment palaces with shops to buy sports clothing, including jerseys featuring the names of baseball players, deluxe restaurants, a parking garage, and of course, high-priced corporate suites and the rent from other sport teams in the off-season. Back when Roy played, Mr. Griffith was able to pay some bills by renting the stadium to the Washington Redskins football team and one of the top black baseball teams in the country, the Homestead Grays, featuring home run slugger Josh Gibson, and did well at the gate. They also added entertainment with pepper games and an invisible ball game with make-believe hitting, fielding, and base running.

Calvin Griffith, who inherited the team from Clark, could afford only one or two stars; the rest were competent players, but not skilled enough to compete for the title. His big attraction was Roy Sievers and, at the same time, Roy was thrilled to be object of attention in this city with the world's great political luminaries.

Griff couldn't afford to give Roy more money, but he did arrange a special night for Sievers at the end of the '57 season. Roy received a brand new car that was presented by Vice-President Richard Nixon, an avid sports fan who called me regularly to discuss his sports questions. He was a great rooter for Roy. After leading the league in homers with 42 and RBI with 114, Roy saw his biggest payday in Washington in 1958 when he received a $36,000 contract. And the applause for the Singing Senators was an added bonus. These were not winning days, but they were happy days. When I think of Roy I still have the urge to break out in a chorus of "Take me out to the ball game."

The game used to be one run at a time. Getting on base and scoring runs were big statistics. Baseball players choked up on their bats and chopped the ball to all fields. Hall of Fame second baseman Nellie Fox went an amazing 98 times in 1958 without striking out, using a light bat. He led the league with 187 hits—not one of them a homer! An amazing record.

Babe Ruth with his high-in-the-air home runs changed all that. Today's thin-handle bats are swung from the bottom, whip-like, in uppercutting homers.

Mickey Mantle also sent baseballs high into the air, either leaving ball parks or smashing into façades close to the top. Mantle could hit them left- or right-handed. He told me he was a right-handed hitter, and hitting home runs was the only thing he could do left-handed. Lefty, he beat out bunts from the left side, though, particularly with a drag bunt when the fielders were playing back.

Roy Sievers was strictly a line drive right-handed hitter, and Hank Aaron the same way. Roy's short, quick, wrist-snapping swing not only hit home runs, but also drove in many runs with voluminous singles, doubles, and the occasional triple. "That's where I make my money," he'd say with a smile.

I was personally delighted to see Roy Sievers rise to stardom in the major leagues and have a chance to enjoy the high-fives, cheers and applause he received from fans and so many well-known government officials.

Baseball is a tough game to succeed in. As a hitter, the pitcher is trying to get you out, and so are the fielders—infield and outfield. And a stadium with distant fences can make it even more difficult. Add injuries and illnesses and there's little time to relax and enjoy one's achievements.

Roy enjoyed both fame and adulation, playing or singing. All in all, he spent 17 years in uniform, some coaching or managing, but his early years in Washington had to be particularly fulfilling in achieving his ambitions.

Roy heard those cheers for 17 years—a privilege that many talented players don't receive.

Today most of baseball's rewards are of a financial nature, designed more for one's wallet than one's pride. Players today ask for and receive larger long-term contracts. But very few should consider baseball a livelihood. There's a time limit for everyone. However, having been part of it means one has shared a special baseball brotherhood. That's something to always be proud of.

Roy Sievers never lost faith in his own ability despite injuries, illnesses, distant fences or baseball slumps. He just tried harder. He ended his first professional season being selected "American League Rookie of the Year," and he kept going upward.

It began with his bonus from the St. Louis Browns when he signed a pro contract with them. He received a pair of baseball spikes. Unfortunately, they didn't fit, but Roy was most grateful for the thought behind the gift.

For Roy, it's been an upward path ever since. He particularly treasures becoming the American League home run leader in 1957, beating out Mickey Mantle and Ted Williams. Roy had 42 homers and 114 runs batted in—the first player in major league history to lead his league in homers and RBIs while playing for a last-place team.

That's something to sing about.

Bob Wolff is the Guinness World Record holder as the longest-running sportscaster in history and is the only broadcaster to have called the championships in all four major pro sports: the World Series, championships in the NBA and the NFL, and the Stanley Cup. He can be seen and heard on News 12 Long Island TV and radio station WHUD.

Introduction

In 1959, the Washington Senators brought something to the DC area that had been missing for a long time: Hope.

Roy Sievers had his "Hall of Fame year" with the Senators in 1957, leading the league with 42 home runs and 114 RBI. His roommate and outfield sidekick, Jim Lemon, had belted a respectable 17 homers with 64 RBI. The 1958 season was nearly a carbon copy of the previous one, with Sievers hitting 39 round-trippers with 108 RBI and Lemon chiming in with 26 dingers and 75 RBI. "The Walking Man," Ed Yost, did what he did best, drawing 73 and 81 walks and posting .370 and .361 on-base percentages. "Scrap Iron" Clint Courtney contributed respectable RBI totals, and 1958 "Rookie of the Year" Albie Pearson earned that honor by literally walking in Ed Yost's footsteps, drawing 64 walks with a .354 on-base percentage and scoring 63 runs.

Then in 1959, Calvin Griffith's offensive-minded moves paid off. Harmon Killebrew, the bonus baby from Idaho, had been seasoned in the minors and was ready to play, and amateur free agent Bob Allison, with his matinée idol good looks and Popeye forearms, was anxious to prove he could be a regular starter after an 11-game "cup of coffee" in 1958. Allison would go on to become the 1959 "Rookie of the Year" and part of the first major league team to post ROYs in successive seasons. Sievers, Lemon, Allison, and Killebrew were dubbed "The Fearsome Foursome," and the balls were flying out of Griffith Stadium with great frequency.

The Senators kept a stranglehold on last place that year, but we didn't care. Mt. Calvary Parochial School had let out in June, and grade schoolers Paul and Glenn Scimonelli were left with long days of playing down at "the mound" with all the neighbor kids, and the inevitable early evening baseball games on Elmhurst Street in District Heights that would stretch on well past the time the street lights went on. After supper, it was a little TV and then off to bed, where we would fall asleep to the dulcet sounds of Chuck Thompson and Bob Wolff calling the Senators' play-by-play on WWDC radio. Being good Catholic boys, our bedtime prayers always included the Senators.

Saturday was always "allowance day." Mother made it known that 50 cents was it for the week. What you did with it was your business, but there would be no more. After finishing whatever chores we had, it was a beeline to the Kay-Cee drug store on Marlboro Pike. If you were frugal, you could stretch a quarter like a rubber band. Five cents for a pack of Topps baseball cards, ten cents for a Superman comic book, and ten cents for a fountain cherry coke. Save the other quarter for after-school Cokes and donuts.

Some weeks, we got lucky. We would do chores or errands for neighbors and earn another quarter or 50 cents. When that happened, it would be **five** packs of Topps cards. Had to build up your stash to play flip cards against the wall at school. Of course, you saved all your Mantles, Mayses, Aarons, Williams, and your favorite Senators players to use as trade bait, but Marv Throneberry? Right into the spokes of your bicycle.

Although we treasured the time away from school, the long summer months would give way to boredom, so what do you do when it's either too hot or too wet to go out and play? Let's call up Roy Sievers!

Well, sure! We'd seen mom and dad use the phone, so how hard could it be? Roy plays for the Senators, right? So he must live in DC! Let's get the White Pages and look him up!

With trembling fingers and trepidatious hearts we ran down the list of "Sievers" to find only one "Sievers, R." in the book. It must be him, we concluded.

Dialing carefully, we heard the phone ringing on the other end, a soft click, and then … the feeble sound of a very sweet old lady saying "Hello?"

Pillared with fear. What do we do?

"Hello?" she questioned again.

We did and said nothing.

"Hello." This time with a little more consternation in her voice.

This can't be our hero Roy Sievers with that feeble little voice! *Wrong number! Hang up!*

Without a word, we sheepishly put the phone back in the cradle and ran pell-mell out of the room. We had been told not to play with the phone. It was important that we keep it open in case our dad got a call from the U.S. Navy Band office, where he served as trumpet and post horn soloist and later as section chief.

But we weren't playing. We sincerely wanted to call our hero Roy.

Several days went by. A strong summer rain was pelting the metro area, showing no signs of letting up. We knew the game would be canceled that night. So obviously, Roy would be home, right?

Surreptitiously meandering downstairs to our father's study, we once again looked up the number and re-dialed.

"Hello?" Again, the nice, feeble little voice.

Again, we said nothing.

"Hello!" This time with more fervor.

Not a word from us.

"I don't know who this is," she exhorted, "but if you call again, I'm calling the operator and the police!"

That was it. Down went the phone, out we dashed, back upstairs to our room, vowing never again to place a call to our hero. Forever to remain a mythic figure, Sievers, R. was not to be called again.

But then, there was always Picture Day at Griffith Stadium.

Bill James, noted baseball historian and statistician, in *The New Bill James Historical Baseball Abstract,* describes Washington Senators slugger Roy Sievers thusly:

> Can you name another player who had a value pattern as Roy Sievers? I'm not sure there is one. Sievers was a standout rookie in 1949 (for the St. Louis Browns), hitting .306 with 91 RBI, and winning the American League Rookie of the Year award. After that, however, he drifted into a prolonged slump, lost his regular status, had two serious injuries, drifted completely out of the Major Leagues, and had to go back to the minors and re-establish himself. He didn't re-emerge as a regular until five years later, 1954, but then became a star, driving in almost 100 runs a year for a decade.[1]

In 1957, playing for the Washington Senators, Roy had a year that most players could only wish for. Hitting .301 while leading the American League with career highs in home runs (42) and RBI (114), he ranked third behind Ted Williams (.731) and Mickey Mantle (.665) with a .579 slugging percentage. He also led the league in total bases (a club-record 331) and was fourth in runs scored (99).

Sievers was on fire that year, for sure. He became the first Senator to win the RBI title since Goose Goslin accomplished the feat with 129 RBI in 1924. He also became the first player in Washington history to win the home run crown after establishing the Senators' franchise home run record each year from 1954 through 1956.

From July 28 through August 3, 1957, he belted a home run in six consecutive games—tying an American League record held at the time by Ken Williams and Lou Gehrig. All this while staying true to a woeful Senators last-place team.

In 1958, Sievers had another big year for Washington. He hit .295 with 39 home runs and 108 RBI. His homer total was third in the American League behind Mantle (42) and Rocky Colavito (41) while his RBI total ranked third behind Jackie Jensen (122) and Colavito (113). Sievers also was fourth in total bases (299) and fifth in slugging at .544.

Roy Sievers, the quiet, good-natured Midwesterner, labored his entire career in the shadows of the likes of Ted Williams, Mickey Mantle, Willie Mays, Henry Aaron, and Stan Musial. Baseball's vomitous "reserve clause" ensured his loyalty to a weak St. Louis Browns team and then to a horribly mismanaged Washington Senators team, led by the miserly Calvin Griffith, who would seldom delve into his pockets to procure any type of baseball talent and who was more concerned with "hot dog money" than with fielding a good ball team.

Griffith also secretly opposed the inclusion of Negro Leagues ballplayers on his club because the Homestead Grays, who played at Griffith Stadium when the Senators were on road trips, outdrew the parent club. The money Griffith made renting the stadium to them kept the Senators afloat. So why kill the cash cow?

So although Roy put up near-Hall of Fame numbers in 1957 and 1958, the parsimonious Griffith wanted to cut his 1959 salary by ten percent—reasoning that Sievers hadn't led the American League in any offensive category and stating categorically, "We finished in last place with you. We can finish in last place without you!"

Frank Howard, the 1968 and 1970 American League home run champion, relates, "There were three people I knew who had the most mechanically sound, picture perfect right hand swings in baseball: Mark McGwire [Sr.] Dick Stuart, and Roy Sievers."[2]

Frank Thomas, former slugger for the Pirates, Reds, Cubs, Phillies, and Mets, made a similar observation. "Roy Sievers was one of the greatest right handed hitters in the game. He had a picture perfect swing and should be considered for the Hall of Fame, but because he played for the Senators, he's ignored."[3]

Ted Williams stated it more succinctly when he called Roy's swing "the sweetest right handed swing in baseball."[4]

Career statistics do not a person make. The colorful, roller coaster life of Roy Sievers is the stuff of Hollywood movies, and Roy actually appeared in one! But the story of his rise to the top, in the face of two significant injuries that would have ended the careers of most of today's players, has yet to be told.

1

Meet Me in St. Louis, Louis

St. Louis, Missouri—the Gateway to the West. If you look at a map of the United States, you will see that St. Louis is geographically located almost exactly in the middle of the entire length of the Mississippi River, literally the "Heart of the Heartland." Founded by French fur traders and populated by the "huddled masses" yearning for all things American, in the 19th century St. Louis skyrocketed to become the commercial powerhouse of the Midwest. It was an ideal environment for building: commerce, industry, aviation, entertainment, and more. And what could be more American than baseball?

By the 20th century, St. Louis had become what every major city in the East already was: a baseball town. Roy Edward Sievers, born and bred in St. Louis, grew up in the heyday of American baseball, saw all the great stars of the day, smelled the beer and the popcorn, and dreamed the adolescent dream of being a big league ball player. "Unlike most kids in town," he said, "I used to root hard for both the Browns and the Cardinals. I was prayin' that someday I'd get a chance to play for one of them, and I didn't want to be disappointed."[1]

The City of St. Louis

The history of St. Louis in the 19th and early 20th centuries is one of growth and vibrancy. Incorporated as a city in 1823, St. Louis grew rapidly in both area and population through the first half of the 19th century. A major factor in this increase was the influx of a large number of immigrants from Germany and Ireland.[2] The city's population grew from 10,049 in 1820 to 104,978 in 1850.[3]

St. Louis remained loyal to the Union throughout the Civil War, even though hostilities and blockades greatly stunted the city's growth. Between 1870 and the mid–1890s, the city expanded in all directions; by 1900 its population exceeded 575,000, making it the nation's fourth-largest city.[4]

The year 1904 marked a major turning point in the history of St. Louis, as the city hosted the Louisiana Purchase Exposition (also called the St. Louis World's Fair). Celebrating the centennial of the Louisiana Purchase, the fair covered 1,272 acres in the western half of Forest Park, transforming the area into a veritable fairyland of white palaces, lagoons, and landscaping. More than 20 million people visited the fair during its seven-month run, and it was immortalized in the hit song "Meet Me in St. Louie, Louie," with lyrics by Andrew B. Sterling and music by Kerry Mills. The song would later become a hit for Judy Garland when she sang it in the 1944 movie musical of the same name.[5]

The Fair, and the 1904 Olympic Games that were held in conjunction with it at Washington University, brought major recognition to the city.

Building boomed in St. Louis after the Fair and through the 1920s. New office building and hotel construction led the way, particularly in the western end of the city. The Jefferson, Statler, Mayfair, and Lennox Hotels sprang up, followed by others. The Grand and Olive district became the theatrical center, with the Orpheum, the American, Loew's State and the Ambassador bringing vaudeville and later "talkies" to the city. The Memorial Plaza project, completed in 1937, added several major buildings to the downtown civic center.[6]

In the Beginning

In this bustling, thriving metropolis the Sievers family saga began. William Sievers, Roy's grandfather, was born in 1849 in Hanover, Germany, and emigrated to the United States in 1865. Settling in post–Civil War St. Louis, William worked in various commercial jobs throughout the city. In 1877, while working as a clerk in the grocery store of Mr. Henry Nortrup, he married his boss's daughter, Emma. William and Emma had six children, including Roy's father, Walter, born in 1892.

Walter thrived and prospered, and in September of 1917 married the lovely Anna Hirt just three months after he had signed up to fight in World War I. Anna, a native German speaker, was born in 1900 and was brought from her native Yugoslavia to America by relatives in St. Louis. Walter and Anna Sievers took up residence at 20th and Angelica Street, on the west side of the river, and gave birth in quick succession to Walter Jr. (1918), Russell (1920), William (1923), and Roy Edward (1926).[7]

Roy Edward Sievers was literally born into a baseball life: his father had had a successful tryout with the Detroit Tigers in 1916. Walter Sievers wanted to be a pitcher, but with his lethal bat, the Tigers wanted him in the outfield to play every day. They offered him $50 a month, but Walter's father said no. He needed to make his money in St. Louis to aid his family.

Roy remembers his father this way: "From everyone I talked to that knew him, my dad was a hell of a pitcher. He had the chance to go away and pitch for the minor leagues [Tigers], but his dad said no, you can't go because you can't make that much money; you need to make the money here in St. Louis. We need you here."

Roy's brother Bill echoed this story: "My dad was offered a contract, but he never signed with the Tigers. He was making more money as a bricklayer than the Tigers were willing to offer him, and my grandfather said he needed to stay here [in St. Louis] and make money."[8]

Walter went on to be apprenticed as a bricklayer and also in an iron foundry, but he didn't like the work. He spent the majority of his adult life working for the Benton Carpet Company of St. Louis. He never lost his love of baseball, however. Roy said,

> I remember most about growing up in Walnut Park. We moved out there to get out of the city. We all lived together in a two bedroom house. My mother and father had the big bedroom, we had one bedroom in the back. My two brothers slept together out there, and I slept on a couch or something like that. We all had a place to sleep. We had a nice time in our family. We did a lot of things together; played Indian ball, cork ball, and all those kinda games like that. We played fuzz ball. My dad would take all the fuzz off a tennis ball and he would pitch to us out in the alley. We enjoyed doing a lot of things together.

Variations on the Ball-and-Bat Game

Since the advent of professional baseball, major league dreams have been nurtured in alleys and sandlots all over America. Beyond television, beyond shopping malls and amusement parks, beyond the constant amusement of the Internet, the long, sunny hours of the spring and summer call for outdoor activity, which baseball provides. But Depression-era Americans could hardly afford food and other basics. Money for real baseball equipment was nonexistent.

But necessity is the mother of invention. Equipment was fashioned from pieces of wood, broom handles, and linen-wrapped pieces of rock, metal, or cork; winter mittens were stuffed with newspaper for cushioning. Baseball variants abounded in the cities: cork ball, stickball, Indian ball, fuzz ball, and more.

Any native St. Louisian will tell you: cork ball was started in St. Louis. The exact date or location of the first game is subject to debate; however, experts agree it started in St. Louis. World War II did much to disseminate the game; Howard Rackley introduced it to non–St. Louisians on the deck of the aircraft carrier *Bunker Hill* during the War in the Pacific.

In cork ball, the bat is approximately the size of a broomstick, 34 to 38 inches long and 1½ inches wide. The ball, originally a cork fishing bobber, weighted with lead pellets and wrapped in electrical tape, is still cork-centered, two inches in diameter, basically a 1.6-ounce baseball. Early cork ball was played with as few as two to as many as six players per team; current cork ball leagues have five members per side.

The field can be anything available: an open field, a parking lot, an alley, or, in the old days, a cage. Rules are relatively simple: three outs per inning, and one swinging strike is an out as long as the catcher holds the ball. Two called strikes is an out. Five called balls is a walk. Caught fly balls or foul balls are an out. A ground ball must travel at least 15 feet in fair territory to be a hit.

Unlike its Eastern cousin, stickball, cork ball has no base runners. Runners are tracked on paper. For example, Batter 1 gets a base hit and is on first. Batter 2 hits a double, man on first advances two bases, now men on second and third. Batter 3 walks to force the bases loaded. If Batter 3 had gotten a single, runners only advance one base so you would have runners now on first and third and one run scored.

St. Louis cork ball is a fast-pitch game. The distance from home plate to the pitching rubber is 55 feet. Pitchers throw overhand, from a mound, utilizing all pitches—fastball, curve, knuckleball, and change-up. In some leagues, substances can be added.[9]

Born in the streets of Philadelphia and New York City, stickball grew to mythic proportions in the mid-20th century. Many a big league player got his start on those city streets. Closely akin to cork ball, stickball is played with a broomstick-sized bat. The ball, called a spaldeen, is a small rubber ball, somewhat similar to a racquetball, supposedly made from the defective core of a tennis ball.

There are three basic types of stickball play:

- In fast pitch, the batter has a wall or fence as a backstop. A rectangle is drawn on the artificial backstop in order to create a strike zone. The rectangle is chalked. If the batter does not swing and any part of the ball has chalk on it when it bounces back to the pitcher, the result is a called strike. If there is no chalk on the ball, the result is a ball. This type of game was predominant in the Bronx, Staten Island, Brooklyn, and Long Island.
- In slow pitch, the pitcher stands 40 to 50 feet from the batter, and the ball is hit after one bounce.
- In fungo, the batter tosses the ball into the air and hits it on the way down or after one or more bounces.[10]

A variant on cork ball and stickball is Indian ball, another supposed St. Louis game. In Indian ball, the pitcher tosses the ball, usually a softball, toward a batter from his own team. If the fielders of the other team fail either to scoop up a grounder before it stops rolling or to catch a fly in the air, it's a single. An out is recorded if they can do either of those or if the batter hits two fouls to the same side of the plate. If a batted ball is fair but doesn't fly or roll past the pitcher, then it's an automatic out: no bunting. Three strikes is an out. There is no catcher, there is no umpire, there are no doubles or triples and, in fact, there are no bases; runs are scored by an accumulation of singles and home runs (hits that go over the fence) using "ghost runners" as in cork ball or fuzz ball. There can be no walks, either, so any ball not swung at by the batter is recorded as a strike.[11]

Fuzz ball has rules more similar to those of baseball; the major difference is the use of a tennis ball with the outer layer or fuzz either worn or burned off. The rules can be revised to fit the situation of playing indoors or outdoors. Players may or may not use a glove.

Bats may consist of broom handles, baseball bats, cork ball bats, or official fuzz ball bats, such as those made by Markwort Sporting Goods of St. Louis. Markwort also makes an official fuzz ball for use in games.[12]

Hand to Eye

All of these ball-and-bat variants were instrumental in making Roy Sievers the hitter he became. He and his brothers, when they didn't have a cork ball, would play with sticks and bottle caps, also known as "top ball."

Bill Sievers remembers it this way:

> We all played ball every day, cork ball, Indian ball, some stick ball. It didn't matter, we all just loved to play ball. We played in the alley right next to our house. My dad played too. None of us ever had to teach Roy how to play. He was one of those natural hitters and just seemed to take to it by heart. He always had those strong wrists from the first time he started playing. He had a strong arm and he could run![13]

In today's baseball academies, young players go through a variety of hand-eye coordination building programs. One of the most effective drills is nothing more than a variation of stickball. Batters are given a broom stick handle or a regulation stickball bat and use this to hit Whiffle-style golf balls into a net. From there, they graduate to hitting tennis balls off a stationary tee. In both instances, the ball is considerably smaller than a regulation-sized baseball.

Many 20th century ballplayers will attest to their love of playing baseball in any way they could. In some instances, predominantly in poor rural areas, kids would fashion bats out of crooked tree limbs and hit rocks. Hitting minuscule objects with either a straight or a crooked bat was the precursor to today's hand-eye skill drills.

Hall of Fame pitcher Bob Feller tells of how he would try to hit fireflies at night with a broom stick handle. Roy said, "Tryin' to hit that little cork ball with that little bat was pretty difficult. You had to have a good eye to get a hit. By the time I got to playin,' that baseball looked like a beach ball to me. That's probably where I got my swing."[14]

Early Baseball

"Baseball is no game for mollycoddles, and the man who makes the best player in the long run is the man who has the most spirit, the most aggressiveness. He has to have spirit and aggressiveness if he is going to make good."[15]

Baseball, in its earliest days, was a rough and tumble sport, populated by hard-drinking, hard-playing men. Baseball games originated as early as 1792; however, it wasn't until 1845, when the New York Knickerbockers Social Club developed "social" rules for baseball play, that there was any kind of organized team play. By 1857, the National Association of Baseball Players (NABBP) was organized, with 16 teams participating in this first amateur league. By the end of the Civil War, there were as many as 400 clubs scattered across America, some as far away as California. It wasn't until 1869, however, that the NABBP allowed professional ball playing, where players were compensated for playing the game.

The years 1900 through 1919 were called the "dead ball" era, and quite justifiably so. Baseballs during that time were handmade, spongy affairs and cost around three dollars apiece, which roughly equals $65 in 2016 currency. Consequently, team owners were loath to provide an abundance of baseballs. One ball was kept in play sometimes for the entire duration of the game. Balls were replaced only if they were hit into the crowd or lost. In some instances, teams employed security guards to go and fetch them back. By the end of the game, these balls were grossly discolored, scuffed, tobacco-stained, and misshapen from being hit so many times.

Home runs were few; the "inside game," where singles, bunts, stolen bases, and the hit-and-run were employed to score runs, was the norm. Superstar pitchers like Walter Johnson, Cy Young, Christy Mathewson, and Grover Cleveland Alexander did battle with hitting greats Ty Cobb, Roger Peckinpaugh, Honus Wagner, and Rogers Hornsby to see who would dominate the field of play.[16]

In 1919 a young, thin pitcher named George Herman Ruth was sold to the New York Yankees. His proclivity for hitting the baseball into the stands would usher in the new "long ball" era of baseball. The home runs of Ruth, Gehrig, Foxx, and Sisler brought fans streaming into the stadiums and a new prosperity to baseball.

Throughout the early part of the 20th century, the majority of National and American League teams prospered around the major industrial cities of the East Coast, and five cities had two franchises, one for each league. St. Louis was the "wild west" of baseball, but St. Louis baseball dominated the lives of everyone up and down the Mississippi. The grade-school-aged Roy Sievers would have reveled in the offbeat exploits of the Cardinals' "Gashouse Gang" as they outlasted the Detroit Tigers in the 1934 World Series and went on to claim pennants and World Series victories in subsequent years. In 1941 a young Stanley Frank Musial burst onto the big league scene. It would be his more than two-decade dominance of the National League as a player for the Cardinals that would make St. Louis the ultimate sports town of the Midwest. Musial was to the Midwest what Joe DiMaggio was to the East Coast.

Play by Play

At the turn of the 20th century, one could only read the daily newspaper box scores or weeklies like *The Sporting News* and *Sporting Life* to learn of the exploits of the baseball greats. But then Harold W. Arlin made radio broadcast history by becoming the first person to announce a baseball game. Sitting behind home plate and using jury-rigged equipment, Arlin announced the Pirates' 8–5 win over the Philadelphia Phillies on August 5, 1921.[17]

Radio would forever change the perception and history of the game, etching the names of Ruth, Gehrig, DiMaggio, Foxx, Greenberg, Dean, Hubbell, and many more into the collective American psyche. Radio, the great "theater of the mind," and all of the famous broadcasters who populated it, would control, cajole, incite, and inform the world until the rise of television. Everyone who listened could paint their very own picture of what their heroes looked like. The nation was soon cemented to the airwaves, and dinner schedules were rearranged around baseball and boxing matches.

In St. Louis, it was KMOX that brought all of these heroes into the Sievers' living room. KMOX began broadcasting Cardinals games in 1927. With its 50,000-watt, clear-channel signal, the mighty CBS affiliate could reach as far as New York City on a cloudless night. As Roy's brother Bill remembers, "When we couldn't get to the games, we would listen to KMOX radio. They were the powerhouse station in town. France Laux was the announcer, did the Cardinals and Brownies games. He made it feel like the next best thing to being there."[18]

Knothole Passes

But radio broadcasts were secondary to seeing games live. Sportsman's Park was literally the heart and soul of the city, accessible by bus, trolley, or on foot. The Sievers boys grew up in the shadow of that venerable stadium, home to the American League St. Louis Browns and the National League Cardinals. The park was within easy walking distance of their Angelica Street home and later their home on Grand and Bissell Streets, almost underneath the "old white" water tower at 20th and Grand.

School would get out at 3:00 p.m., and the ballgames would start around the same time. With their 25-cent "knothole gang" passes, the Sievers boys would hustle up after school to make the game by the end of the first inning. Once school ended for the summer, they would spend their afternoons sitting in the bleachers, where Roy would watch all the greats: Musial, DiMaggio, Williams, Foxx, Greenberg, and many more.

"We would sit in certain sections at the park with our knothole passes," Roy remembered. "Wheaties Cereals would sometimes do a promotion and throw baseballs up into our section. I got to see all the great players during the 30's. Gehrig was a big favorite of mine, but my idol was Joe 'Ducky' Medwick. He was a heck of a hitter. I sort of copied his swing a little bit. I used it to find my own swing."

During the Great Depression, softball became a cheaper alternative for cash-strapped Americans, and there was a lot of softball played around St. Louis during that era. The Sievers lived only a block away from Sisler's Northside Park, located at the corner of Grand and Florissant Avenues. For a dime, the boys could see a doubleheader, the women playing at 7:00 p.m. and the men at 9:00 p.m.

"It was great entertainment during the summer, spending a dime and seeing a double header," Bill Sievers remembers. "Sometimes Roy and all us brothers would stand outside the park and scramble for foul balls. In those days, you could get as much as a dollar for a ball in good condition. One year, me and my brothers got 66 softballs. Made over ten dollars, which was pretty good money in those days. Those balls was our spending money for the summer."

It was a Spartan life, but the Sievers boys wanted for nothing. Baseball would be their solace for as long as the summer lasted.

2

"A pair of spikes, and they were too big!"

Early Education

Eventually, after many years living in North St. Louis, Walter Sievers decided it was time for a change, so the family moved to Walnut Park. Nestled between Riverview Boulevard and West Florissant Avenue, Walnut Park was almost idyllic and was blessed with good schools.

Roy attended Walnut Park Elementary School, located at Robin and Thekla Avenues, where he excelled more in sports than in his studies. He then went to the Cyrus P. Walbridge School on Davidson Avenue for eighth and ninth grades. When asked what his favorite subject was, he replied, "Recess!"

"I was never really good in school," said Roy. "I mean, I was all right, my grades were all right. I never achieved anything great, but I got through it!"

Beaumont High

In those years, students from the Walnut Park area were required to attend Beaumont High School on Natural Bridge Avenue.[1] This made for a long trip daily between home and school. "It was a little bit of a hike to get to Beaumont," Roy remembered. "I'd have to take a streetcar down to Grand Avenue and walk across Natural Bridge to get to school."

Named after Dr. William Beaumont, a prominent St. Louis surgeon, Beaumont High opened in 1926. The school had five stories, including a basement and an attic, which housed the rifle range. Within 20 years, it became a veritable wellspring for major league talent.[2]

During Roy's three years at Beaumont, the baseball team, coached by

A young Roy in his 1945 graduation picture from Beaumont High School (used with permission of the Saint Louis Public Schools).

Ray Elliott, produced four players who would go on to play Major League ball: Bobby Hofman, Jim Goodwin, Jack McGuire, and Sievers. Other alums from Beaumont include Hall of Fame managers Dick Williams and Earl Weaver, and MLB players Chuck Diering, Bud Blatner, Pete Reiser, Bob Miller, Bob Wiesler, and Lloyd Merritt. In addition, alums Bud Schwenk and Ken Iman played pro football, and Gene Barth was an NFL official.[3] And 1953 Beaumont graduate Lee Thomas, who had a distinguished MLB playing career with the Yankees and the Angels, went on to become general manager for the Philadelphia Phillies and an integral part of the front office for the St. Louis Cardinals, Boston Red Sox, and Baltimore Orioles.[4]

At Beaumont, Roy found the perfect conduit for his physical talents. The lanky, 6'1" sophomore made All District and All State in both basketball and baseball. "I could have played basketball: I was scouted by the University of Illinois," he said. "But I loved baseball more, and my dad wanted me to play."

Besides baseball and basketball, Roy also excelled in football at Beaumont. He got scouted and received offers from colleges and pro teams alike. "I could punt 50 to 60 yards. I was fast then, and I had the good hands an end needs. One night the whole Beaumont football team come to my house, trying to get my dad to sign so's I could play football, but he made me choose between football and baseball."

The Great Nickname Controversy

It was at Beaumont that Roy earned the nickname "Squirrel." Much has been written about the source of this sobriquet. Roy himself, of his own volition, has spurred the debate by telling different stories at times.

Roy (first row, #21) with his high school basketball team (used with permission of the Saint Louis Public Schools).

Roy played basketball for three years at Beaumont. During that time, the term "cager" was still used as a nickname for basketball players, harkening back to the era when basketball courts were actually caged in order to protect fans from the many fights that would erupt when players went for balls going out of bounds. (Once the rules were changed, the cages were removed but the name endured).[5] Roy said they used to call him "Squirrel" because he played like a squirrel running around in a cage.

But Roy's brother Bill insists that he got the name because he could jump so high. "Roy played against [future Boston Celtics star] Ed Macauley at Beaumont High," said Bill. "Ed was six foot eight. Roy was only six foot one and he could outjump him. That's how he got the nickname."

From Roy's own lips:

> In high school, when I come out on the court, I was always a little goofy. I always sort of stirred up a lot of crap and did goofy things, you know, just to try and loosen us up. One day, a friend of mine come up to me and says, "You know what, Roy? You're

really squirrelly!" I said "What?" And he said, "You're squirrelly!" Well, you know high school kids. From that day on it was, "Hey Roy, hey Squirrel, how's yer nuts!" and so on. So that's how it got started.

American Legion and Beyond

While still in high school, Roy played in the city's highly competitive American Legion league for the Fred W. Stockham Post 245, coached by Leo Browne. American Legion baseball got its start in 1925 when Major General John L. Griffith, then collegiate commissioner of the Big 10, proposed the creation of an organization to promote youth training and development through sports, at the Legion's convention in Milbank, South Dakota. The convention agreed and resolved to inaugurate baseball leagues throughout the country, to compete in departmental, sectional, and regional tournaments, culminating in a national championship.

Leagues, teams, and tourneys were organized, and the first Legion World Series was held in Philadelphia in 1926. It seemed to be a success, but the Legion's funds were depleted and they couldn't fund a World Series in 1927. In 1928, the Legion's American Commissioner, Dan Sowers, went to MLB Commissioner Kenesaw Mountain Landis, American League President E. S. Barnard, and National League President John Heydler and presented the Legion's nationwide program for junior baseball. Stressing that the program would serve not only as a training ground for young ball players but also as a powerful weapon against juvenile delinquency in the nation, Sowers asked that MLB co-sponsor it. Barnard heartily agreed and suggested that the majors contribute $50,000 annually (about $750,000 in 2016 dollars) to the program.

Organized Baseball initially funded the program, but the Depression intervened and OB had to pull its funding in 1933. Sowers sought and received funding from several large newspaper publishers throughout the country, and Legion baseball continued. OB resumed its funding, although reduced, in 1935, and continues to fund the program to this day.

True to its calling, American Legion ball produced some of the greatest stars the game has ever seen. Ted Williams played for the San Diego post. Frank Robinson led his Oakland, California, team to the only back-to-back national championship in the program's history. Mark Teixeira played in the league's 1997 World Series. Other Legion baseball greats include Sparky Anderson, Jeff Bagwell, Dusty Baker, Johnny Bench, Dominic DiMaggio, Al Kaline, Greg Maddux, Ryan Sandberg, Pee Wee Reese, Warren Spahn, and Carl Yastrzemski.

Babe Ruth spent the final years of his life promoting the program as its

Director of Operations. Bob Feller, the first Legion alumnus elected to the Baseball Hall of Fame, cut his teeth playing for the Variety Post 313, saying the experience taught him as much about life as it did baseball. Feller became an outspoken endorser of Legion baseball.[6]

Roy Sievers' cohorts on the American Legion Post 245 team included longtime friend Bobby Hofman, who would go on to play for the New York Giants, and Russ Steger, who became a standout football star for the University of Illinois. Alums of this team also include Yogi Berra and Joe Garagiola.[7] Roy showed great promise there, and the team won the state championship in 1943.

Playing in the outfield, Roy was attracting scouts as early as age 16. The Cardinals' area scout, Wally Shannon, was at every one of his games, urging him to sign with the Cardinals. "Wally Shannon come out to my house almost every day for a year. At that time we weren't really interested," Roy recalled. The Cardinals had a mammoth farm system, with dozens of teams, and Sievers and his dad were cagey about the prospect of battling his way through an army

Caduceus

BASEBALL—1945

Roy (first row, 4th from the left) with his high school baseball team. He played outfield, shortstop and pitched occasionally! (used with permission of the Saint Louis Public Schools).

of minor leaguers so Roy could try to break into a Cardinals outfield held by the likes of Stan Musial, Johnny Hopp, Harry Walker, and Enos Slaughter.

Lou Magoula, scout for the St. Louis Browns, persuaded Jacques Fournier, head of the Browns' farm system, and Browns executives Bill and Charlie DeWitt (later owners of the club) to go out, see the young Sievers and sign him. Bill DeWitt remembers it like this:

> One afternoon in 1944, I walked over to Fairground Park, about four blocks from Sportsman's Park, to watch a Beaumont High boy who had been recommended to us. Beaumont was playing Webster Grove High School for the district championship. About the fifth inning, the coach called a kid off the bench and sent him to third base. I quickly observed he was the best player on the field. Who was he? Roy Sievers.

DeWitt hustled back to his office, summoned Fournier from the West Coast, and ordered him to sign young Sievers, although Fournier had never seen Roy play. But before Fournier arrived in town, DeWitt asked Bob Bauman, the Browns' trainer, to stroll over and see if he could spot any prospects on the Beaumont High club. Bauman spotted Sievers in a prep game. When he returned to DeWitt's office, DeWitt asked him if he saw anything. "Only one—he's outstanding—a kid named Sievers!"[8]

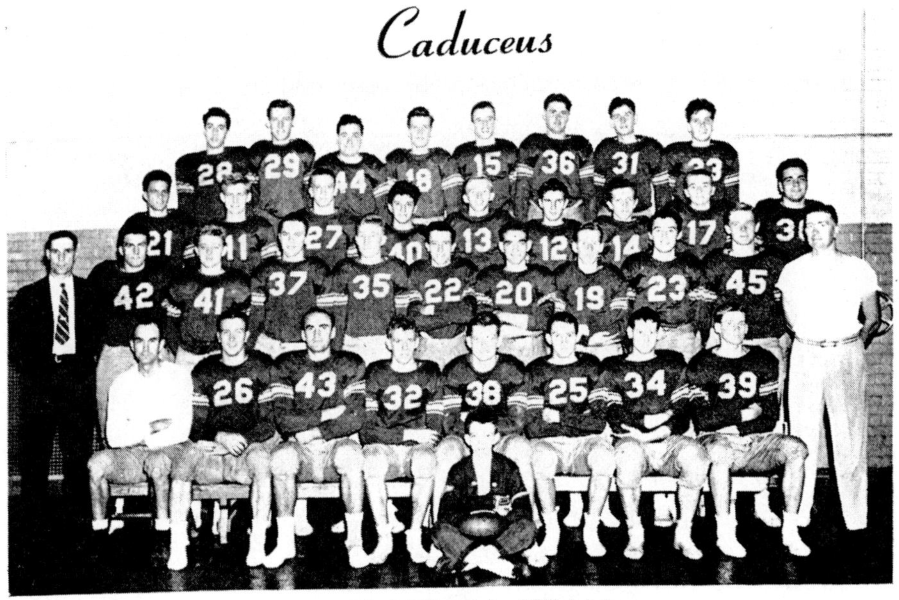

Roy (middle row, #22) poses with his high school football team. He played end and occasionally punted (used with permission of the Saint Louis Public Schools).

The young St. Louis Browns "Rookie of the Year" complete with game face (National Baseball Hall of Fame Library, Cooperstown, New York).

Said Roy, "Jack Fournier called my house and we ended up signing with the Browns, but he never saw me play." Sievers signed with the Browns in 1945. The signing bonus? A pair of spikes.

> Jack Fournier had a little better sales pitch than the other scouts, so my dad and I figured I'd have a better chance of making it into the big leagues by playing for the Browns. It's true the Browns didn't give me an elaborate bonus, because I was just thrilled to get the opportunity to play ball. Jack Fournier noticed that the baseball shoes I was wearin' were pretty well worn, so he presented me with a brand new pair of [spikes] as my reward for becoming a Brownie. But they were too big! So I had to stuff 'em with paper up at the toes so I could wear 'em.

Roy's brother remembers: "It was a great thrill for us, the whole family [having a brother in the major leagues.] We were all very proud of him. I only wish I coulda played as good as he did!"[9]

Those spikes would be only the first of many awards Roy would receive during his playing career.

3

"I thought, hell, this is easy!"

This is the Army, Mr. Sievers

After Roy Sievers signed with the Browns in 1945, Uncle Sam came calling. The 18-year-old was drafted into the Army in June and was stationed at Fort Knox, Kentucky, as a military policeman. Like many other war-time players, Roy found that his baseball skills led to an easy assignment.

> About a month or so after I reported, the captain of the post called me into his office. He said, "I see here you play some ball." I said yes sir, and told him about being signed by the Browns. He said he wanted me to play for the post team. I tried out and made the team, and from then on, I didn't pull no more guard duty. I would just go out and play ball, then come back to my bunk and relax. Boy, some of the guys were really pissed!

However, Roy did pull some duties while stationed there.

> Part of my duty was to break up the dice games at the horse race tracks in Louisville. We'd watch all the servicemen go into the men's rooms and when they didn't come out after ten or fifteen minutes, we knew they were up to something. The captain told us to go in there and scoop up all the money and roust 'em all out of there. I asked him what we should do with the money and he said just keep it. I didn't think that was right, so I would just tell 'em to pick it all up and git.

The Journey Begins

Mustering out on February 7, 1947, Roy came back home and reported to the Browns' spring training camp, fully expecting to make the parent ball club. However, he was assigned to the Class C Central Association Hannibal (Missouri) Pilots, where he played the outfield and third base, and even pitched in two games.[1] He had an outstanding freshman year with the Pilots:

in 125 games he batted .317 with a league-leading 159 hits, 21 doubles, 3 triples, 34 home runs and an amazing 141 RBI.

> I got sent first to Pine Bluff, Arkansas. I was there with about 400 other fellers. They put us up in an old Army barracks. Worked us out every day, we did some drills and hitting. Then they whittled down a lot of players and then assigned us to different teams from there. That's when I was assigned to Hannibal.
>
> I had a great year in that league. We played in this old ball park, Clemens Field, in Hannibal. I think I led the league in home runs that year. I hit one out of that park, people say went nearly 500 feet. Went across the street, over a bluff, and landed on the street on top of that bluff. I thought, hell, this is easy, but I found out otherwise later.

(In 2013, Hannibal resident Jay Draudt began a petition to erect a plaque or a marker on the site of Roy's home run, citing that it could potentially be one of the longest home runs in baseball history. The plaque was dedicated in July of 2016.)

In 1948, Roy was again invited to the Browns' spring training. Initially assigned to the Class AAA Toledo Mud Hens, he was moved down to the Class A Elmira Pioneers in the Eastern League, where he briefly shared the field with future stars Irv Hall and Pete Gray. Here was were baseball reality set in. "I wasn't hittin' real good down there [Elmira]. I learned real quick these guys could throw! Packy Rodgers, my manager, had to send me down."

After just 16 games, ten hits, two home runs and a minuscule .179 batting average in Elmira, Roy was sent down to the Springfield (Illinois) Browns in the Class B Illinois-Indiana-Iowa League. He missed a month of play due to a shoulder injury (a harbinger of bad things to come), but still managed to find his swing. In 96 games, he batted .309 with 106 hits, 15 doubles, and five triples. Battling with teammates John Novosel and future major leaguer Don Lenhardt, Roy came in third in home runs with 19 and total bases with 188.

In 1948, the entire Browns team hit only 68 home runs and was in dire need of power hitters, as well as pitching. Jack Fournier stated thusly for *The Sporting News*: "Just remember this name: Roy Sievers. He's a former Beaumont High boy from St. Louis now knocking down the fences with our Springfield Three-I league club. He's hitting .300 and has driven out 15 home runs. [He] can't miss."[2]

With such platitudes, it was easy to see why Roy made it to the parent club in 1949.

"I should have made it to the big leagues in 1947 or '48. I had two great springs with the Browns, but they always tell you, 'you need more seasoning,' so they kept sending me down. When I went to Springfield I promised myself I ain't gonna be sent down no more."

There was another great accomplishment in Roy's life in 1948: he met the lovely Joan Colburn of Springfield, Illinois, while playing for the Springfield Browns. Roy and Joan were married on November 12, 1949.

That Rookie Season

Roy reported to the Browns again in the spring of 1949. He was originally slated to go to the team's AA club in San Antonio; however, he so impressed manager Zack Taylor and his assistants with his tremendous hitting, throwing, and running that it was decided to keep him with the parent club.[3] Playing for the league minimum $5,000, Sievers debuted on April 21 as a pinch-hitter in the ninth inning against Cleveland and struck out. "I struck out my first two, three times at bat, and I thought for sure they were gonna send me down again. But my manager Zach Taylor told me, 'You go up there and do your best.' Next time I got up, I hit a double and that was all she wrote."

In the 12th game of the season, Taylor started Roy in the first game of a doubleheader. Roy went 3-for-4 and soon made it into the starting lineup, where he would stay for the rest of the season. He hit his first home run, a two-run shot, on May 14 in the sixth inning against Fred Hutchinson, adding a double and driving in four runs in an 8–3 win over the Tigers.[4] "My first home run? Hit it off Fred Hutchinson. Boy, what I thrill! I'll never forget that one. He threw me a good pitch and I just swung as hard as I could. I guess I got lucky. It went over the left field wall like a shot."

Roy literally clubbed his way into the Browns lineup. In his first 19 major league games, he had 21 hits in 59 at-bats, including seven doubles, a triple and a home run, and he drove in 14 runs. Manager Zack Taylor said,

> He looks like a natural hitter to me. He's got great wrists. He stands well back in the box, somethin' like Rogers Hornsby used to do, and gets his hands in there the last fraction of a second. I've watched this kid improve day by day. He has great power, can run like a deer, and is one of the sweetest flyhawks in the league. Everywhere we go, players on other clubs tell me this boy looks like a future Joe DiMaggio. I can't name another first year man that could carry Roy's glove.[5]

Roy just seemed to be an RBI machine that first year. He liked the Athletics, hitting five homers against them; he had three each against the Yankees and the Red Sox, two against the Senators, and one apiece against the Tigers, the Indians, and the White Sox. Eight times that year he went 3-for-4 or better. On July 17, he went 5-for-7 in a doubleheader sweep of the Senators. On September 20, he went 4-for-6 with a single, two doubles, and a home run for six RBI.

For a youngster, Roy showed he could hit big league pitchers, hitting homers off the likes of Philadelphia ace Bobby Shantz, Cleveland great Bob

Lemon, and Yankees legends Eddie Lopat and Tommy Byrne. Bobby Shantz, a Phillies teammate with Roy in 1962–1963, recalled,

> That damn Sievers! He was one of the toughest hitters I ever had to get out, and I don't know why. I threw every pitch I had, and he hit every one of them. He just seemed to know what I was going to throw at him all the time. I don't know if I ever struck him out in 16 years!
>
> The last time I got him out, he hit a line drive right at me. He yelled, "Look out!" and I tried to get out of the way of it. I threw my glove up and the ball stuck in the webbing of my glove and knocked it off my hand! I picked my glove up, run a few feet over and threw the glove, ball and all, over to first base, and he's still standin' at home plate. He never left the plate! After the game, he said, "I thought I killed you!" If he hadn't of hollered, I might have gotten nailed by it. He was really one of the nicest people I ever met, but a fierce competitor.[6]

Roy went on to grand slam Shantz in the first game of a twi-night doubleheader on July 21 of that year, as he and his teammates put together an 11-run sixth inning to beat the A's, 15–2.[7]

> That one was pretty good, but my best one was against Cleveland. I was sent in to pinch hit in the top of the ninth, two men on, against Bob Lemon. Whu! Was he fast! We was up one to nothin' and I hit one out and we took the lead four to nothin.' But the Indians came back in the bottom of the ninth and put two runs across before Ned Garver finally got the side out. That was the only homer I got off Cleveland that year, but it was enough for the win.

By the end of the year, Roy's bat was striking fear in the heart of the American League. In September, he received a dubious honor that would become a mainstay for such sluggers as Mickey Mantle, Ted Williams, Willie Mays, and Barry Bonds. In a game with the Yankees, with the bases loaded and two out in the ninth, Yankees ace reliever Joe Page walked Sievers intentionally to force in a run, so he could pitch to Browns catcher Sherman Lollar.[8]

On the season's final day, October 2, 1949, the Browns pulled one of their many wacky promotional stunts. In the first game of a doubleheader, manager Zack Taylor used a different pitcher in each inning against the White Sox and almost pulled it off. The Sox won, 4–3, but Roy went 5-for-5, including his 16th home run. The nine pitchers used set a major league record. All the Browns pitchers used (save for Al Papai) gave up at least one hit![9]

By season's end, Roy had become a hitting machine, driving in much-needed runs for the perennial AL doormat Browns.

A Rookie's Luck and Glory

It would seem that Roy, like Ebenezer Scrooge, would be visited by numerous "what if" ghosts throughout his career, events which would go on to have a major impact on his life. The first of these came on September 29, 1949. Roy and his friend Bobby Signaigo, an outfielder in the Three-I League Quincy Gems, had driven together to Hannibal, Missouri, where Roy was to speak at a banquet for a local amateur team. Signaigo asked Roy if he could borrow the car to make a quick trip to Quincy to see some friends. While on the road to Quincy, Signaigo got into a head-on collision, suffering a concussion and a broken jaw and ankle. The driver of the other car survived, but his passenger did not. Remembering that night, Roy explained that if Signaigo had stayed for the speech, they would have driven to Quincy together.[10]

Roy's 1949 season was capped when, with a career-best .306 batting average, 16 home runs (which led all rookies), and 91 runs batted in (ranking sixth in the league), he was named the first American League "Rookie of the Year" by the Baseball Writers' Association of America. The BBWAA had initiated the award in 1947 with the naming of Dodgers great Jackie Robinson as the first "Rookie of the Year" in the National League. Alvin Dark of the Braves received the honor in 1948. In the winter of 1948, the BBWAA decided to name an award for both leagues. There were 24 voting members of the Association at the time; Roy received ten votes, Alex Kellner drew five, Jerry Coleman four, and Mike Garcia, Johnny Groth, and Bob Kuzava got one each. There were two abstentions. Roy won the American League crown, and Brooklyn's Don Newcombe the National League one.[11]

Thinking back on his teammate's rookie year, St. Louis Browns pitching ace Ned Garver spoke about Roy in glowing terms:

> He was just wonderful. He had a great attitude and was full of enthusiasm. When you were on the St. Louis Browns and you got an addition like [him] you were really tickled! He was a valuable addition to our ball club. In the spring of 1949, they tried to change his batting style [stance] to where he would pull the ball more. Well, that hurt him for a while, until they realized they didn't know what they were doing, so they let him go back to hittin' [his own way].
>
> He looked like a Joe DiMaggio up at the plate. He just stood there real quiet and didn't make a move until he started his swing. Oh! He was something to see!
>
> Roy and I were just good friends. We didn't room together, but we spent a lot of time together on the long train trips to and from the towns we had to play. He was just a good guy to be around.[12]

Roy's brother Bill also recalled the glory of those early years: "When Roy was with the Browns, the family was given season passes to Sportsman's Park, which meant we spent countless nights supporting the team. Roy was a joy to watch and we were so proud of him, especially our dad."

Roy's rise from the unknown drew considerable attention from the other ball clubs in the league. Connie Mack of the Athletics reportedly offered the

Browns $250,000 for him.[13] But the front office resisted. Browns President Bill DeWitt went so far as to say,

> We are not interested in any offers for him. Sievers will be a Browns star for a long, long time. You hear reports that several of the better clubs in the American League have expressed a desire to make a deal with us for Sievers. Well, that's ridiculous, because we wouldn't entertain an offer for him. He's going to be a fixture with the Browns—like Dick Kokos. I've even heard it said that the Yankees, for instance, hold an option for first call on Kokos' contract. Maybe in 1959, but not now![14]

Things seemed to be going easily for the young man from Beaumont High School.

Reality would soon set in.

4

The Sophomore Jinx

Sievers the Stormer

The term "barnstorming" came into use in the United States in the 1800s to describe various forms of traveling showmanship. Theater companies would travel about rural areas presenting impromptu shows, often in a barn. Politicians and sports figures would "storm" about the country promoting themselves or their sporting events, first on trains and later on buses.[1] The most spectacular form of barnstorming was made famous during the Roaring Twenties by airplane pilots, men and women alike, promoting themselves and the sturdiness of airplane flight. Charles Lindbergh got his start by barnstorming throughout the Midwest as one of the first "wing walkers," climbing outside the cockpit onto the wing of the plane and waving to the crowds below.[2]

Baseball barnstorming had its heyday from 1901 to 1962 as a way for professional players to augment their incomes before, during, and after the regular season. Until 1947, players did not receive any money from their ball clubs from the day one season closed until the day the next season opened. The club paid for the player's trip south to spring training in late winter, paid for his hotel and food while he was there, and let him pay for the rest: movies, laundry, shoeshines, shaves, and sundries. Only after the first two weeks of the new season had passed, for a period of about 165 days did a team member have money put in hand.

Consequently, once the season ended, ball players needed to find work in any way they could. It was not uncommon to find players in banks, shoe stores, and construction firms, or working as policemen, printers, ranchers, farmers, jailers, or undertakers. In the 1950s, Washington Senators slugger Jim Lemon worked at the famous Tick-Tock Liquor Store (still in existence in Takoma Park, Maryland) before he tried running for mayor of the town.[3]

Early in the 20th century, a barnstormer could take home an extra $100 or $200—and if very successful, much more—for a week or two of playing.

This was equivalent to taking home ten to 20 weeks of average pay, so the money from barnstorming might be able to get a ball player through the long winter months before spring training. That is, of course, if bad weather and low attendance didn't wreck his paycheck. If they did, the problem became what to do for the next 200 days?[4]

Barnstorming continued to be an important source of income for ball players through the middle of the 20th century. By the 1940s, a major league rookie could make approximately $2,500 for a season, about $1,000 above the average American household income level at the time. That might seem like a huge amount of money, but the player would be responsible for ALL his expenditures: mortgage and family support at home, hotel or room rent during the season, travel clothes, all of his sports gear with the exception of his uniform and cap, shoeshines and shaves, entertainment, and any other miscellanea. His salary might have been high, but so were his expenses.[5]

Baseball barnstorming was the "television" of sports during the nascent years of the 20th century. Babe Ruth's famous "Bustin' Babes" and Lou Gehrig's "Larrupin' Lous" frequented sandlots and stadiums throughout the country during the late 1920s, giving life to the mental images provided by the great baseball radio broadcasters.[6] In those years, the Cardinals were the "wild west" of baseball, and there was essentially nothing west of the Mississippi. Ruth almost singlehandedly "franchised" baseball, even as far away as Japan, by bringing himself and many other greats of the game, including Lou Gehrig, Walter Johnson, Sam Rice, Joe Judge, Jimmie Foxx and the Waner brothers, to perform in hundreds of small towns, some of which still had no telephones or running water.

When baseball began to be televised, players were little more than white cotton balls on a fuzzy, eight-inch screen. Barnstorming continued to be the way to see your heroes up-close and personal, to see how big they were in real life, how they swung the bat or threw their fastball. Early 1950s televised baseball had a limited market, almost exclusively centered in major Northeastern cities. Fans in the far North, Midwest, and South attended the barnstorming games until the advent of color TV and the resulting growth of the TV market eventually led to the demise of barnstorming altogether.[7]

With his Rookie of the Year status, Roy Sievers became a good draw for the barnstormers. His first tour came at the end of his 1949 season with the Dizzy Trout All Stars, traveling throughout the Midwest and the Great Lakes region. Fellow stormers included Cass Michaels and Bob Kuzava from the White Sox, Pete Suder and Elmer Valo from the Athletics, fellow Brownie Sherman Lollar, and Virgil Trucks from the Tigers, among others.[8] In 1950, he went out with the Birdie Tebbetts All Stars. The team included Roy, Dom

DiMaggio, and Vic Wertz in the outfield; Johnny Pesky, Phil Rizzuto, Cass Michaels, and Mickey Vernon in the infield; Art Houtteman, Ray Scarborough, Mel Parnell, and Joe Coleman on the mound; and Tebbetts behind the dish.

In 1954, Roy went out with a team headed by his old Browns teammate Ned Garver, which featured "Moose" Skowron, "Bullet" Bob Turley, Bill Tuttle, Clint Courtney, and Jim Delsing. They played against the "Cool Papa" Bell All Stars, featuring Negro Leagues greats Satchel Paige and Ernie Banks. In 1956, he traveled with his Senators teammates Jim Lemon and Clint Courtney, as well as Milt and Frank Bolling, Willard Nixon, and Dave Philly. In 1957, he toured again with Lemon and ace hurler Jim Bunning on a team headed by the Bolling brothers.[9]

After his tremendous year in 1957, he and Willie Mays headlined a team that traveled to Mexico early in 1958, making about $450 for the trip.[10] Roy enjoyed barnstorming so much, he traveled regularly with barnstorming teams up until the early 1960s.

The Sophomore Jinx

There are myriad theories concerning the so-called "sophomore jinx" or "sophomore slump," where a second year or season does not come up to the level of the first.[11] Its prevalence in higher education has led numerous colleges and universities to provide guidance for students on what the slump is and how to manage or overcome it. As the Muhlenberg College website puts it,

> Sophomores experience a whole new set of stressors as they return to the college campus. Unlike freshman, they receive fewer warnings about the do's and don'ts of college life; they are expected to know how things work. Combine this with the push to declare a major, find an internship, and decide whether or not to study abroad can lead sophomores to fall into the "sophomore slump."[12]

The jinx is not limited to college students, however. It can affect television shows in their second season and sequels to great films. And there's an old rock-and-roll saying that is sadly close to the truth: You get your whole life to make your first album, and two weeks to make your second. The music industry is rife with artists and bands who have had disastrous second albums, some of which have led to their demise altogether. Fortunately, many artists have been able to overcome their unsuccessful second offerings and have gone on to long and full careers.

The list of major league baseball players to suffer the sophomore curse is long and varied. To name just a few:

A contemporary of Roy's, 1950 Rookie of the Year Walt "Moose" Dropo from Moosup, Connecticut, had one of the best rookie seasons in baseball history. He batted .332, hit 34 home runs, and had a league-leading 144 RBI. He and Johnny Kling (1902 Chicago Cubs) are the only two players to hit safely in 12 consecutive times at bat in the major leagues; however, Dropo did so in his first 12 plate appearances in the majors. In his sophomore season, however, Dropo slumped to a .239 average and 11 home runs.[13]

The 1979 National League Rookie of the Year, Rick Sutcliffe, went 17–10 and posted a 3.46 ERA for the Los Angeles Dodgers. In 1980, he plummeted to 3–9 with a horrible 5.56 ERA.[14] And 1980 American League Rookie of the Year Joe Charbonneau, who hit 32 homers and posted a .289 average in his first season, suffered a disastrous second year with only four homers and a .210 batting average, and was out of the game by 1983.[15]

Such was the case with Roy Sievers. His first year was marked with superlatives wherever he went: "looks like DiMaggio," "the best fly chaser we've ever had," "the boy can't miss," and so on. There have been many players in sports history who have failed to live up to such hype, but it was even more so for Roy because of his situation with the Browns.

Bob Broeg, writing for *The Sporting News*, summed it up:

> By the sale of Gerry Priddy and Bob Dillinger [in 1949] and by pushing the under-28 movement, the front office had eliminated the last big names from the roster. For St. Louis writers, for visiting press services and major league scribes, Sievers represented the one touch of glamor, the one source of ready copy. Roy would have [received] his share of attention as Rookie of the Year if the Browns had had other big names, but this way he was lionized.
>
> I'd say that the second season trouble frequently experienced by ball players is a human reaction to successes that have come too rapidly or too easily. They just don't bear down to get ready. When the pitchers start throwing the ball at them … they smile and assure everyone they'll get going. Finally when the slump is prolonged they get alarmed and panicky. Then they try too hard.[16]

Sievers slumped badly at the opening the 1950 season. He went 1-for-4 on Opening Day, then was 0-for-5 the second day, dropping his average to .111. He went 5-for-26 with three walks for the month of April, giving him an average of .192. He finally reached .200 on May 28, but was unable to stay there, bouncing over and under .200 for another five weeks. On July 2 he was batting a dismal .196. He lost his starting center field position and split time with Ray Coleman. Later in the season, he moved to left field and third base. That must have been the impetus he needed. By July 7, he had upped his average to .218, and it climbed steadily from there.

Despite the eventual improvement, Roy's 1949 career-best .306 average and rookie-leading 16 home runs in 1949 dropped to just .238, with 88 hits,

57 RBI and ten homers in 1950. "I'm not 'down' worrying about this thing," the big center fielder maintained. "I'll come out of this [slump] and when I do, you'll see there's nothing wrong with me."[17]

To their credit, all the coaches and the front office stayed behind Roy. His manager, Zack Taylor, said, "Sievers is too great a ball player to be a flop this year. He'll come out of it, sophomore jinx notwithstanding."[18] Owner Charles DeWitt, commenting on trade rumors for Roy, said, "I'll predict that he'll be making a lot of other clubs moan very shortly. He's a great ball player and we're counting on him to help the Browns—not somebody else."[19]

The Hoax on Top of the Jinx

As if his lagging performance were not enough, Roy had to suffer through a very disturbing hoax during the 1950 season. His wife Jo had had a premonition that she was going to be involved in an auto accident. The Browns left for Chicago and a series with the White Sox, and Jo went to Springfield, Illinois, to visit her parents.

The July game between the Browns and the White Sox had just gotten underway in Comiskey Park when the clubhouse telephone rang. Trainer Bob Bauman answered it, and a woman's voice asked to be connected to manager Zack Taylor. Bauman explained that Taylor was on the field and couldn't leave the bench. The woman insisted on speaking with Taylor and said that it was an emergency. Explaining that he was the club trainer, Bauman finally convinced the woman that he would carry the message to Taylor "providing it is as important as you say."

The woman went on to claim that Sievers' wife Jo had suffered a heart attack and had been taken to a hospital, and that manager Taylor should remove Roy from the game and send him immediately to the hospital to be with her. Bauman asked the woman the name of the hospital, and she replied, "The State Hospital. I'm looking after her, I'm Nurse Jenkins."

Bauman, a 25-year resident of St. Louis, began to smell a rat. He knew there was no State Hospital in St. Louis, but to be on the safe side, he asked for the telephone number for the hospital "so we can telephone Mrs. Sievers' doctor." She answered, "It's DE5–3904. I must hang up now. The doctor is calling me."

Bauman also remembered that there were no five-digit numbers in the Delmar telephone exchange in St. Louis, but he called the long distance operator just the same and tried to contact the number or the hospital in St. Louis for verification, only to find that both were fictitious.[20]

Most self-respecting baseball fans have seen the movie "The Natural," with Robert Redford and Glenn Close. The movie is based upon the novel written by Barnard Malamud, which was, in turn, based upon a real incident. On June 14, 1949, Eddie Waitkus, first baseman for the Phillies, was staying at the Edgewater Beach Hotel in Chicago during a series with the Cubs. He received a note, which he would later discover came from a deranged, 19-year-old secretary, Ruth Ann Steinhagan, saying she urgently needed to speak with him. After briefly speaking with her by phone, he went up to meet her, whereupon she shot him in the chest with a .22 caliber rifle. In one of the first cases of celebrity stalking, Ms. Steinhagan was declared criminally insane, committed to a state mental hospital, given shock treatments, and released in 1952. Waitkus, suffering from post-traumatic stress disorder from both the shooting incident and his World War II service, died of esophageal cancer at age 53.[21]

Bauman remembered the Waitkus case from the summer before, so he immediately called Browns president Bill DeWitt in St. Louis. DeWitt said he would investigate in St. Louis and call back with any findings.

Meanwhile, the incident was referred to traveling secretary Bill Durney, who passed it on to Taylor. The Browns manager, not wishing to disturb Sievers since he believed the report to be a hoax, pulled Roy aside in the seventh inning and reported the incident to him. Naturally, Roy was upset and wanted to contact Jo as quickly as possible. He knew she had been visiting family in Springfield.

> It's absolutely true. We [Durney, Bauman, and Sievers] burned up the phone lines all over the Midwest, Springfield, Chicago, and St. Louis, trying to find my wife. We called every hospital we could think of in all those places and left messages with them and all the family. Around 11 or 12 that night she finally called me at the hotel [Hotel Del Prado] to tell me she was all right. She had gone out with her parents to visit some relatives in Springfield. It was probably gamblers trying to get me out of the game or something. I was pretty shook up, though.

Though it was disconcerting, the incident would prove to be the least of Roy's worries.

Desperate Moves

Bill Veeck and the Browns would provide director Barry Levinson with more fodder for his movie version of "The Natural," as the following will attest:

In 1950, the team was in desperate need of help. But rather than find a solution through trades or promotion of minor leaguers, the Browns turned to David Tracy, a psychologist, who was hired to hypnotize the team into winners. After a few sessions, Tracy announced that the Browns were suffering from "loser's syndrome." Being traded to the Browns was the psychological equivalent of being shipped to Siberia, he said, adding that new players arrived in a dejected frame of mind. Fans and players, none of whom had psychology degrees, already knew this. Like most everything else the Browns tried, Tracy's hypnosis didn't improve the team. The "whammy man," as the press labeled him, was summarily dismissed.[22]

"Absolutely true," said Roy. "The team hired this hypnotist to come down and talk us into winning. We all knew it was a bunch of hooey, but we had to sit and listen to it. It didn't help much!"

Levinson incorporated this story into several scenes in the movie, most famously with Robert Redford, playing the mythical Roy Hobbs, angrily walking out of the session.

Contingency Plan

In March 2014, Bill James wrote a wonderful article for his online magazine called "Four Sluggers." In it, he outlined the year-by-year careers of four of the most-feared sluggers of the Golden Era: Ted Kluszewski, Joe Adcock, Vic Wertz, and Roy Sievers. Herewith an excerpt from his description of Roy's 1950 season:

> In any case, Sievers finally started to hit in July, had a good month and was having a decent August until the Browns, in a move that defines how organizations struggle, decided to move Sievers to third base. It appears that the "decision" to make this move may have been made in the middle of a game; I do not believe there was any planning or preparation involved. The Browns had been unable to find a third baseman. A rookie named Bill Somers had been playing third for them and posted a nice .370 on-base percentage, but he wasn't very good defensively and then he got hurt. They played Owen Friend at third base for a week, but Friend was worse defensively than Somers, and the Browns were losing every game; by August 25 they had lost ten out of eleven. On August 26 they were trailing the Yankees 2–0 going into the ninth. In the top of the ninth the Browns used four pinch hitters, and rallied to tie the score 2–2. That was good, and surprising, but the Browns had pinch hit for Friend, and there was nobody left to play third base. The manager, Zack Taylor, told Sievers to go play third base, or else Sievers volunteered; in any case Sievers, with no experience at third base, took the position.
>
> Fair enough; you have to do that sometimes. We've had to do similar things with the Red Sox in my era; sometimes it just happens. The Browns lost the game in the bottom of the ninth, and lost the next game 8–0 to Washington. Sievers sat out that game. In the second game of the double header the Browns once again used a string of pinch hitters, and this time rallied to take the lead, 8–6 in the seventh inning. Sievers again went in to play third base.

The Browns immediately gave back the three runs they had scored in the seventh. So Washington led 9–8 after seven innings; but Roy Sievers then drove in the tying run with a ninth-inning single and scored the winning run after reaching on an error in the tenth. That ended a seven-game losing streak.

On August 28 Sievers went back to the bench while the Browns lost 9–3, Friend making his 27th error of the season, one of four Browns errors leading to three unearned runs. On August 30, after an off day, Sievers started at third base. The Browns won the game, 2–1; Sievers walked and scored one of the two runs and handled three plays cleanly at third base. Roy Sievers was now the Browns' third baseman. If you are wondering how any organization could be stupid enough to make Roy Sievers their third baseman after the rookie season he had, that's how it happened. Exigent circumstances led to a contingency plan; a tiny bit of success converted the contingency plan into the new reality. Exactly the same way that an 18-year-old boy finds himself married to a girl he just met, with whom he has not yet had his first fight.

So Roy Sievers, who had opened the 1950 season as the Browns' center fielder, wound up the season as their third baseman. He had a poor season but salvaged something of it, finishing at .238 with 10 homers, 57 RBI; he hit .284, .240 and .298 over the last three months after hitting no better than .203 in any of the first three.[23]

In an interview, Roy explained: "Yeah, Zack [Taylor, his manager] asked me to play third base. I didn't mind it. Hell, I was just happy to be playin' ball is all. But it was hard tryin' to learn a new position in the middle of the season."

Hitting Woes

Despite the improvement in his average during the latter part of the 1950 season, Roy continued to struggle with hitting. One theory concerning his lack of hitting power came from former Browns great George Sisler. He passed along a tip to manager Zack Taylor, a tip that the manager appreciated.

He told me to watch the front shoulder, not the feet or the tail, of a hitter having trouble with the curve ball. Sisler's theory is that a hitter who flinches or even eases his front shoulder away from the direction of a breaking ball is off balance and therefore unable to hit the hook with authority. It's fear of getting hit in some cases, but in others it's just a bad habit developed overnight or over a period of time. Stopping to think of George's shoulder idea, I can just see Roy Sievers doing that last year when he was having so much trouble at the plate. The kid wasn't leaning his shoulder into the ball the way he did in 1949.[24]

In a phone interview, Roy said, "I don't know why it took me so long to find my swing during [spring] training. I'd work out a lot in the off season, but I just didn't click too well when I'd get back to camp. Just don't know why."

It may well be that Roy's front shoulder was "flying open" and robbing him of his power and balance; however, he was determined not to have a repeat of 1950.

Spring Training 1951: The Date That Changed His Life

In the Golden Era of baseball, players negotiated their own contracts with the owners, one on one. Roy went to see Browns owner Bill DeWitt in February of 1951. After playing for the league minimum of $5,000 in 1949, his salary had been doubled in 1950 after his spectacular rookie season. Eager to show he was not a flop, he settled for a $1,000 pay cut for the 1951 season.

"Roy's willingness to take what he was offered is further proof he intends to go out and show that he just had an off-year," *The Sporting News* reported.[25] As Roy himself remembers it, "I was anxious to get back out on the field and prove I could do it. I trained three or four times a week with Bob Bauman at the St. Louis University gym, lost some weight, and worked on my coordination with Bob. I was rarin' to go."

Roy began spring training playing third base again. He worked hard at making the defensive shift, but it just wasn't in the cards. He had trouble throwing across the diamond with consistency and in starting the double play to second base. An error-filled March led Zack Taylor to move Roy back to the outfield and put Johnny Berardino at third.

Taylor told *The Sporting News*, "Understand, Roy gave it a good try, and in a pinch I wouldn't hesitate to play him a few days at third base, but he's a better outfielder, and I wouldn't want worry over the new position to affect his hitting." Taylor went on, adding emphasis, "I don't care about the batting slump he had last year. Sievers is a hitter, a natural, and he'll be in there regularly barring bad luck."[26]

Hitting .273 on May 15 but without power, Sievers fell into another slump that dropped his average to .225 by June 10, with only one home run. In desperation, the Browns, weary of his long slump, sent him to San Antonio with instructions for him to become a real third baseman. They were hopeful that he would regain his confidence and his "swing" with more minor league experience. "Yeah, I was havin' a bad time startin' the season in '51," Roy said. "Zack Taylor sent me down to San Antonio. Said I needed more 'seasoning.'"

After about a month in the Texas League, Roy showed signs of breaking out of the slump. On July 22, he went 5-for-6 and boosted his average up to .323. He did very well out there: 42 hits, two home runs, 17 RBI, and a .297 average. Then manager Jo-Jo White took him aside one day for some fielding drills. "Jo-Jo showed me this new way to catch a low fly ball by laying out and tumbling over on my shoulder [like the old Marine Corps shoulder roll]. I guess I thought I knew how to do it, but I was wrong."

Trying out this new technique in a night game on August 1, Roy made a sensational diving catch for a ball and separated his shoulder. The shoulder was snapped back into place; however, it separated once again after Roy fell in the clubhouse shower. His arm was taped to his side and he was flown back to St. Louis for further treatment.[27] "Chronic dislocation is what the doctors called it. It just kept poppin' out. I had to get surgery on it to get it to stay in there," Roy said.

Roy was out for the rest of the season, but he knew he had a friend in the club's new owner, Bill Veeck. After spending that off-season doing Little League and Boy Scout benefits around the St. Louis area, he found winter work selling jewelry in suburban St. Louis. However, he was anxious to get back to baseball, this time with a new manager at the helm, the great Rogers Hornsby.

Rooming with a Legend

Roy was fortunate to play with one of the finest players ever to wear a baseball uniform: Satchel Paige. Paige was signed by Bill Veeck in 1948 to play with the Cleveland Indians, then followed Veeck to St. Louis to play with the Browns from 1951 through 1953. For one particular road trip, they asked if someone would room with Satch. As Roy recalls:

> They needed somebody to room with him for a week or two. I don't know why. I said, "I'll room with him. I don't give a damn." He was unbelievable, just unbelievable. Satch was just a fantastic person. He was extremely intelligent. And he was a marvel at that age, still pitching in the big leagues.

As a roommate, Paige had one drawback.

> He used to answer his fan mail himself. He took his own typewriter with him on trips. One time, we was ridin' a train out the Midwest somewhere. I'm in my bunk and I hear this tap-tap-tap-tap and I say, "What the hell is that!?" So I get up and hear it comin' from the next bunk and he's sittin' up, using a one-finger system, just tattooing on that typewriter, answering his mail.

There were some other oddities as well.

> I don't know how they knew, but when we would come through a lot of these small towns, there would be dozens of [African-Americans] standin' along the tracks with signs and wavin' to Satchel. To this day, I don't know how they found out it was us, but there they were.

It's probably safe to call Paige a pitching genius. And like many geniuses, he was eccentric.

> Satch never liked to run. He'd walk slowly everywhere. Know how pitchers are supposed to do laps and sprints to keep their legs in shape? Satch didn't believe in it, he never put out one more ounce of energy than he needed to, except on days he pitched. Didn't seem to hurt him none. Plus, Satch had more damn ointments than you can shake a stick at. He'd put 'em on his arm. And they must have worked. He probably had the greatest, the liveliest arm in the history of baseball. I don't know how old he really was—nobody did—but he must have been at least 60 when he was still pitching.[28]

Baseball's color line had not been crossed until Jackie Robinson broke it in 1947. Paige was one of a handful of black players who followed immediately in Robinson's tracks.

> Satch loved pitchin' against guys like Luke Easter and Larry Doby. The rivalry was there from the old Negro Leagues. He'd tell us, "They aren't gonna hit me," and most of the time he'd get them out. He was one of the nicest people I ever knew.[29]

Roy spent the off-season nursing his bad shoulder, anxious to get back to spring training in 1952 and show his new manager he could help the team. But such would not be the case.

5

Bad Breaks and Small Wonders

Bill Veeck and the Browns

Perhaps there has never been a more storied baseball team owner than Bill Veeck. Literally raised in a ballpark, Veeck grew up in Wrigley Field after his father became president of the Cubs in 1918.[1] Described by many as the P. T. Barnum of baseball—perhaps because his first wife, Eleanor, had been a performer in the Ringling Brothers and Barnum & Bailey Circus[2]—Veeck became legendary for his ballpark stunts and promotions.

Veeck bought his first team, the Double-A Milwaukee Brewers of the American Association, in 1942, and they went from last to first in a matter of a few years. Veeck joined the Marines in 1943 and spent two years in the Corps. Upon his return to the States, he bought the Cleveland Indians, bringing them to a pennant in 1948.

Veeck's baseball dealings were a success, but not so his marriage. When his first marriage broke up in 1950, he was forced to sell the Indians. Anxious to skipper another team, he turned his sights on the St. Louis Browns. "The Browns, whose attendance was in the range of three to four thousand fans a game, were the only team left that Veeck could afford."[3] He bought the team in 1951.

Veeck felt that going to the ballpark should be fun, and he would do anything to make it so. When he took over the Browns, he vowed three things: to run the Cardinals out of St. Louis, to make the Browns a pennant contender, and to put Browns fans back in the seats. Largely to irritate Cardinals owner Fred Saigh, he hired Cardinals baseball greats Rogers Hornsby and Marty Marion as managers, and legendary Cardinals pitcher Dizzy Dean as an announcer. He dressed up Sportsman's Park in nothing but Browns merchandise and memorabilia. On his first night as owner of the club, he handed out a free beer or soda to everyone in the stands. He held a "Grandstand

Managers Day," allowing the fans to raise placards and vote on in-game strategies such as walk, bunt, hit-and-run, and so on. It turned out to be a good idea; the Browns won the game, ending a four-game losing streak.[4]

Veeck's most famous publicity stunt with the Browns involved the hiring of 3'7" Eddie Gaedel. Gaedel, a midget by his own admission, had worked as an aviation riveter during World War II. Due to his diminutive stature, Gaedel could get into small spaces like the interior of the engines and wings to check the riveting and any structural defects.[5]

Veeck decided to hold a "birthday party" on August 19, 1951, to celebrate the 50-year history of the American League. For good measure he included his main sponsor, the Falstaff Brewing Company. He planned to give away a free beer and birthday cake to all in attendance.

Between games of the Sunday doubleheader, the entertainment started with Gaedel popping out of a seven-foot birthday cake. However, Veeck had promised a "spectacular" promotion, and the representatives of the beer company were neither amused nor impressed. Veeck pleaded with them to hold on; they wouldn't be disappointed.

In the bottom of the first inning of the second game, Gaedel, wearing the number "1/8" on his back, went in to "pinch hit" for Frank Saucier. Umpire Ed Hurley objected, but manager Zack Taylor produced a copy of Gaedel's contract, duly signed by all parties. Hurley then called for Tigers pitcher Bob Cain to pitch to the batter.

Gaedel was under orders from Veeck "not to swing at anything," and it was purported that Veeck had hired a sniper to shoot Gaedel if he as much as *looked* liked he would swing.[6] No danger of that, though; Cain's first two pitches came in at about Gaedel's eye level, and the next two floated by over his head. Gaedel jogged down to first, then surrendered the base to pinch-runner Jim Delsing, shook hands with the first base coach, waved to the cheering crowd, and departed the field.[7]

Ned Garver had pitched the opener of the double header. As he recalls it, "I was in the club house, showering up and getting my clothes on, in a leisurely way 'cause I knew I wasn't goin' in for the second game. I was listening to the radio and I heard the announcer talkin' about this midget coming to bat and all the commotion outside. So I got dressed up as quick as I could, but by the time I got to the dugout, he had already been up to the plate and had left the park."[8]

Roy remembers it this way:

> We had a runway through the stands; he come through the runway, up to the dugout and he was settin' against the wall and he had this little uniform on and I said, "Who the hell is that?" you know. Then he come up and sat on the bench next to Zack Taylor,

our manager, and [Zack] says, "That's Eddie Gaedel. Bill Veeck signed him to a contract." And I said, "What??!!"

So he gets up to pinch hit, Bill Veeck is up in the press box hollerin' down, "Don't swing the bat! Don't swing!" He walks on four pitches. Then [Zack] took him out of the game, he come in [to the dugout], said goodbye to everyone, walked up to the clubhouse, and we never saw him again.

Bob Buckholtz, our batboy, says to me, "You know, I got four baseballs here, I should get him to sign them." But by the time he thought about doing it and all, [Gaedel] was gone. Can you imagine what those autographs would be worth today?

American League President Will Harridge was furious when he heard the story and immediately voided Gaedel's contract. Veeck had mailed the contract to the league office as required, but he had posted it on Friday afternoon. With Gaedel "scheduled to play" on Sunday, and the contract unlikely to reach the league office until Monday, Veeck had a copy made so manager Zack Taylor could show it to the umpire when Gaedel came up to bat. As a result of this stunt, Major League Baseball enacted a rule requiring that all trades, sales, and signings be approved by the league president BEFORE a player had his first at-bat.[9]

This was only one of the many stunts and promotions that would wreak havoc on professional baseball throughout Bill Veeck's long and storied history as an owner. Although his detractors said he made a mockery of the game with his stunts, Veeck was what was referred to as a player's owner. He treated his players with dignity and respect. Many are the stories of the $100 bill or the new suit winding up in the locker of the guy who hit the winning home run in the big game. And Veeck wasn't afraid to spend money to make money.

With regard to Roy Sievers, Veeck's largesse seemed boundless.

Sievers' shoulder injury was extremely serious, and it appeared likely that it would end his career. Under the laws and rules that governed the situation in 1951, Veeck could simply have cut Sievers from the team; he had no legal obligation to him, as he would today. (Now, when a player gets hurt, the team has an obligation to pay for any surgery that the player needs to try to get back to where he used to be.) Not so in 1951—but Veeck did pay for an experimental surgery that doctors thought might possibly save his career.[10]

Veeck also kept Roy on the payroll at $7,500, a significant sum of money for those years. "I worked hard all that winter with Bob Bauman again," said Roy. "He and his brother Frank were the best trainers in baseball. I don't know what I would have done without their help."

In 1952, Roy reported to early spring training in El Centro, California, on February 1, hoping to make proud his new manager, Rogers Hornsby. Veeck, who had hired the baseball legend to manage the 1952 team, had run

Bill Veeck, flamboyant owner of the St. Louis Browns, circa 1952, is presented with a "loving cup" by Ned Garver, Brown's ace pitcher, for firing manager Rogers Hornsby, who had become a source of great friction in the club house (courtesy Roy Sievers).

into a buzz saw. Hornsby, a veteran of the old school of Ty Cobb baseball, made it abundantly clear that he wouldn't put up with any of Veeck's odd promotions. He went so far as to personally run out of camp several publicity-seeking midgets purportedly trying out for the team.

"He was tough," said Roy. "One of the toughest managers I played for. No fooling around on the field with him. He showed me a lot. I think he believed that I could be a big hitter again, although my shoulder was still giving me fits."

Working slowly, Roy started to regain the strength in his throwing arm, and in the easy soft-toss batting practices, he was crushing the ball into the left field seats, looking very much like the Sievers of 1949. But again, injury would strike. "Raj [Hornsby's nickname was The Rajah] put me out at third during our first fielding drills and I was doing pretty well, I thought. Then I tried to put some speed on my throw to first and wham! It popped out again. That was it for the spring."

Roy collapsed in a heap. His teammates thought he was just clowning around, but Roy didn't move. He had blacked out from the intensity of the pain. With his arm in a sling, Roy was flown back to St. Louis for medical examinations on February 27.[11]

Dr. George Bennett

Roy was sent to Dr. George Bennett at Johns Hopkins University Hospital in Baltimore, Maryland. Dr. Bennett, a renowned orthopedic surgeon, is regarded by many, including Dr. Michael Jacobs, current orthopedic specialist for the Baltimore Orioles, as one of the founders of sports medicine. Born in Claryville, New York, in 1885, he was forced to work while still in school because both of his parents died when he was 11 years old. He played semi-pro baseball when he was 16. After high school, he worked in part-time jobs around the Midwest until he had saved enough money to attend the University of Maryland Medical School. He graduated in 1908 and joined the staff at the Johns Hopkins Hospital in 1910, where he remained until his resignation in 1947. Dr. Bennett became the eighth President of the American Academy of Orthopedic Surgeons in 1939, President of the American Orthopedic Association, and an Emeritus Professor of the School of Orthopedic Medicine at Hopkins.[12]

When Dr. Bennett died in 1962, a photograph was found in his desk drawer. It showed Joe DiMaggio, Tommy Henrich, Charley Keller, and Frankie Crosetti in their Yankees uniforms and was inscribed "To Dr. George, the man who made this picture possible." Dr. Bennett had performed procedures on each of those Yankees greats, surgeries that saved and ultimately lengthened their careers. Among his patients in his earlier years were Dizzy Dean, Allie Reynolds, Lefty Gomez, Pee Wee Reese, Red Rolfe, Eddie Arcaro, and many more.[13]

As a former semi-pro ball player, Dr. Bennett had a detailed understanding of the motions involved in playing baseball and the causes of baseball injuries. He treated ballplayers as real human beings who were susceptible to many types of ailments.[14] George Weiss, creator of the Yankees' farm system and later the General Manager, spoke of Dr. Bennett in glowing terms:

> Dear Doctor:
>
> If I have achieved anything worthwhile in the baseball world, it was the part I had in inducing you to interest yourself in the treatment of injured or disabled baseball players when it was my good fortune to operate in Baltimore. As a result, the careers of many fine athletes have been lengthened and the game of baseball is very much in your debt.[15]

Dr. Bennett saw Roy in March of 1952 and found strained nerves in the shoulder. He ordered Roy back to St. Louis for a period of rest and healing before surgery.[16] Some weeks later, Dr. Bennett operated on Roy by drilling a hole into his shoulder bone and tying one of his bicep tendons through the hole. Orthopedic specialist Dr. Richard Brand explained the procedure as follows:

> I know of at least three old procedures [Henderson, Joseph, Nicola] that involved drilling holes in the humeral head, but only one that used the biceps tendon [the operation described by Toufick Nicola in 1934 in the *Journal of Bone and Joint Surgery*]. In that operation, the long head of the biceps tendon is divided distal to the transverse humeral ligament, and the proximal portion reflected proximally to its insertion. A hole is drilled from the greater tuberosity into the superior articular surface. The proximal tendon is then threaded from proximally to distally through the hole and reattached to the distal portion of the tendon. Why such an operation—or one of many described in the past—might prevent further dislocation is beyond me, although many have explained their success—presuming they were—to the large amount of scar tissue that formed from the extensive exposures. In other words, they created a "scar bomb" that prevented further dislocation.[17]

Several years later, Oscar Ruhl, writing for *The Sporting* News, reported the immediate outcome of the surgery as follows: "Dr. Bennett reported to Bill Veeck that no one had ever recovered enough freedom of arm swing following such an operation to throw normally again. In fact, Dr. Bennett told Sievers that if he ever threw in any manner except side-arm, his career would certainly come to a tragic end."[18]

In a taped interview, Dr. Michael Jacobs, the current orthopedic specialist for the Baltimore Orioles, reviewed the aforementioned procedure and commented:

> My best guess is that his arm was popping in and out of the joint. And in fact there are about 20 or so operations to treat that. And until the last 25–30 years, many of them worked okay; not many of them work great. In the last 15 years, in particular, there has been a bit of a revolution in doing [these operations] arthroscopically. And now most of these kinds of things are treated mostly successfully using arthroscopic techniques that will allow you to more accurately recreate the anatomy that is abnormal. And in the old days, what they would do, was to not fully understand how to do that. So, they would borrow from other parts of the body and move things around to try to supplant what was wrong. So basically, in a very general sense, you would have one deformity and they would create another deformity to fix the first one. So, it's easy to understand why that [Roy's throwing motion] was an inconsistent result. As they said here [in Dr. Bennett's report] they never expected him to do much with that arm after surgery.
>
> Obviously he played many, many years, 'cause I remember seeing him play in the '60s, so it worked reasonably well. But no doubt it affected his power as a hitter as well. The fact that he was a long time player and had some All Star appearances speaks highly of him, but he certainly would have been even better as a hitter if he had two

good arms. There's no other way to look at that. It's very unusual that he recovered from that kind of operation. And to be able to play at that level [All Star], that's a tribute to him.[19]

The Lost Season

The 1952 season may have been a wash for Roy, but it wasn't a complete bust. On June 18, his oldest son, Robin, was born. Rob would go on to have a three-year minor league career in the Cardinals' farm system, from 1970 to 1973.

In September, Roy managed to play 11 games with 30 at-bats, collecting six hits with three doubles and five RBI. But challenges persisted. Bill James describes it this way:

> Even after the surgery, Sievers couldn't throw, and now had no defensive position, so Bill Veeck told him to learn to play first base—and went to the park with Sievers, day after day, to hit ground balls to Sievers, trying to get him ready to play first base. Veeck would stand at home plate on his wooden leg and try to line the ball past Sievers at first base, shouting encouragement all the time.[20]

Roy also worked out daily with coach Bill Norman on orders from Veeck. When the weather turned too cold, they went indoors to the Missouri Stables Arena to work, but had to leave due to the preparations for the Joey Maxim-Archie Moore light heavyweight championship title fight in December. So they moved to the St. Louis University gym, where Roy worked with Norman and Bob Bauman.[21]

Years later, Roy remained grateful:

> I don't know what I would have done if Bill Veeck hadn't helped me out. I don't know what it was; he must have seen something in me. I was the most awkward guy you ever saw around the bag. My feet kept getting in the way. I was always trying to find the bag with my foot and I groped around like somebody in the dark.
>
> It was hard, tough work for Bill and me. Veeck and [coach Bill] Norman would work me out for hours at a time at first base, throwing to me, hitting grounders to both sides of the bag, and all that stuff. He was probably one of the best owners I ever played for. He had confidence in me, and I just couldn't give up. I'd wanted to be a big league player all my life, and I wasn't going to be cheated.
>
> He [Veeck] did a lot for the ballplayers and a lot for the fans. For example, if you got a winning hit against a top, first division club, at the end of the game when you're going through your locker, you'd find a check for $250 or $500 for you to buy a new suit or a nice coat or whatever you wanted. He was just a super guy.

By January of 1953, Norman remarked,

> I'm not given to going overboard on any player, but in this case, I'll have to admit that Sievers is about 200 percent better than he was late in the season when the Browns tried him out at first base. The kid's in great shape, he wants to play and, most impor-

tant, he likes his assignment at first base. Roy's arm is in great shape. I want him to keep working so as to keep his weight down. I don't know how long [Veeck] plans to keep working him this winter, but I'd recommend he go straight through until spring training. To me, it's surprising, almost unbelievable, the way Sievers has improved. He's quite agile, has learned to shift beautifully, and is handing off the ball well on the plays where the first baseman is supposed to toss the ball to the pitcher covering the bag. Of course, we'll have to wait and see how it goes under game conditions, but I'm ready to predict right now that he'll click. If Sievers can make it at first it would mean a tremendous lift for the Browns, for Roy wields a potent bat.[22]

1953: The Era of New Hope

Roy began 1953 with renewed optimism. On January 6, he and seven other players went "to lunch" with Bill Veeck, where Veeck served them their contracts on a silver platter.[23]

On January 29, the arm felt good enough to get in a little basketball. Catcher Del Rice, a former pro basketball player himself, put together a group of "St. Louis All Stars" to play a St. Louis semi-pro team in a benefit for the March of Dimes. Along with Roy, Dick Sisler, Don Lenhardt, Jim Delsing, Del Wilber, Kurt Kreiger, Bill Jennings and future Frick Award winner Joe Garagiola all participated in this fun event.[24]

Roy reported to early spring training with the Browns' new manager, Marty Marion, on February 12. Marion had high hopes for the new Browns and wasn't afraid to tell them so. In his first locker room talk with the players, Marion told them they would "be a first-division team, there would be no golf because there would be no time for it; the players would be in bed by midnight and on the field by 10 AM, and the healthiest drink was California orange juice."[25]

Coming out of spring training, the players had high hopes and some interesting encounters. Roy remembered:

> We was comin' back from spring training with the Browns. We're out in California, getting' on the bus to go back to St. Louis, when this big Cadillac car comes up to the bus. Stops in the middle of the street and who gets out but Bob Hope. He comes up to the bus and says, "Oh, you guys the St. Louis Browns? Gettin' ready to go home?" and he starts talkin' with all of us. He was a part owner of the Cleveland Indians back then. So he's got traffic all backed up and he's talkin' with all of us and I got to talk with him for awhile myself. So he says, "So you guys think you're gonna beat Cleveland?" and I says, "We sure as hell hope to!" So he says, "I wish you boys all the luck in the world but you're not gonna beat my team!" Nice guy and a really great man.

Versus Cleveland in 1953, the Browns won five games and lost 17.

Roy beat out six other players to win the starting first base position, and his comeback began to gain traction. A major part of the comeback was due to a change in his choice of bat. Roy described the change in an interview with Ray Gillespie for *The Sporting News*:

> I was going pretty bad for awhile early in the season and Marty [manager Marion] even benched me because my hitting fell off. I guess I had a lot of things on my mind, trying to play a new position—first base—and also hold my own as a long ball hitter. Then one day I saw Harry Brecheen, our veteran pitcher, fooling around with a Red Schoendienst bat. [He liked] to experiment with everything possible to improve his pitching, his hitting, his fielding and his general all around play. Well, Harry noticed his old Cardinals teammate, Schoendienst, was having a big year at bat, so he decided to look him up and borrow one of his sticks.... I sort of liked the idea myself, so I asked [him] if I could use it the next time I went up to the plate and he told me go ahead.
>
> Well, it seems phenomenal, for I've been hitting line drives all over the league parks ever since. I've discarded the bats I had been using and now that our traveling secretary, Bill Durney, got me a shipment of Schoendienst bats, I feel like I'll continue to improve my hitting.
>
> I hope I can soon pass the .300 mark.... Maybe I only imagine the Schoendienst bat has made a big difference in my hitting. The difference between Red's bat and the K-55 I was using was not in the weight but in the handle. The Schoendienst model has a skinnier handle. It feels a lot better to swing than my old bat.[26]

Once Roy seemed to get his swing back, manager Marion decided to use him full-time again. Roy fell into a brief slump on a road trip in mid-July, so he was platooned again at first base with Dick Kryhoski: Roy versus left-hand pitchers and Kryhoski against right-handers. But overall he had the best season since his rookie campaign of 1949. Playing in 92 games, he hit a respectable .270 with eight homers, 15 doubles, 77 hits, 35 RBI and 116 total bases. Respected hitters around the league like Mickey Vernon and Phil Rizzuto both remarked that he was looking like the rookie of 1949 all over again.[27] This in spite of playing a new position and with a shoulder that wasn't 100 percent.

The Brawls

Baseball has always been a colorful game, and rough-house baseball was still prevalent in the 1950s. The shadow of the 1934 Cardinals' rowdy "Gas House Gang" was omnipresent in St. Louis.

The Dickson Baseball Dictionary describes a "red-ass" as "a fierce competitor, someone who hates to lose."[28] This is the textbook definition of Clint Courtney. The American League Rookie of the Year in 1952, Courtney was one of the toughest players ever to hail from Hall Summit, Louisiana. He had scrapped his way through the minor leagues. Fiercely combative, he was a natural left-hander who taught himself to use his right arm to throw. Also extremely myopic, he is considered the first catcher to wear glasses in the major leagues.

Courtney made it up to the Yankees for a cup of coffee at the end of the 1951 season and played one game with the team, then was unceremoniously pushed out by Yogi Berra, who was firmly ensconced behind the plate. (Berra was, after all, referred to by Casey Stengel as "my man.") Courtney was traded to the Browns on the request of then-manager Rogers Hornsby, who admired his pugnacious attitude after managing him in Beaumont of the Texas League. "Scrap Iron" Courtney would go to the Orioles when the Browns were sold to Baltimore at the end of the 1953 season, and hit the first home run in Memorial Stadium in 1954.[29]

Courtney, who held grudges fiercely, wanted to get back at the Yankees for not keeping him on the club. On July 12, 1952, the Browns were playing the last game of a three-game series with the Yanks in New York. In the second inning, Courtney got on base with a single. Bob Nieman hit a grounder to second baseman Billy Martin, who went to force out Courtney at second; however, Courtney kicked the ball out of his mitt, much to the fiery Martin's chagrin. In the sixth inning, Courtney came in hard against Yogi Berra on a ground out/fielder's choice. The *mishegas* came to a head in the eighth inning. Courtney tried to steal second base, but was gunned down by Berra to Martin, who tagged the runner less than lovingly. Courtney sprang to his feet to go after Martin, who decked him, not once, but twice, sending his glasses flying. The dugouts emptied, two umpires got knocked down, and by the time the dust settled, Courtney was thrown out, but not Martin.[30]

J. W. Porter was a Browns' backup catcher and utility infielder in 1952. In an interview at the St. Louis Browns alumni reunion in 2015, Porter remarked, "Those things always looked a lot worse than they were. Sure, there was some pushin' and shovin' but not a whole lot happened. But with Courtney and Martin, their reputations preceded them."[31]

In retrospect, very few Yankees ever got thrown out of games. Their haughty position as perennial world champions gave them a luster envied by almost every other team in both leagues. And the Yankees kept up this mystique by treating most everyone else as a "red-headed step child."

It obviously stuck in Courtney's craw.

In April of 1953, the Browns showed they could give as good as they got. It happened on April 28 during a night game at Busch Stadium. The world champion Yankees were in town for a series, and the Bombers were in their prime. It seemed it would be a laugher of a game, but it turned out to be more than either team had bargained for.

The Yanks got it started in the top of the first. After Phil Rizzuto flied out and Billy Martin doubled, Hank Bauer took Bob Cain deep for a two-run homer, leaving the Browns trailing, 2–0. There it remained until the top of the third. Cain walked Yankees pitcher Vic Raschi, got Rizzuto and Martin to pop out, and walked Hank Bauer.

Phillies pitcher Curt Simmons once said, "Trying to get a fastball past Hank Aaron is like trying to sneak a sunrise past a rooster." In 1953, the same could have been said about Mickey Mantle. In the throes of one of his finest seasons, Mantle got into a Bob Cain fastball and drove it 500 feet over the right-center field wall for a three-run homer. Cain, after walking Gene Woodling and Berra, was replaced by Hal White, who got Gil McDougald to force Woodling at third. The Browns now trailed, 5–0.

The Yanks put one run up in their half of the fifth, and the Browns answered with three in the bottom half of the inning. Then the Browns exploded.

Bob Elliott led off the bottom of the sixth with a double. Courtney flied out, and Billy Hunter got hit by a pitch. Utility man Dixie Upright hit for pitcher White and walked to load the bases. Yankees manager Casey Stengel had seen enough and pulled Raschi for right-hander Ray Scarborough. Hank Edwards, pinch-hitting for Johnny Groth, got into an off-speed pitch for a single, scoring two runs and leaving Upright on third. Second baseman Bobby Young singled home Upright and knotted the game, 6–6. Stengel yanked Scarborough for Johnny Schmitz, who pitched out of the inning.

The Browns tried to mount a come-from-behind win in the bottom of the ninth, and the strategizing began. Schmitz got Edwards to fly out, then walked Bobby Young on four straight balls. Stengel decided to walk center fielder Jim Dyck and hard-hitting Vic Wertz. With the bases loaded, Casey opted for his masterful closer, Allie Reynolds. Manager Marion decided to go with his strength and sent Sievers up to hit for Kryhoski. The stage was set, the drama heightened. Unfortunately, on this night, Reynolds won the fight and fanned both Sievers and Elliott to end the inning.

Regulation was over, but the ballyhoo was about to begin.

In the top of the tenth, Berra grounded out, McDougald doubled and Collins was walked intentionally. Reynolds hit a blooper that was fielded at deep second by Young, who forced Collins at second; however, McDougald raced around third to try to score. Shortstop Billy Hunter relayed the throw home, and McDougald was out by a mile. But this was Yankees baseball. McDougald crashed into catcher Clint Courtney, jarring the ball loose and scoring the go-ahead run. Blasting catchers was an age-old tradition, and this evening would be no exception. It was probably a comeuppance stemming from the brawl in 1952.

So Courtney, who was a good catcher, understandably was miffed at himself and his tormentors on the Yankees bench. He was still burning when he came up in the bottom of the tenth and lashed a drive off the right field wall.

Head down, Courtney tore for second base, and when he saw that he would be out, he slammed into Yankees shortstop Phil Rizzuto, spikes high. Rizzuto dropped the ball, and umpire John Stevens changed the call from out to safe.

Evidently the Yankees would rather be the bully than be bullied. The benches emptied. Allie Reynolds (6', 205 lbs.) was the first to get to Courtney and punched him in the jaw. Bob Cerv (6'1", 204), a reserve outfielder, dashed from the dugout to land another one on Courtney's face. Billy Martin, no stranger to being a red-ass himself, jumped on Courtney's back.[32]

Roy remembers it this way: "All hell broke loose when Clint went into Rizzuto. I knew I had to do something or the Yankees would have killed him [Courtney was 5'8" and weighed 180]. I got into the mess and pulled everyone off him and got him out of the pile. I saw Don Larsen gettin' into it with someone over by the Yankees dugout. We didn't think it was a big deal but the league thought otherwise about it."

Pitcher Don Larsen upheld that story: "Oh! That one. We had another one with Detroit that year too. It wasn't any big deal. Courtney, our catcher, hit a single and tried to stretch it into a double, and came hard into Rizzuto. Then all hell broke loose. I dived into the pile trying to pull everyone off, so's they wouldn't kill Courtney, and I eventually got into it with somebody else. Hell, that's how it was in those days. You protected your players, both teams did."

When asked if there were any repercussions when he got traded to the Yankees in 1955, he said, "Not a bit!"[33]

When the smoke cleared, Rizzuto was on the ground having a minor spike wound fixed; Courtney was bruised and battered; and umpire John Stevens had suffered a separated shoulder and was receiving first aid from Browns trainer Bob Bauman. However, the decision at second base had been reversed, and Courtney was called out. Curiously, no one was thrown out of the game.

The incident produced a league record $850 in fines, including $250 for Courtney. The ensuing hail of bottles directed at the Yankees and the umpires caused the town council to pass a city ordinance banning glass bottles from the stands and to substitute paper cups, much to the dismay of the concessionaires.[34]

Little Hope for a Pennant

The Browns had been slipping into oblivion since their only World Series appearance in 1944. The "streetcar series" matching the Cardinals and the Browns, both sharing venerable Sportsman's Park, was the first inter-city Series in the Midwest since the 1906 Series between the White Sox and the Cubs in Chicago, and it garnered the attention of the nation.

Both ball clubs were so seriously depleted by wartime conscriptions of major players that the Browns resorted to a one-armed outfielder, Pete Gray, in 1945. Great names like DiMaggio, Bob Feller, Hank Greenberg, Joe Gordon, and Ted Williams in the American League and Warren Spahn, Gil Hodges, Pee Wee Reese, Johnny Vander Meer, and "The Big Cat," Johnny Mize, in the National League, all saw service to the nation, as did dozens more from every ball club in both leagues, as well as many minor league players. The major leagues were so bereft of first-string players that the Browns actually became the strongest team in the American League in 1944, edging out the Detroit Tigers on the last day of the season.

The Cardinals, the "class" of the National League, winning 105 games and running away with the 1944 pennant, were expected to win the Series in a laugher. But the Browns put on a good show, although ultimately losing in six games. They had a good year in 1945, but eventually found their way back to the cellar by 1946 and never again saw a winning season.[35]

And so the Browns sat, languishing in or near last place for nearly a decade, with little hope of attracting the quality players necessary to win a pennant. When a bright young slugger like Roy comes into such an organization, and *wants* to play for the organization, one can see how all will stand up and take notice. Hope springs eternal.

However, all of Bill Veeck's stunts and promotions notwithstanding, the Browns and Roy Sievers would not last much longer in St. Louis.

6

Big Bat and Short Fences

Veeck Bids Good-bye ... Again

Bill Veeck succeeded in achieving one of his three goals: He brought more fans to watch Brownie baseball. He never did get a contender, but he did come very close to running the Cardinals out of town.

In early 1953, Cardinals owner Fred Saigh was compelled to sell the team due to his conviction on charges of income tax evasion. At first it looked as though the club would go to an out-of-town buyer; Veeck started to celebrate. But at the last minute, Saigh agreed to sell the team to August A. Busch Jr., owner of the Anheuser-Busch brewery, who wanted to keep the team in St. Louis. As Warren Corbett puts it, "Veeck knew his game was over: 'I wasn't going to run Gussie Busch out of town.'"[1]

Strapped for cash to run the Browns, Veeck was forced to sell Sportsman's Park to the Cardinals, who had been his tenants there, as well as his Arizona ranch and several players. He then struck a deal to move the Browns to Baltimore. However, the other baseball owners rejected the plan.[2] Veeck had tweaked their noses too many times with his stunts and with his idea, put forward after the 1952 season, that home and visiting teams should split the radio and television revenue—a suggestion that the other owners regarded as "socialistic."[3]

Defeated, Veeck finally sold the Browns to a syndicate in Baltimore in a deal that was immediately approved. "The vote against me was either silly or malicious," he said, "and I prefer to regard it as malicious."

"They didn't care whether they bought him out or froze him out," John P. Carmichael of the *Chicago Daily News* wrote, "just so they got even with him, after five years, for disturbing the old, established order of things."[4]

The Fresh Start

Roy Sievers had his bags packed to go to Baltimore and was looking forward to the new opportunity. However, he had forgotten one thing: Dr. Bennett's letter. The letter, saying in essence that Sievers would never be able to throw "normally" again, had found its way into his file. When Orioles manager Jimmy Dykes found the letter, he told the front office that Roy was "damaged goods" and suggested they trade him. On February 18, 1954, the new Orioles traded Roy to the Washington Senators for outfielder Gil Coan.

Coan, playing for the Chattanooga Lookouts, had been a minor league phenom like Sievers, but managed only two .300 seasons during his eight-year tenure with the Senators, hovering in the low to mid .200s the rest of the time. The Senators felt they were doing Coan "a favor" by trading him away.

"He wasn't doing us or himself any good," said Senators owner Clark Griffith.

> In Baltimore, he might take a new lease on life in new surroundings. We didn't get what we wanted from Coan, but we felt we owed him a chance to get started with another club. He gave us a good try and that counted with us. The fans were on him and I wanted him to have a fresh start in another town....[5]
>
> We always liked Sievers, and maybe we were impressed with the fact that last year with the Browns, on their trip to Washington, Roy clouted a pair of home runs in one game off of Bob Porterfield. We have to respect a hitter who can get two off of a pitcher like Porterfield, especially when they're hit into our left field seats.[6]

Remembering the trade, Roy said, "It turned out to be a blessing for me. For some reason they thought I couldn't throw no more. Jimmy Dykes, the manager of the Orioles, thought they should get rid of me, so they traded me to the Senators. Turned out to be my biggest break."

The trade was a blessing, and a lopsided one at that. Sievers turned out to be an All-Star, while Coan was traded twice more and left the major leagues in 1956.

1954: Where Will I Play?

When Roy got to Washington, he was unsure as to where he would play. He was certainly not going to unseat All-Star first baseman Mickey Vernon, deep in the prime of an outstanding career year in 1953. Vernon had just won the batting crown, barely edging out the Indians' Al Rosen (.336) with a .337 average.

"When I come up to Washington, I asked [manager] Bucky Harris, 'Where'm I gonna play?' I told him I still couldn't throw too good, so I couldn't play the outfield. He just said, 'You get rid of the ball quick as you can. I need your bat in the lineup.' So he put me in left field. Back then, I would just kinda loop the ball to the shortstop best as I could."

Harris was determined to have Sievers in the lineup even after March X-rays showed that the shoulder was still not healed enough to allow Roy to throw overhand.[7] Bucky told *The Sporting News*: "Roy Sievers is heaven-sent as far as bench strength is concerned. He can play first or third in an emergency, and right now we have him in the outfield. He won't throw anybody out at the plate, but how many left fielders do?"[8]

Bucky Harris was as good as his word. Roy played in a total of 145 games in 1954, 133 games in the outfield and eight games at first base.

There's another great baseball saying concerning good hitters that goes: "He's so good he can hit in any park, including Yellowstone!" Griffith Stadium might as well have been Yellowstone to Roy that year. With its irregular dimensions, the stadium was one of the largest in baseball. It boasted a 388-foot power alley in left field, a sloping 408 to 421-foot center field (complete with an enormous oak tree that jutted out because the original land owner refused to cut it down for the construction of the stadium), and a right field power alley measuring 373 feet with a 31-foot-high concrete fence. The stadium gave everyone trouble, with possible exceptions being Babe Ruth, Mickey Mantle and Josh Gibson.[9]

ROY SIEVERS, Washington Senators

The newly minted Washington Senator. Roy in his 1954 uniform (from the collection of Carmen Arroyo Mendoza).

It was an adjustment for Roy, as well. Although he slumped a little in the spring, as he always did, hitting just .198 by May 15, Roy finally figured out the ballpark's quirky fences. By mid–August, he had raised his average to .246 and had taken over sole possession of left field. He ended the year with 119 hits, 26 doubles, and 102 RBI, and he set the Senators' franchise home run record with 24 dingers, besting Zeke Bonura, who had set the record at 22 in 1938. Roy was voted "Comeback Player of the Year" by *The Sporting News*.[10]

Roy recalled that year well: "'54 was a tough year for hitters. The Indians had Bob Feller, Early Wynn, Mike Garcia, and Bob Lemon. If you weren't careful, you could go 0-for-20 in a weekend!"

When asked if he got knocked down a lot, he responded, "As a hitter, you figure you're gonna get knocked down once, maybe twice, during a series. That's if you're a 'fairly good' hitter. If you're the best hitter on the club, they won't pitch to you, they're not gonna give you much to hit." His memories of Early Wynn were particularly vivid: "Wynn was always high and tight on everybody. He was just mean." He quoted a story that Mickey Mantle recounted about Wynn: When asked if he would knock down his own mother, Wynn replied, "Only if she was diggin' in."

Asked about his strategy back then, Roy said, "As a hitter, I tried to figure out, whoever I faced, what his best pitch was, 'cause in a given situation in a ball game, I'm gonna get their best pitch just once, fastball, curve ball or slider. There's not too many pitchers today who throw a good curve. Most of them are all sliders. Wynn had a good curve, along with Dizzy Trout and Hal Newhouser. Camilo Pascual, on the other hand, had a hell of a curve ball!"

Besides being the Comeback Player of the Year, Roy was also one of only two players to homer in every park in the American League circuit that year; the other was Larry Doby.[11] And Roy hit another milestone in 1954: His daughter Shawn was born on November 9.

1955: The Beat Goes On

The 1955 season seemed to start out just fine for Roy and the Senators. On Opening Day, April 11, President Dwight Eisenhower, along with 26,683 paying customers, watched the Senators beat the Orioles, 12–5, in new manager Charlie Dressen's inaugural outing. The glory was short-lived, however, as they went to New York for the Yankees' home opener on April 13 and were soundly beaten, 19–1. Whitey Ford lost his shutout bid because he slipped off the wet mound pitching to Roy and balked in Mickey Vernon from third base.[12]

The Opening Day batting order went as follows:

Ed Yost	third base
Jim Busby	center field
Mickey Vernon	first base
Pete Runnels	second base
Roy Sievers	left field
Tom Umphlett	right field
Bruce Edwards	catcher
Bobby Kline	shortstop
Bob Porterfield	pitcher

After the 19–1 debacle in New York, it didn't take long for Dressen to shake things up. By the second week of the season, the lineup went something like this:

Umphlett	Sievers	Runnels
Busby	Yost	Kline
Vernon	Ed Fitz Gerald (catcher)	Pitcher

Ed Yost, nicknamed "The Walking Man" for his prodigious ability to draw walks (his 1,614 career walks put him 11th all-time), was dropped down to hit behind Vernon and Sievers. Dressen was relying on Yost to increase his long ball production (in every park in the league except Griffith Stadium), as well as putting Sievers in the coveted cleanup position. Roy agreed: "I wanted to be the cleanup man. I was feeling better, and I felt I was gettin' some good wood on the ball back then. Ed Yost was a hell of a hitter, beside his ability to draw walks, and I thought the change would do us good."

The shakeup only worked for a short time. Try as they might, Senators pitching, along with poor run support, mired the team in the second division once again. By mid–May, Roy was in another slump, going 0-for-24 and watching his batting average drop to a paltry .128. Dressen had no choice but to bench him and put in big Cuban Carlos Paula in left field. Paula, the first black player for the Senators, had a better arm than Roy, but was notorious for chasing bad balls out of the strike zone.[13] "I had always been a slow starter. I knew I would come back," said Roy.

Trade talks began to circulate. In May, Frank Lane, general manager of the White Sox, made a bid for Roy, offering Johnny Groth, Ed McGhee, and cash. But Calvin Griffith said no. He was busy working on deals for Mickey Vernon and Ed Yost. By June 25, things changed. Griffith, in a trade planned by manager Dressen, traded fan favorite Jim Busby to the White Sox for outfielder Johnny Groth, catcher Clint Courtney, and reliever Bob Chakales.[14]

True to form, as the temperatures rose in the nation's capital, so did Roy's batting average and home run output. Hitting two homers in April, three in May, and four in June, Roy smashed seven in July, six in August and three in September. He ate up Kansas City pitching, hitting ten against them for the year, three in July alone. He and Carlos Paula turned a devastating one-two punch.[15]

In 1954, the Nats had been knocked around by the AL champion Indians, not winning a game against them for the entire season. But as the saying goes, "revenge is a dish best served cold." Washington took three out of four in a series against the Indians in June of 1955. Roy hit homers off Bob Lemon and Bob Feller, whom Roy described as "one of the toughest pitchers I ever faced."

Roy played some third base and some first base that season, as well as patrolling the outfield, and managed to increase all his stats. By the end of the season, he had brought his average up to .271, driven in 106 runs, moved up in the MVP voting from 26th to 17th, and once again broken the Senators' home run record by increasing his own 24 homers in 1954 to 25 in 1955.[16] The heat and humidity of Washington, D.C. seemed to agree with him.

On July 30, before the Senators' Red Cross benefit game with the Red Sox at Griffith Stadium, Roy, Mickey McDermott, and Frank Shea gathered around a microphone at home plate and sang "You Gotta Have Heart," from the Broadway musical "Damn Yankees."[17] It would prove to be a harbinger of things to come.

1956: The Changing of the Guard

Calvin Griffith, "adopted" son of "The Old Fox," Clark Griffith, officially took over the helm as owner of the Senators after the passing of the elder Griffith. Calvin was the last of the "bunt and steal" dinosaurs of the Deadball era. He and his sister Thelma had been taken in and raised by their uncle Clark when their biological father died. Calvin, who then took the Griffith name, became the Senators' batboy, and he watched Walter Johnson win the seventh game of the 1924 World Series against the New York Giants. After attending George Washington University and catching for its baseball team, he became an executive, manager, and part-time player in the Senators' minor league organization, then returned to Washington in 1941 to run the concession operation at Griffith Stadium.

When Clark Griffith died in October 1955, Calvin and Thelma gained control of the team, and Calvin was named president. In the reorganization, Joe Haynes, former Senators pitcher and Thelma's husband, was named roving minor league pitching instructor. His brother, Sherry Robertson, became assistant farm director, brother Billy Robertson assumed the position of supervisor of Griffith Stadium personnel and maintenance, and brother

Jimmy Robertson remained as director of concessions. It became a true "mom and pop" organization, staffed primarily by family members, and remained that way until Griffith sold the (then Minnesota Twins) franchise in 1984.[18]

The Cuban Connection

No book on the Senators would be complete without mention of the renowned scout, Joe Cambria. Cambria, a former Baltimore laundry store owner, became Clark Griffith's most active talent scout when Griffith owned the Albany, and later the Trenton, franchises in the International League. The Senators assigned him to be their first scout in Latin America. Cambria would filter a succession of low-cost Cuban players through Washington, starting with Bobby Estrella in 1935. By 1944, 12 Cuban players had been invited to spring training teams, but none ever made the parent club.

In 1946, Cambria founded the Havana Cubans, which became a Senators affiliate. The Cubans, along with five other teams, played in the Florida International League, winning the league championship in 1947 and 1948.

In 1954, Griffith realized he had to integrate the team and asked Cambria to provide a suitable candidate. Cambria's choice turned out to be Carlos Paula, a hard hitting, 27-year-old outfielder from Havana. Paula didn't last long in the majors, but several other Cambria finds had excellent major league careers, including Jose Valdivielso, Julio Becquer, Camilo Pascual, and Pedro Ramos. Cambria's two diamond gems were 1964 AL "Rookie of the Year" Tony Oliva and 1965 AL "Most Valuable Player" Zoilo Versalles. All played significant roles in the fortunes of Senators baseball during the 1950s and 1960s.[19]

Hispanic players were not a novelty to baseball. Many Latinos played for American-affiliated ball clubs before the turn of the century; however, the first true Latino players were Raphael Almeida and Armando Marsans, who played with the Cincinnati Reds in 1911 (signed, incidentally, by then-manager Clark Griffith). The first true Latino "star" was Adolfo "Dolf" Luque of the 1923 Reds.[20]

In his biography of Cambria for the Society for American Baseball Research (SABR) BioProject, Brian McKenna notes,

> Cambria supplied the Senators with talent for two decades. When Griffith needed a ballplayer, he called Cambria and a player was soon headed to Washington. The Griffith/Cambria relationship was unique in sports history. Cambria lived frugally, almost completely relocating to Cuba in the mid 1940's. His loyalty to Griffith was such that he turned down significantly higher offers for Mickey Vernon and George Case, among

others, and relinquished them to the Senators for considerably less cash. Such a relationship didn't exist anywhere else in sports.[21]

Cambria gave the forever tight-fisted Griffith low cost players, and in return gave those players a new future. Some maintained that he took advantage of the impoverished young men he recruited. However, in a 2010 radio interview for the Twinstrivia blogsite, Julio Becquer stated differently:

We called him "Papa Joe." He did everything he could to help out his players. I am very thankful to him for getting my wife out of Cuba. I don't know how he did it, but he handled all of the paperwork and all of the legal matters to be able to get my wife to this country. My wife was a professional person in Cuba. (She was a pharmacist by profession. Castro did not want people in essential positions to leave the country after the revolution and banned their travel.) If we had a problem, we all said, "Go see Papa Joe."[22]

Hope Springs Eternal

Chuck Dressen, ever the optimist, saw that he had the makings of a powerhouse team—if he could move the right players. Opting to go for youth rather than experience, the Senators made enormous trades during the winter of 1955–1956 so that Calvin Griffith could fulfill his promise to the fans that "there will be new faces on this club."[23]

First on the block were veteran first baseman Mickey Vernon (now 38 and considered a baseball "dinosaur"), pitchers Bob Porterfield and Johnny Schmitz, and outfielder Tom Umphlett, traded to the Red Sox for Karl Olson, Neil Chrisley, Al Curtis, Dick Brodowski, and "Tex" Clevenger. Pitcher Mickey McDermott and shortstop Ron Kline went to the Yankees for southpaw Bob Wiesler, catcher Lou Berberet, outfielder Dick Tettelbach, infielder Herb Plews, and Whitey Herzog as the infamous "player to be named later."

Young Cuban Jose Valdivielso, who was brought up for a look-see in 1954 and 1955, was finally dubbed the team's starting shortstop, with veteran Pete Runnels moving to second base, Ed Yost to third base, and Sievers to first base. Chrisley, Olsen, veteran Jim Lemon, rookie Whitey Herzog, and Carlos Paula were slated for the outfield slots, which left new acquisition Lew Berberet and Ed Fitz Gerald to battle Clint Courtney for the starting catcher's slot. Julio Becquer, another Joe Cambria find from Cuba, was brought up to spell Sievers at first and add left-handed hitting power to the lineup. The only fly in the ointment: what to do with the 19-year-old bonus baby from Idaho, Harmon Killebrew. Dressen would work him at first and third base, along with Whitey Herzog as an experiment. At least that was the plan at the beginning of spring training, 1956.[24]

In a phone interview, Hall of Fame manager Whitey Herzog, a 24-year-old rookie in 1956, summed it up this way:

> Playin' for Washington, I was just glad to be in the big leagues, don't get me wrong. But our pitching was terrible! We had Stobbs (15–15), Pascual (6–18), Ramos (12–10), Dean Stone (5–7), and Bob Wiesler (3–12), and not a lot of relief pitching. But we had some pop [at the plate]. We had Sievers (29 HR) and Lemon (27 HR) and Pete Runnels (179 hits), who about led the league in hitting every year. And we had a kid named (Jerry) Snyder, who played short and he did a good job (.270 average), and we had Carlos Paula. He had a good year at AA ball the year before, could hardly speak any English, and couldn't catch a ball! I'd be playin' center and he'd be playin' left sometimes, and every time a ball was hit he'd yell, "I got it! I got it!" and damn near run me over all the time! Most of the time he'd drop it!
>
> You didn't hear 'em talk much about winning, you understand. I mean it just wasn't there. Most clubs enter a season, they all think they have a chance to win [the pennant] before they find out just how horseshit they really are. But you didn't hear them talk much about winning with the Senators.[25]

Roy's Good Start

Roy got off to a fine start in the 1956 season. On March 18, in his first plate appearance in the first exhibition game, Roy went yard to help beat the Athletics, 7–5. He hit two against the Reds on April 3 and one against them on April 8.[26] "I had a good exhibition season that year. The ball just seemed to be poppin' off my bat. My shoulder felt better, and so did I," said Roy.

The Sporting News tagged Roy as "Best Bet" to win the home run and the RBI titles for the Senators that year; however, Roy, true to form, started slowly once again. After eight days of regular season play, he was hitting an anemic .172 with only three RBI and one extra-base hit.[27]

Opening day, April 17, 1956, turned out to be another Washington, D.C. "3-D day": dreary, drizzly, and disappointing. Over 27,000 fans showed up to watch veteran right-hander Dwight Eisenhower do his comedy routine. Pretending he was going to chuck his ceremonial first pitch into the outfield, he motioned the boys to pull back almost to the foul line, then proceeded to lob a laugher to Gil McDougald in the front of the pack. He threw another one, this time caught by Senators coach Cookie Lavagetto. Both men walked away with a presidential autograph.[28]

Once the festivities were done, the former general and his entourage settled back to watch a slugfest as the Senators took on the Yankees. Opening Day starter Camilo Pascual's famous curve ball didn't seem to be working against the Bronx Bombers. In the top of the first, Mickey Mantle, in what was surely the precursor to his Triple Crown season, took a Pascual slider and put it over the top of the big oak tree 500-plus feet into deep center field, then followed with another blast in the sixth. Not to be outdone, Yogi Berra put one in the right field bleachers in the third inning.

But the Senators, although on the losing end of this game, would not go gently into that good night. Dick Tettelbach, in what he would later describe as "the greatest thrill of my life," cemented himself into Senators baseball history. In the bottom of the first inning, batting second in the lineup, Tettelbach connected on a Don Larsen fastball and took it down the left field foul line for a home run in his first at-bat as a Senator. It would prove to be his only major league home run.[29]

But the Senators were not done. Karl Olson, a big part of the Vernon–Porterfield deal with Boston that year, made amends for his terrible exhibition season, connecting for two dingers off Larsen, one in the fifth inning and one in the seventh. Tettelbach and Olson provided the only offense the Senators could muster that day, driving in all four of the Senators' runs. All the other veterans, including Roy, would go 0-for every at-bat for the afternoon.

New Faces, Same Story

The Opening Day lineup went like this:

Ed Yost	third base
Dick Tettelbach	left field
Whitey Herzog	right field
Roy Sievers	first base
Pete Runnels	second base
Lou Berberet	catcher
Karl Olson	center field
Jose Valdivielso	short stop
Camilo Pascual	pitcher

The only three familiar faces were Yost, Runnels, and Sievers. Dressen and Griffith were determined to revamp their perennial cellar dwellers into the first division with the crop of new, young faces acquired from the nemesis Yankees and Red Sox. Clint Courtney, the only Senator to hit .300 in 1955, was platooned with Berberet at catcher; this in turn led to a seething feud between Courtney and Dressen.[30]

Ted Abernathy, the side-arming submarine pitcher, was sent down to Louisville to work on his control. Carlos Paula, who had been named to *The Sporting News'* All-Rookie Team in 1955, proved to be too fun-loving on the road for the otherwise conservative Dressen, and was also sent down to the minors. Two others would also be let go before Opening Day: Johnny Groth, obtained from the White Sox in the Jim Busby trade, and slick-fielding, light-hitting Julio Becquer, who was widely looked upon to become Roy Sievers' heir apparent, as Roy had been for Mickey Vernon.

As the season progressed, many of the other winter experiments did not bear fruit. Shortstop Jose Valdivielso had "trouble with the curve" and was benched for Jerry Snyder. Pitcher Bob Wiesler developed his usual control problems and became ineffective on the mound. All of the Senators' starters that year wound up with terribly high ERAs.

Shorten Up the Fences, Loosen Up the Wallet

Roy started to come around, though. In 1955, it had taken him 54 games to bat in 15 runs and hit four homers. In 1956, it took him only 13 games to have nine RBI and three homers.[31] On April 29, Roy, along with Wally Post, Jack Shepard, Vic Wertz, Al Smith, and others combined to set a major league home run record for ten games in one day, belting 34 homers, 20 in the National League in six games, and 14 in the American League in four contests.[32]

Roy continued his domination of Kansas City pitching, hitting seven long balls off them and eight off the Detroit staff in 1956. All told, Roy hit three homers in April, nine in May, and five in June. He had a bit of a slump in July after being reassigned to the outfield when Pete Runnels became the new first baseman, and hit only two homers that month. The summer heat seemed to do the trick, though, and he exploded again in August with seven, with three more in September to finish up the season with 29. Roy also started to develop a reputation as "Mr. Clutch," as he hit nine of his dingers in either the eighth or the ninth inning.[33]

Roy's success that year was due in large part to management finally getting wise to Griffith Stadium's dimensions. Calvin Griffith pulled in the left field fence to 350 feet down the foul line and pulled the other fences in 15 to 20 feet, admitting that he was making the changes to help home run production and appease the fans' penchant for them.[34]

It obviously helped; Roy responded by hitting 29 home runs, once again a franchise record. He and Jim Lemon, who had 27 homers, became the AL's most potent 1–2 punch behind the Yankees' Mickey Mantle and Yogi Berra. The left field fence was christened "Sieversville" in honor of Roy's prodigious blasts.

The Senators set a team record with 112 home runs that season, but coughed and sputtered to a seventh-place finish at 59–95. (Manager Dressen had vowed at the beginning of the season that "we won't end up in last place again!") Fans showed their displeasure by staying away in droves, with fewer than 432,000 in attendance for the season; however, Roy's three steady years of run production and homers led to his being named to his first American League All-Star team.

When asked what was different about being in Washington and why he was developing into such a long ball hitter, he responded:

> Well, my shoulder finally felt good. I felt like I had my old strength back. And it makes a difference when you're playin' every day. You get your timing back and everything. Plus it also helped that the managers had enough confidence in me to hit me third or fourth all the time; you see more pitches when you're in that situation.

Whitey Herzog remembers those days with fondness:

> Roy was my first big league roomie. I roomed with him my first year in Washington. I knew he had grown up outside of St. Louis like me, and I followed the Brownies a lot. And I can tell you right now, I wasn't a scout back then, but being a young fan of baseball, he was a helluva ballplayer. He was such a disciplined hitter. When we roomed together, he talked a lot about RBI. That's how he got his money. He wouldn't hit a ball above his waist, so everybody would pitch him low, so he became a really good low ball hitter. And Dressen would make them let the grass grow real high out in left field so Roy wouldn't have to go to deep, and the ball would slow down so's he could catch up with it and toss it into short, 'cause he couldn't throw that well. But boy! What a helluva player he was![35]

Roy's steady run production was also paying off in his wallet. After making a paltry $9,000 in 1954, his salary had increased to $13,000 in 1955. Realizing that he had the makings of an All Star, Calvin Griffith let the moths fly out of his wallet and paid him a staggering $18,500 in 1956. However, even after breaking the franchise home run record for three straight years, in 1957 Roy was offered only a miserly $500 raise, making his salary $19,000.[36]

But, to paraphrase a great Frank Sinatra classic, the best was yet to come.

7

“The sweetest right-handed swing in baseball”

In the spring of 1957, Roy decided he was being undervalued by the Senators and held out from signing his contract. He wanted more than $20,000. He figured that if the stadium could be remodeled for the benefit of his hitting talents, he deserved more than the very small raise Calvin Griffith was offering him.

But Roy was up against one of the most parsimonious club owners since Connie Mack. As Roy remembers it, Griffith countered that Roy's average had slipped to .253, his RBI totaled a “mere” 95, and he had failed to deliver a single walk-off homer all year. He then cribbed some lines from Branch Rickey: “We finished next to last with you; we can finish next to last without you.” Roy settled for the paltry $500 raise that he had been offered.

To make matters even more interesting, rumors were circulating about a Sievers trade. Charles Comiskey, owner of the Chicago White Sox, told the press that he had offered to trade Minnie Miñoso and “Jungle” Jim Rivera for Sievers and Clint Courtney, but the offer had not been accepted. When he was advised of Comiskey's proposed trade, Griffith shrewdly replied that it was the first he had heard about it. Griffith purportedly tried to contact Comiskey, but by the time they connected, Miñoso was tearing up the Mexican Leagues in home runs and Comiskey called off the “deal.”[1]

Owners often used such tactics, true or not, to cajole and intimidate players, especially during trade talks, and Griffith was a master of this sort of deception. However, Griffith admitted that during the winter months he had “made strenuous efforts to deal Sievers off and that he was included in almost every deal that was broached” by the Senators.[2] “That made me pretty mad,” Roy recalled, “but it also made me determined to do better so's I could get better money the next year. Griffith was a tough old bastard to deal with.”

True to his word, Roy began to up the ante on Griffith by turning in his best spring performance to date. During spring training games in March and

April, he put up excellent numbers and was getting solid hits. As a result, Griffith changed his tune: "The price has gone up on Sievers. In fact, he's one of the players we won't trade now. Sievers and Lemon are going to give us one of the best one-two punches in the major leagues."[3] On April 3, in particular, the Sievers-Lemon duo sang a merry tune on the Cincinnati Reds, hitting back-to-back homers off Warren Hacker in a 4–3 exhibition win. After that game, Reds manager Birdie Tebbetts opined that the Senators could surprise the American League and reach the first division on the power of Sievers and Lemon.[4] Loyal Senators fans surely thanked him for his optimism, but deep in their hearts, they knew better.

Avoiding his traditional poor start, Roy had ten hits in his first 30 at-bats over a seven-game span and was hitting at a torrid .370 clip. He had 12 RBI in his first eight games and hit four homers in April, the first one on April 16 against "The Chairman of the Board," Whitey Ford. Roy would have good luck against the Yankees' ace lefty, taking him deep three times in 1957 and five times throughout his career.

On April 23, Roy hit the first of his five dramatic walk-off home runs of the year against Johnny Kucks as the Senators bested the Yankees, 3–1. "I just seem to feel better," Roy said, "and anybody can see I'm getting better wood on the ball."[5]

In their April 15 edition, the sages at *Sports Illustrated* gave this analysis of the 1957 team:

Analysis of This Year's Senators

Strong Points

Senators have two low-average but powerful sluggers in Roy Sievers and Jim Lemon, and it's a good thing they do. They also have steady hitter in cheerful Pete Runnels, a versatile ballplayer who shifted around infield and finally ended up as first baseman. There's veteran Eddie Yost at third, who has an uncanny ability for making pitchers walk him, despite his .231 average; three fairly good catchers in Lou Berberet, Clint Courtney, Ed Fitzgerald; one superb starting pitcher, name of Chuck Stobbs, and one good relief pitcher, name of Bud Byerly.

Weak Spots

Poor fielding and awful pitching. If it weren't for Stobbs (15–15, 3.60 earned run average) and Byerly (2.94 earned run average), Washington pitching staff would have established all sorts of records for absolute futility. Dressen prides himself on ability as instructor of pitching, but performance of Washington hurlers is not good testimonial, to put it mildly. Even when fine work turned in by Stobbs and Byerly is included in statistics, Senators' pitching staff had combined earned run average of 5.33 per game, which is almost unbelievably bad. Senator pitchers gave more bases on balls than anybody else, more home runs than any staff except Baltimore's (despite the spaciousness of Griffith Stadium playing area), made more wild pitches and more balks. They were even softest touch in league for run-scoring sacrifice flies. Part of blame for this aromatic record could be attributed to fielding. Neither Lemon nor Sievers is a first-class outfielder, Runnels is not a first baseman by trade, Yost is slowing up some at third. Shortstop and second were passed back and forth among half dozen aspirants last year, and that fluid situation was never really solidified, though Jerry Snyder and Herb Plews were about the best to appear at short and second. The trouble is, Senators have no one who makes the big pitcher-saving play.

Rookies and New Faces

Most of young players on this squad have been up and down a few times between parent club and minor leagues. Lyle Luttrell and Jose Valdivielso, for example, have both played long stretches at short with Washington. Both have looked brilliant at times, awful at other times. Outfielders Carlos Paula, who hits hard but who doesn't seem too interested in baseball, and Dick Tettelbach, who cares very much but who doesn't hit hard, were in camp for another look. Outfielder Neil Chrisley is a genuine rookie, and hopes are high he'll repeat with Washington the good year he had with Louisville. Management also fondly hopes that some of young pitchers (Abernathy, Brodowski, Clevenger, Hyde, Wiesler, for example) will do something to improve mound situation. Bonus Player Jerry Schoonmaker, who played on U.S. baseball team in 1955 Pan-American Games, is hope for future.

The Big Ifs

It seems reasonable to assume that established players such as Lemon, Sievers, Yost, Runnels, Stobbs, Byerly and the three catchers will do about as well this season as they did last. This is cheering, but not cheering enough because both Kansas City and Baltimore, Washington's immediate rivals, seem considerably improved over last season. In order for Senators to stay with Athletics and Orioles, pitching (which in Washington is spelled I-F) absolutely must get better. Pedro Ramos and Camilo Pascual, two Cuban right-handers who have endeared themselves to Dressen, are being counted on very heavily. Last year Ramos gave up 5.27 runs per game, Pascual 5.86. The Senators have reasonably fair hitting, but they're not a six-run-per-game team by a long shot. Q.E.D.: Ramos and Pascual had best improve. Then, too, young pitchers must take up more of the slack.

Outlook

Two years ago, as he began his first season as manager of Senators, Dressen talked so optimistically about potential his sharp eyes had spotted in his young players that he conned at least one New York baseball writer into picking Senators to finish well up in first division. The Senators finished last, the writer's enthusiasm vanished, and so did Charley's. This season Dressen is working just as hard, but the scales seem to have dropped from his eyes. No longer does Dressen feel bullish about his boys. On paper club is not improved. Prospect: eighth place.

Sports Illustrated was spot-on: the Senators finished eighth that year.

The Times, They Are A-Changin'

On April 15, 37,872 fans crowded into Griffith Stadium to see their Senators take on the nearly new Baltimore Orioles on Opening Day. President

Eisenhower did his usual "schtick," tossing out another long ball to the guys on both teams.

The Senators battled bravely. The O's were up 2–0 until the bottom of the fourth inning, when the Senators exploded. Roy hit a two-bagger (going 2-for-4 for the day), and pitcher Bob Chakales helped the cause by hitting a triple, putting the Senators ahead, 5–2. It seemed the team might be destined for a winner.

But no lead is ever safe. The O's scored two runs in the fifth and two in the seventh to take the lead, 6–5. In the bottom of the eighth, Courtney drove in Ed Yost with a double to tie the score and send the game into extra innings.

Pascual was called in to hold onto the game in the top of the eighth and used his famous curve ball to keep the Birds at bay through the tenth inning. But the O's' Dick Williams doubled to start the 11th; Al Pilarcik's bunt put Williams at third, and rookie Carl Powis sacrificed Williams home. Billy Loes, who replaced a magnificent Mike Fornieles in the bottom of the tenth, shut down the Senators in their home half of the 11th, thus sealing another Opening Day loss for the Senators.

On opening day, the Senators' lineup went like this:

Whitey Herzog	center field
Herb Plews	second base
Pete Runnels	first base
Eddie Yost	third base
Roy Sievers	left field
Jim Lemon	right field
Clint Courtney	catcher
Lyle Luttrell	shortstop
Bob Chakales	pitcher

But it wouldn't stay that way for long, as manager Chuck Dressen tried to piece together a team with some sort of consistency. Herb Plews and Lyle Luttrell were anemic at the plate and were shuffled with Jerry Snyder and Rocky Bridges. Herzog failed to produce the way he was expected to; hitting an anemic .167, he was sent down to the AAA Miami Marlins, never to return that year. Dressen was forced to platoon him with Dick Tettelbach. The middle of the order, Runnels, Yost, Sievers, Lemon, seemed to be the only ones who were consistent, with Roy being the most consistent of the group. His hits and RBI were up, and he had ten homers by the end of May.

There was no disguising the fact that Dressen's major worry was the pitching staff. Starters Ted Abernathy and Russ Kemmerer were struggling to find wins. Camilo Pascual and Pedro Ramos, two great Joe Cambria acquisitions from Cuba, were inconsistent, with Ramos giving up the long ball frequently. Veteran Chuck Stobbs (15–15, 3.60 ERA in 1956), was the only one

Noted for his slugging, Roy Sievers also possesses one of the best glove hands in baseball. Here he makes a leaping catch in left field and robs a rival of a homer.

The Senators' famous No. 2, waits in the on-deck circle for his shot at the pitcher.

Retired former heavyweight champion Rocky Marciano admires the muscles of another great slugger, the Senators' Roy Sievers.

A trio of photographs from the 1959 Senators Yearbook. Roy plays with his bat in the on deck circle; Roy robbing someone of extra bases up against the left centerfield wall; Roy mixes it up with former heavyweight champ Rocky Marciano.

able to go the distance in his first six starting assignments. Bud Byerly, a New York Giants acquisition, Tex Clevenger, and submariner Dick Hyde seemed to be the only hope in the bullpen. The pitching staff's earned run average would end up at 4.85 for the season, the worst in both leagues.

Three weeks into the season, on May 7, Calvin Griffith broke his Uncle Clark's firm position, fired Dressen, and replaced him with third base coach Cookie Lavagetto. Lavagetto was forever etched into baseball history as the player whose pinch-hit double in Game 4 of the 1947 World Series—his last hit in a Dodgers uniform—broke up Bill Bevens' bid for a no-hitter.[6]

Cookie Lavagetto was a loyal friend to Chuck Dressen. After his playing days in Brooklyn ended, he played with the minor league Oakland Oaks under managers Casey Stengel and Dressen. When Dressen was hired to manage the Dodgers in 1951, Lavagetto quit playing and hired on as a coach with him. When Dressen was hired to manage the Senators in 1954, he took Lavagetto with him.[7]

At first, Lavagetto refused to take the manager's job, wanting to remain loyal to his friend. "It's sickening," he said. "They want me to take the job and I won't. I'm still with Chuck wherever he goes." It was Dressen who convinced him to stay in DC, saying, "Look, Cookie, this is your big chance. This is the way it happens in baseball. I got my first job as a manager when one of my friends was fired. Nobody is a better friend of mine than Bucky Harris, but I also took his job in Washington when he was fired."[8]

Roy, Jim Lemon, Chuck Stobbs, Pete Runnels, and Ed Yost were a chorus of veterans, all decrying the rumor that it was a "rebellion" by the players that forced Dressen out. In an interview for Bob Addie of the *Washington Post*, published in *The Sporting News*, Runnels stated, "I learned more baseball under Dressen in two years than I did all my life under other managers. Charlie wasn't tough. He was enthusiastic about all he did and I think the general feeling of the players was he was always working for the good of the team. I'll tell you flat. There has never been any 'rebellion' or anything like that."[9]

A Manager in Spite of Himself

The transition was not an easy one.

Lavagetto never thought of himself as anything but a coach, and he had a tough time at first adjusting to the position. He was used to being out of the spotlight and had always deflected sportswriters' questions to Dressen. He liked playing cards with the players and enjoyed his anonymity.

That all changed when he became a manager. The life free of mental strain was gone, and he was thrust into the limelight. People now wanted to hear what he had to say. On the road, he was given a suite in the team's hotel. He did not like being alone and missed having a roommate. He also did not like deciding the batting order and the pitching rotation, and making decisions during games. What bothered him most was dealing with the losses of a last-place team. Eventually the constant worrying took a toll on him, and he began to have trouble sleeping and eating and even broke out in hives.[10]

After a while, though, Lavagetto became more confident. Although the team finished in eighth place in his first three seasons as manager, in 1960 they improved to fifth.

Roy remembered, "Cookie was a real player's manager. He enjoyed just being with the guys. He was always good to me. He could be firm when he had to, but he treated us all with respect." Broadcaster Bob Wolff also remembered Lavagetto with fondness: "Cookie was a great personal friend of mine. He handled his players very well. He was a great baseball man."[11]

Television talk show host Maury Povich, son of Spink Award-winning sportswriter Shirley Povich, spent three years as a batboy for the Washington Senators during the tenure of Bucky Harris. In 1955, he "graduated" to become Bob Wolff's production assistant. Maury would take notes, go for coffee, or just be available to do anything Wolff or the players needed. In a phone interview, he reminisced fondly about his days in Washington:

> My friend was Cookie Lavagetto. First of all, his door was always open to everyone. He was so unkempt in terms of his hair. It always looked like he had never slept, and he was always taking his hand and rubbing it through his hair. He had this nice mane of gray hair, and he would just rub his hand through this mane of hair trying to think of what the hell to do to make things better! Cookie was good to me because his door was always open, I can't remember one instance when Cookie's door wasn't open. And he might have had a little pint of liquor in there, yea, a little somethin' to tide him over after the game! I don't think there was anything "politically incorrect" about having a pint or a half pint there on the table of a manager after the game.[12]

The Great Year Begins

Once Lavagetto took over, things settled down and Roy began his incredible home run tear. He had a respectable May, hitting six homers. On May 16, he hit two in one game off his friend Billy Pierce of the White Sox. That put his total at eight, and his average at .299 for the month.

June was another good month, with Roy going yard eight times. He seemed to like White Sox pitching ... a lot! He took pitcher Jack Harshman deep twice in June and once in August. By the end of June, he had upped his average to .302. He would finish the month in grand style: on June 30, he got a dinger in each game of a doubleheader against (who else?) the White Sox, the second one a walk-off homer off Dixie Howell.[13]

Roy, who liked the hot Washington weather, caught fire in July, hitting nine round-trippers, spreading them out over every team in the American League. Each homer seemed to be higher, farther, and more dramatic than the last.

Roy's daughter Shawn remembered those days well. "We would love coming to Washington," she said. "School would let out sometime in June, and Momma would pack us all up for the trip to DC. We, of course, loved seeing Daddy and watching him play. But we would secretly hope for a rain out. Then we would all go to Glen Echo Park. I loved the big swimming pool and the bumper cars especially!"

When asked if it was a big deal to see her dad play, Shawn responded, "In my mind, baseball wasn't such a big deal. I was very little and didn't really understand it all. I just knew it kept Daddy away from us."[14]

Stuffed Boxes and an All-Star Snub

In July 1957, for the third time in the then-24-year history of the All Star Game, St. Louis hosted the summer classic. A total of 30,693 paying customers would file through the turnstiles at the newly refurbished Busch Stadium, formerly Sportsman's Park, just a stone's throw from the Sievers residence. Among the fans that year would be Roy's parents, his wife and children, his brother Bill and his family, and many of his hometown friends.

The 1957 All-Star Game started out mired in controversy. The rumblings had begun in 1956, when five of the starting nine National League All-Stars were from the Cincinnati Reds. Questions were raised, but nothing was said. The 1957 voting would be another story altogether. Reds fans stuffed the ballot box and elected nearly their entire team, with the exception of first baseman George Crowe.

The *Cincinnati Times-Star* published an already filled-out ballot for the ease of the fans. Many local bars and taverns purportedly made it a prerequisite to fill out a ballot before ordering a meal. Another story told of a local tavern receiving ballots from Reds sponsor Burger Beer and leaving them on the counter in stacks. One young girl came by, took 1,400 home, filled out all of her favorite Reds players, and returned the stack to the tavern, to be returned to the beer distributor the next day, who then mailed them in to the league office. The Z-Bar in Cincinnati accounted for over 10,000 ballots.

A late deluge of over 550,000 ballots from Cincinnati raised the prospect that seven of the starting nine players would be from the Reds. All of this was perfectly legal at the time. Any other Major League city could have done the same, but none did.[15]

An investigation instituted by Commissioner Ford Frick revealed that over half of the ballots cast had come from Cincinnati. Not wanting the game to be turned into a "mockery," Frick stated, "An overbalance of Cincinnati ballots has resulted in the selection of a team which would not be typical of the league and which would not meet with the approval of the fans the country over."[16] In an effort to achieve some semblance of parity, he removed Gus Bell and Wally Post from the starting nine and inserted Hank Aaron and Willie Mays on his own authority. The following year, he transferred the responsibility for All-Star voting to the players, managers and coaches; it would stay that way until 1970, when the vote returned to the fans.

Told he would be used as a pinch-hitter, an excited Sievers bought 21 tickets for family and friends to watch the game. Unfortunately, his seats were relegated to some far-flung section of the stadium next to several old beer signs. And to add insult to injury, Sievers, along with five others, did not play in the game. Manager Casey Stengel kept the team "Yankee heavy," keeping Yogi Berra and Mickey Mantle in for the whole game and subbing in pitcher Bob Grim, shortstop Gil McDougald, and first baseman Bill Skowron.

Roy said:

> Casey had a job to do and he did it. Certainly I was disappointed I didn't get to play in the All-Star Game, but I guess my biggest disappointment was in disappointing my home-town folks. My mother, my dad and all my friends were there.
>
> Casey told me he meant to use me for a pinch hitter for Billy Pierce in the ninth, but then Billy was going so good that Casey left him in there—and I didn't blame him. I wanted to see us win.
>
> But I just wish I could have had one lick for everybody back home. It was a big kick for me to play in my own home town—at least, I mean appear with the All-Star squad, even if I didn't play. It was a chance-in-the-lifetime shot because the next time St. Louis gets an All Star Game I'll be too old. Casey wanted to win and I didn't blame him … still…[17]

The manager gets paid to make the tough decisions. In the eighth inning, Stengel chose to replace Ted Williams with Minnie Miñoso in left field instead of Roy. It turned out to be a propitious choice. Miñoso's double in the top of the ninth scored Al Kaline and put the American League up, 6–2.

However, the National League came back with a vengeance in the bottom of the ninth. The White Sox's Billy Pierce walked Stan Musial. Willie Mays tripled to right, scoring Musial. Mays scored a moment later on a wild pitch to Hank Foiles. Foiles singled, and Gus Bell walked. Don Mossi replaced

Pierce and struck out Eddie Mathews for the first out. Ernie Banks singled, scoring Foiles and making it 6–5. When Bell tried to go to third on the play, Miñoso fielded the ball and fired to Frank Malzone, getting Bell for the second out. Banks went to second on the throw. Gil Hodges was chosen to pinch-hit for pitcher Clem Labine as Bob Grim came in to pitch for the AL. Hodges sent a shot to left-center, but Miñoso made a spectacular running catch to end the game.[18]

It's a sure bet that Roy would have loved to have had that chance.

Hot Fun in the Summertime

After the All-Star Game break, Roy continued to punish American League pitching: he hit 22 of his record-setting 42 home runs from July 17 to the end of the season. But Roy's bat was not the only thing on fire. As the temperature rose in Washington, so did his fielding. In an article published in *The Sporting News*, Dr. George Resta, the Senators' physician, concurred that Dr. Bennett's experiment on Roy's shoulder was bearing fruit. "He's the only man I've ever heard of who has gained so much free use of his arm following such surgery," he observed.

Roy's vastly stronger throwing began to command respect from the runners in the league. "I can cut loose from a three-quarters position once in a while and get pretty good distance," Roy said. He developed an extremely quick release that ensured that base runners would not take chances with him.[19]

August turned out to be just as hot as July, both literally and figuratively. Starting with the Saturday game on July 27 against the Athletics, Roy connected for seven home runs in eight games. Starting with a blast in the second game of a doubleheader on Sunday the 28th, Roy homered in six straight games, tying the mark set by Ken Williams of the 1922 Browns and Lou Gehrig with the 1931 Yankees.[20]

It was almost seven in a row, however. Playing the Tigers at home on Sunday, August 4, Roy came up for his last at-bat in the bottom of the eighth inning and drove one to deep center field.

"My six straight games with a home run were quite an accomplishment," Roy maintained.

> On the seventh day, Paul Foytack [of the Detroit Tigers], who I liked to hit all the time, was pitching. The wind was blowing out a little in Washington. I popped out the first three times and then in my last at bat, I hit it pretty good and I thought it was going out of the park, but Bill Tuttle, the center fielder, jumped up and caught the ball against the fence. I thought I would break the record. Good catch on his part, though.

Roy's most dramatic walk-off homer of the year came on August 3. Only 4,600 die-hard fans came out on that sweltering, 98-degree August Saturday night to see the Senators and the Tigers battle for four hours and 24 minutes in a 17-inning pitcher's duel. The Senators got things going in the bottom of the first. After Ed Yost's groundout to start the inning, Bob Usher doubled into the left-center field gap. Jim Lemon popped one up to second baseman Frank Bolling for the second out. Then Tigers manager Jack Tighe did the smart thing; he intentionally walked Sievers. Roy strayed a little too far off the bag, and pitcher Billy Hoeft pegged a perfect pickoff throw that would have ended the inning, but first sacker Ray Boone let it get by him. Usher scampered to third and Roy took second on the error. Art Schult singled to center, bringing home the first two runs of the game, and Ed Fitz Gerald ended the inning with a groundout.

The Senators kept their 2–0 lead into the top of the sixth. Russ Kemmerer gave up only one hit in that inning, but that was a solo homer by "Mr. Tiger," Al Kaline, bringing the Tigers within one.

In the top of the seventh, Kemmerer, tiring in the heat, gave up singles to catcher Red Wilson and pinch-hitter Charlie Maxwell. Pitcher Billy Hoeft's sac fly scored Wilson to tie it up. After Kemmerer gave up another single to Harvey Kuenn, manager Cookie Lavagetto decided he had seen enough. He brought in Tex Clevenger, who promptly closed out the inning.

And there is where it stayed. Each manager sent in relievers after the seventh inning until Tighe settled on Harry Byrd and Lavagetto sent in steady Bud Byerly. Byrd and Byerly dueled for five innings in the sweltering evening heat, allowing the occasional hit but following it up with groundouts and pop-ups.

Lavagetto brought in submariner Dick Hyde in the top of the 16th. Steve Boros singled to start the inning, Red Wilson bunted him to second, and Johnny Groth singled him in. Hyde retired Harry Byrd and Ron Samford to end the top of the inning, but the Tigers were up, 3–2.

But our hero Roy Sievers would have none of that. He singled to start the bottom of the 16th. Julio Becquer bunted him over to second. Jack Tighe replaced Byrd with Al Abner, but the Senators smelled a rally.

Catcher Lou Berberet singled Sievers home, then took second on Kaline's long throw from right field. Milt Bolling hit a grounder to third baseman Steve Boros, who threw it past Ray Boone at first, and Berberet took third on the error. Rocky Bridges hit a comebacker to Al Abner, who threw Berberet out at home. That put Bolling on second and Bridges on first. Lavagetto sent in Jerry Schoonmaker to pinch-hit for Hyde, and he drew a walk to load the bases. Up came "the walking man," Ed Yost.

Could he do it? Not that night. Yost struck out to end the inning, leaving the bases swollen with Senators.

Lavagetto decided on young Ted Abernathy to try to hold the Tigers at bay. Abernathy, 24 years old and in only his third season of pro ball, had been manager Chuck Dressen's go-to guy in 1955, appearing in 40 games and posting a 5–9 record, mostly in relief. He languished with Washington from 1955 through 1957, then was sent down to the minors for 1958 and 1959. After resurfacing with the Senators in 1960, he would go on to have a distinguished career after the 1961 expansion, spending seasons with the Indians, Cubs, Braves, Reds, and Cardinals, and closing out his career with the Kansas City Royals, posting a fine lifetime 63–69 W/L record.[21]

But on the night in question, Abernathy did what he was supposed to do: three up and three down.

The way the Senators started the bottom of the 17th, it looked like they'd be playing into Monday morning. Faye Throneberry flied out to Kaline in right, and big Jim Lemon grounded out meekly, second to first.

Up strode our hero, Roy Sievers.

He had had enough, as had all those who had stayed and sweltered until the wee hours of Sunday morning. He took the first Al Abner fast ball he saw and sent it into the steamy night air, deep into the left field bleachers, sending everyone home happy ... except for the Tigers, of course. Roy's solo home run in the bottom of the 17th would give Bob Addie, Shirley Povich and all of the *Washington Post* and *Evening Star* beat scribes volumes to write about over the weekend.[22]

"Yeah, I remember that one!" said Roy. "Boy, was it hot. We'd been playin' for hours and I just wanted to get in and take a shower. By that last inning, I figured, now's the time, and just went up there tryin' to end the thing." It was the third of Roy's five walk-off homers for the year, and it turned him into the Senators' greatest gate attraction since Walter Johnson. Washington became one of four teams to show an increase in attendance for the 1957 season.

With that August 3 dinger, his 30th of the year, Roy was well into his record-setting 42-homer season. Finishing August with seven homers, Roy unleashed his September fury on Whitey Ford and Art Ditmar of the Yankees, and in particular on Ray Moore of the Orioles, whom he took deep three times in the month, twice on Saturday, September 21, at Memorial Stadium in Baltimore. Roy's biggest blow came on September 14, when he tagged a Ned Garver fastball for a home run in the bottom of the tenth inning to give the Senators a 3–2 walk-off victory over the Athletics.

Hall of Fame third baseman Brooks Robinson remembers that big year: "Roy Sievers was one of the nicest guys you'd ever wanna meet and one hell of a hitter. I was still playin' part time in 1957, but Roy just hit the heck out of us, especially Ray Moore. I think he hit him deep about three or four times that year. What a great swing he had."[23]

The Race Is On

Nothing pleases newspaper reporters more than a story "with legs": a story with human interest that keeps readers engaged and sells newspapers. What captures readers' interest more than anything are the great sports streaks and rivalries. DiMaggio's 56 game hitting streak, along with Ted Williams's equally quixotic attempt to hit over .400 for a season, gave American sportswriters fodder for an entire summer and well into the fall of 1941. Grandfathers today can still tell their grandchildren exactly where they were in 1951 when the Dodgers began their late-season slide and "The Giants win the pennant, the Giants win the pennant!!" And even though Baltimore's Camden Yards officially holds 45,971, the entire population of Maryland will swear they were there in 1995 when Cal Ripken, Jr., broke Lou Gehrig's seemingly unbreakable streak of 2,131 straight games played.

In 1957, Roy Sievers' prodigious home run output was the stuff of legend for American sports writers in general and the DC scribes in particular. Washington had not had much but the perennially cellar-dwelling Senators to read about since their last pennant in 1933. But this was a legitimate streak. The *Washington Post* and the *Evening Star* were harkening back to the DiMaggio era, posting Sievers,' Williams,' and Mantle's home run accounts day by day to go along with the usual American and National League standings. The three heroes' stats were pretty evenly matched throughout the entire season. The monthly tallies looked like this:

	Sievers	**Williams**	**Mantle**
April	4	4	2
May	6 (10)	7 (11)	8 (10)
June	8 (18)	9 (20)	11 (21)
July	9 (27)	9 (29)	7 (28)
August	7 (34)	4 (33)	6 (34)
September	8 (42)	5 (38)	0 (34)

Mantle had a torrid June, belting 11 round-trippers to pass the other two after his slow April start. Each man seesawed through each month, keeping pace with the others.[24]

September became the telling month, though. It is quite possible that Roy would have been out-slugged by both Mantle and Williams if fate had not intervened.

Mickey Mantle had famously struggled with leg problems throughout his career. His battle with osteomyelitis kept him out of military service. His famous near-knee shattering injury in Game Two of the 1951 Yankees-Giants World Series should have ended his career then and there. And his severe thigh injury, sustained when he crashed into the bleacher wall in Boston in September of 1955, kept Casey Stengel up at night.[25]

Mantle's legs never stopped taking a pounding, and 1957 was no exception. Fighting shin splints throughout August and relegated to pinch-hitting roles, he finally succumbed and was admitted to Lenox Hill Hospital on September 6. He stayed for five days and was thereafter used sparingly by Stengel, who opted to save his star for the upcoming World Series. This might have cost Mantle the home run and RBI crowns in 1957, but he still walked away with the American League MVP trophy.[26]

At almost exactly the same time, Red Sox slugger Ted Williams, suffering from a severe chest cold, was ordered to bed by team physician Dr. Ralph McCarthy. The cold worsened into pneumonia and kept Williams sidelined for over two weeks. He was able to recover enough to give a good showing in September, but ultimately he lost out to Roy.[27]

By the time the last out was recorded, Roy had achieved another milestone. His league-leading 42 home runs and 114 RBI would give him the dubious distinction of being the first person in MLB history to win the home run and RBI titles with a last-place team. He also led the league in total bases (a club record 331), came in fourth in runs scored (99), and came in third in the MVP Award voting for the year.

Respect must be given to Roy's worthy opponents. Mantle ended the regular season with 34 homers, 94 RBI, and a .365 batting average. Williams finished with 38 home runs, 87 RBI, and a league-leading .388 average, along with a new record. From September 17–23, he reached base in 16 consecutive plate appearances. Roy's, Ted's, and Mickey's numbers were the "stuff that dreams are made of" for many modern-day players.

By the end of the season, the Williams-Mantle-Sievers triumvirate would lead the league in 13 out of 44 statistical batting categories, with Roy winning four outright: home runs, RBI, extra-base hits, and total bases. Even sweeter, from Roy's perspective: Ted Williams proclaimed that Roy had "the sweetest right-handed swing in baseball."

Can't Get Enough of That Good Thing

With the baseballs flying out of the stadiums with great frequency, the Senators needed to keep the team in the plus side of the headlines for as long as they could. Enter Herb Heft.

Heft, the director of promotions for the Senators, had the dubious job of making a silk purse out of a sow's ear, and he did so with panache. Having had a successful career as a sportswriter for the *Washington Post* from 1943 to 1954 and then for *The Sporting News*, he had returned to Washington in 1955 to work for the Senators. He subsequently moved with the team to Minneapolis in 1960, and then became the first PR director for the New York Mets in 1963. He later went on to become Executive Vice President for the Baltimore Bullets, later to become the Washington Wizards.

Heft, in a precursor to today's All-Star Game home run derby, arranged for a head-to-head home run contest between Mickey Mantle and Roy Sievers on the night of September 6, when the Yankees came to DC to play the Senators in a three-game set. Mantle had to work overtime, hitting in both the right- and left-handed contests. Mantle and Bill Skowron were paired up with Sievers and Jim Lemon in the right-hand contest, and Mantle and Yogi Berra were matched with Clint Courtney and Lou Berberet for the left-hand contest.

Sad to say, Mantle took the home run exhibition that night, but the Senators won the game, 4–3.

The Big Night

In a gesture of magnanimity, the Senators decided to give Roy a "night" in his honor. Local businessman Edward R. Carr chaired the Roy Sievers Night committee and arranged a joyous and varied program on September 23.

Mr. Carr, a successful home developer in the area, was an energetic civic leader within the metropolitan community and also the president of both the National Home Builders Association and the DC Board of Trade. A dedicated Senators fan, Mr. Carr was instrumental in securing housing for many of the Senators players, including Roy and Harmon Killebrew.

The evening began with several songs presented by "The Singing Senators." This a cappella vocal group was started in the mid–'50s by Senators broadcaster and future Ford Frick Award-winner Bob Wolff, who had been a big band singer in his college days and played a mean ukulele. He started the vocal group as a means of relaxation on the long road trips. Players would come and go, but the group, with our own Roy Sievers as lead baritone, rose to such prominence as to be featured for several hours on the nationally syndicated "Dave Garroway Show" in 1959.[28]

After the vocal stylings of the Singing Senators came the hilarious baseball antics of Nick Altrock. A veteran coach with the Senators from 1912 to 1953, Altrock frequently teamed up with Al Schacht, the "Clown Prince of

Baseball," to perform comedy routines in dozens of stadiums throughout the United States.

Following Altrock's hilarity came the Senators' version of "shadow ball." Shadow Ball had been a mainstay of the Negro Leagues for decades. The team would take the field, the pitcher would throw an imaginary ball to the batter, who would hit, and everyone would scurry around like there was a real ball in play, throwing to bases, tossing it over their shoulders, and performing many other spectacular feats of legerdemain. The fans sat in amazement as the players went about their drills as if there were a real ball in play.[29]

After that came a comic "footrace" between Clint Courtney and Pedro Ramos. A lightning-fast runner, Ramos (with the Yankees in 1964) would constantly challenge Mickey Mantle to a $100 sprint race. (Mantle always declined.) On this night, however, Courtney would start at second base and walk to home plate, while Ramos had to run the bases at full speed and try

Vice President Richard Nixon, an unabashed Roy Sievers fan, hands Roy the keys to his new 1957 Mercury station wagon on "Roy Sievers Night," September 23, 1957, as more than 20,000 fans pay tribute to the American League home run and RBI champ (National Baseball Hall of Fame Library, Cooperstown, New York).

to beat him to the plate. Courtney, with a little "cheating jog" every once in a while, beat Ramos to the plate. Following that came an egg-throwing contest, with its usual messy results, won by pitcher Art Schult.

The feature of the evening was the home run derby. Roy, along with teammates Faye Throneberry, Lou Berberet, and youngster Harmon Killebrew, went head to head with Boston's own Ted Williams and his mates Dick Gernert, Jackie Jensen, and former Senators first baseman Mickey Vernon. Appropriately, Roy won the contest, hitting two out of five right-handed, and Ted Williams hit one out to win the left-handed contest. The Senators generously gave a $1,000 check to Roy and gave Williams a check for $250, which he donated to his favorite home town charity, the Jimmy Fund for Cancer.

The coup de grace occurred when the Master of Ceremonies, Vice President Richard Nixon, an unabashed Sievers fan, appeared on the field to make presentations to Roy and his family. The Vice President gave Roy and his wife Joan the keys to a new 1957 Mercury station wagon and complimented the 17,800 fans by saying, "This proves Washington is one of the most loyal baseball cities in the country."

Next, Joan was given a beautiful mink stole, and Roy's children Robin, 5, and Shawn, 3, were given new tricycles. Then the "showering" began. Roy was presented with a full set of Sam Snead golf clubs, a Motorola clock radio, a tape recorder, a television set, free haircuts from a local barber shop, and an engraved wrist watch, along with dozens of other gifts donated by his teammates.[30]

"Oh yeah, I remember," said Roy's daughter Shawn. "I had my little checkered dress and my Buster Browns on. They gave Daddy a car and Momma a pretty mink coat. Then they gave my brother a bicycle and gave me a tricycle, and I just took off around the bases. I didn't know any better; I just wanted to ride my new bike!"[31]

Also viewing the festivities that evening were Jack Dunn, assistant general manager of the Baltimore Orioles, and Lum Harris, one of the Orioles' coaches. Talking with columnist Bob Addie a few days later, Dunn described the evening thusly: "First, Mrs. Sievers wept, then Roy shed a tear of happiness, then I noticed several of the fans were crying as well. Then Lum Harris looked at me and we reminded each other that the Orioles had traded him away. Then we both decided that maybe we should be crying as well!"

Roy's wife and family, his parents, Walter and Anna, his brother Bill and his family, as well as thousands of great Washington fans watched as Roy, overcome with emotion, lowered his head and sobbed as he shook the Vice President's hand. In an interview, Roy remembered it this way: "That was the most memorable night of my life. They gave me a car and all kinds of things.

I'm not ashamed of it, I wept like a baby, all those fans cheering for me and my folks come up all the way from St. Louis. I'll never forget it."

True to form, however, the Senators lost to the Red Sox that evening, 9–4. Ralph Lumenti, the Senators' new bonus baby who was still attending college at the University of Massachusetts, had rushed back to Washington to pitch to his "neighbors." The 20-year-old Lumenti had just made his Major League debut against the Yankees three weeks earlier, and the Senators held high hopes for this fireballer.

But Lumenti, who hadn't worked out or pitched since his previous start because of attending classes, was also nursing a heavy cold that evening, and it surely affected him. After striking out Jimmy Piersall to start the game, he gave up six hits and two runs and hit one batter in one and one-third innings. Pedro Ramos was brought in to relieve Lumenti in the top of the second. Inheriting two runners, Ramos gave up RBI singles to Frank Malzone and "The Golden Boy," Jackie Jensen, before finally getting Dick Gernert to ground into an inning-ending double play.

Behind 6–0 in the fourth inning, the Senators brought in former Red Sox Russ Kemmerer to relieve Ramos. Kemmerer fared no better, though. In only two innings, he gave up a walk, a two-run homer to Frank Malzone, a single to Ken Aspromontc; and an RBI double to Sammy White. White, trying to stretch his double into a triple, scored, unfortunately, on a throwing error by the honoree of the evening, Roy Sievers.[32]

Besides the genuine outpouring of affection for Roy, the only other bright spot of the evening for the Senators was a tremendous pinch-hit home run by their youngest bonus baby, future Hall of Famer Harmon Killebrew. Roy managed two hits in four at-bats.

Charlie Brotman holds the distinction of announcing every Presidential Parade in Washington, D.C., since 1957. He was the Senators' public address announcer and director of promotions from 1956 to 1971 and was invited to be the Opening Day announcer when the Washington Nationals returned to DC in 2005. He remembers Roy's evening this way:

> It was a really special night. The Vice President was there, and Roy's kids and his folks. It was a very special night for all of us. Roy was everybody's favorite ball player; his personality, the way he handled himself. He was always everybody "superhero" 'cause he would come up with the big [hit] that would win the game. He never had the attitude that he was "above and beyond" anybody else. It wasn't like he was a superstar and used it to his advantage. He was just a regular guy![33]

It would have been nice if the team could have rallied behind Roy to make his evening a sweeter success.

High Praise from High Places

Remembering that night, Roy mused, "Yeah, I was Nixon's favorite player. Nixon liked me, and Eisenhower liked my roomie Jim Lemon. He had me over to the White House several times. See that picture there? [Referring to a large, affectionately signed photo of President Nixon which hangs in Roy's living room.] He gave that to me personally."

Vice President Nixon was a *big* Roy Sievers fan and held him in deep regard. He was also an avid Washington sports fan and sincerely enjoyed throwing out the traditional Opening Day first pitch every year when he was President.

In a letter sent to Edward Carr, Nixon wrote:

> Dear Eddie,
>
> I am enclosing a modest contribution to the Roy Sievers Fund which I understand you are handling.
>
> No man in baseball more deserves recognition than Roy. The fact that he is leading the league in both home runs and runs batted in is, of course, in itself outstanding but, in addition, the determination which enabled him to overcome the effects of an almost disastrous injury is an inspiration to our young people all over the country.
>
> I think the highest compliment I've heard paid to him was expressed by my 11-year-old daughter Tricia. After she had seen him hit his thirty-seventh and thirty-eighth home runs against Kansas City on television, she exclaimed that "Washington shouldn't even trade Roy Sievers for Mickey Mantle."
>
> This note brings my best wishes for what I know will be a very memorable evening on Roy Sievers night.[34]

The Slight at the End of the Tunnel

One would think that, for a humble Midwestern boy to be mentioned in the same breath with deities such as Ted Williams and Mickey Mantle, to battle with them tooth and nail for 152 games and best them in two out of three categories, it would be enough. Enough to earn the respect of fans and sportswriters alike. Enough to garner the most esteemed crown in baseball, the Most Valuable Player Award.

One would be wrong.

Singlehandedly providing the only offense for a perennial cellar-dwelling team like the Senators was considered not valuable enough for the Baseball Writers' Association of America. In 1957, Mantle won the MVP crown for a second time with 233 votes, followed by Williams with 209 and Roy with 205.

Vice President Richard Nixon tries to get a hold of the big bat of Roy Sievers before the August 2, 1957, Senators-Tigers game. Nixon and Republican Senator Leslie Arends (left) hoped to see Roy hit one out. Roy obliged with his 29th homer of the season (AP photograph/Charles Gorry).

Bob Addie, a dean of Washington baseball writers, was chagrined, as he wrote in a *Washington Post* article in October of 1957:

> Looking at the past selections for the Most Valuable Player in the American and National leagues, it's obvious that, despite what individual heroics he performs, Sievers will have no chance for the top award. Why? I don't know. But the award always goes to a player with a first-division club, usually the player with a pennant winner and rarely to a player with a club as low as fourth. That, of course, would eliminate Roy.

Addie explained that since 1931, when the award was established, the National League had had 17 players from pennant-winning clubs take the award; three from second-place teams; one from a third-place club; four from a fourth-place team; and one from a fifth-place team. The American League nearly mirrored that average, with 16 players from first-place clubs, seven from second-place clubs, one from a third-place club and two from fourth-place clubs.

Addie reasoned:

> This brings up the old question as to what constitutes the most valuable player. Literally, it undoubtedly means the player who is most valuable to his club. It doesn't mean the club MUST win the pennant—else only the flag winners would have the MVP boys. I suppose it all means the without the MVP, a club would not have done as well as it did. ...Certainly, the Washington Senators could not have done as well as they did without Sievers.
>
> But this premise is never accepted by the voters among the baseball writers. They'll argue, logically, that the Yanks couldn't have won the pennant without Mickey Mantle, and the Red Sox couldn't have finished third without Ted Williams. Both have contributed outstanding performances. But what happens to the poor man's hero, Sievers, who beats out these more famous stars in two departments—homers and RBI? Can you shunt Roy aside?
>
> Sievers figures to be no better than third in the voting this year. That's a distinction in itself. But who can say he doesn't deserve the top spot if he succeeds in winning two crowns? Is a man with a first division club who hasn't performed as well as Sievers entitled to be named the most valuable player because he was surrounded by better players? It's something to think about.[35]

For Roy, the third place he achieved in 1957 would be as high as he finished in the MVP balloting. He got votes in MVP balloting seven times in his 17-year career (even in his rookie year), and was an American League All-Star four times.

"Yeah, I had a helluva good year," said Roy, "best I ever had. And I was gonna make them pay for me the next year!"

8

The World Is His Oyster

Bon Vivant and Raconteur

Flying high after his tremendous season and his big night in Washington, Roy Sievers was golden.

Right after the season ended in September, he appeared along with Joe DiMaggio, Mickey Mantle, and Willie Mays on the "Ed Sullivan Show." Ed paid tribute to Roy for winning two-thirds of baseball's Triple Crown in 1957. As Roy recalled: "Boy, what a thrill that was for me. They flew me and Joan up to New York City and put us in a nice hotel. I was sure proud to be on that stage with Willie and Mickey and DiMag. Ed was real nice to me. I'll never forget that night."

Roy spent most of October earning some much-needed off-season money, barnstorming with the Bolling brothers (the Senators' Milt and the Tigers' Frank), Jim Bunning, his roomie Jim Lemon, and many other baseball colleagues. Roy, along with Tigers center fielder Bill Tuttle and Orioles catcher Gus Triandos, entertained the crowds in Texas, Arizona, and Mexico with booming home runs.[1]

Roy may have been snubbed by Casey Stengel in the All-Star Game and by the Baseball Writers' Association of America, but he became the toast of Washington during the winter of 1957–1958. He joined the "Knife and Fork League" to gain a few extra dollars (and a few extra pounds!), speaking at and receiving a host of awards from organizations all over the country.

On October 25, he was named the American League's Most Outstanding Player at a banquet given by the Home Plate Club of Washington. Sharing the dais with him at the Continental Hotel on Fourteenth Street in downtown DC were former Senators and Redskins greats Joe Judge, Sam Rice, Ossie Bluege, George McQuinn, Bozie Berger, Bill Jurges, Ben Cantwell, and Jim Castiglia.[2] After that, it was a short trip across the Potomac River to Arlington,

Roy and infielder Rocky Bridges clown it up in the dugout with Hollywood legend Jerry Lewis. Lewis would don a Senators uniform and take batting practice, no doubt tutored by an appreciative Mr. Sievers (National Baseball Hall of Fame Library, Cooperstown, New York).

Virginia, where Roy, along with stars Robin Roberts of the Phillies, the Pirates' Dick Groat, and the Red Sox's Frank Malzone were honored at the annual Better Sports Club banquet on November 14.[3] Then it was a quick trip home to St. Louis to receive the Elks Lodge No. 9's Outstanding Sportsman of the Year award on November 21.[4]

On December 14, Roy was once again honored, this time by Maryland University's "M Club," at a lavish dinner held at the Statler Hilton Hotel in downtown Washington. The M Club, started in 1923 by legendary football coach Dr. H. C. "Curley" Byrd, was used as a way to promote the development of excellence in the individual student through sports. William Cobey, University of Maryland Director of Athletics, presented Roy with the Outstanding Athlete Award, and Dr. Wilson Elkins, President of the University, presented the Distinguished Service Award to General Curtis LeMay, Chief of Staff of the U.S. Air Force and Commanding General of the Strategic Air

Command. Roy and General LeMay also received honorary induction into the M Club.[5]

Baseball and football stars, as well as the biggest politicos in the nation's capital, came out to the 23rd annual Touchdown Club awards banquet at the Sheraton Park Hotel on the evening of January 11, 1958. The Touchdown Club had been started in 1935 by Arthur "Dutch" Bergman as a way of recognizing outstanding athletes and raising money for children's charities and scholarships throughout the metropolitan area. At the 1958 banquet, baseball broadcasters Red Barber and Joe Garagiola acted as toastmaster and featured speaker respectively. John Crow, Texas A & M halfback, received the Walter Camp Memorial trophy as outstanding college back, and Lou Michaels, a tackle for Kentucky, received the Knute Rockne Memorial trophy as outstanding college lineman.

But the biggest hand of the night went to our own Mr. Sievers. Roy was presented the Clark Griffith Memorial Trophy in honor of his outstanding contributions to baseball in 1957. He was the third winner of the trophy, following Ted Williams in 1955 and Sal Maglie in 1956. After expressing humble and heartfelt thanks, Roy took his seat on the dais next to his old friend Richard Nixon and Supreme Court Justice Tom Clark.[6]

On January 13, Roy was invited to share the dais with a throng of the game's greatest for the Maryland Professional Baseball Players' Association's annual "Tops in Sports" banquet at the Lord Baltimore Hotel in Baltimore, Maryland. On hand for the evening were Braves pitcher Lew Burdette, Orioles star Billy Gardner, Yankees great Gil McDougald, Senators and Colts broadcaster Chuck Thompson, Cleveland first baseman Vic Wertz (soon to be Roy's teammate), Cardinals legend Stan Musial, Tigers ten-time All Star George Kell, *Baltimore News-Post* sports editor Roger Pippin, and the Splendid Splinter himself, Ted Williams. For his impressive .388 batting average, which led both leagues in 1957, Williams received the Babe Ruth "Sultan of Swat" crown, a beautiful, gold-filled crown lined in red velvet, from Musial; *The Sporting News* noted that "Ted even wore a tie as a concession to the occasion."

But all these greats, and the 1,100 fans packed into the Grand Ballroom, had come at the behest of the organization to honor 73-year-old orthopedic specialist Dr. George Bennett, who had singlehandedly rebuilt the careers of many of the decade's greatest sports heroes, Roy Sievers included. Many came to the microphone to offer their praise, but it was the ever humble Roy who brought tears to many an eye as he gave his heartfelt tribute to Dr. Bennett, saying, "Without the operation you performed on me in 1952, I wouldn't be here tonight. God bless you, sir."[7]

"[Bennett] always said it was the best operation he'd performed on a ballplayer," Roy remembers. "I ended up playing 15 more years with that shoulder. I was very fortunate."

When asked to pick an All-Star lineup of players he had treated, Dr. Bennett named the following:

First base: Dolph Camilli, Eddie Robinson, and Tommy Henrich

Second base: Max Bishop

Shortstop: Frankie Crosetti, Pee Wee Reese, and Phil Rizzuto

Third base: Red Rolfe and Cookie Lavagetto

Outfield: Joe DiMaggio, Charlie Keller, Ted Williams, Whitey Lockman, and Roy Sievers

Catcher: Stan Lopata

Pitchers: Lefty Gomez, Dizzy Dean, Whit Wyatt, Vic Raschi, Billy Pierce, and Bobby Shantz

Also in attendance that evening was toastmaster extraordinaire Joe Garagiola. He was in fine form, needling his many friends on the dais and in the audience. But he brought down the house when he quipped, "After listening to that all-star list of players Dr. Bennett has mended, I'm sort of sorry that I didn't break my leg!"[8]

From Baltimore, it was on to Manchester, New Hampshire, on January 15 to attend the Union Leader Charity Fund's tenth annual baseball dinner, sponsored by the *Manchester Union Leader* newspaper. Roy would kid it up with his pals Stan Musial and Joe Garagiola once again, and be honored for his baseball accomplishments along with baseball legend Ty Cobb; Hank Aaron and Lew Burdette of the Braves; Al Kaline of the Tigers; and Yankees great Bob Turley.[9]

Roy got himself into a little hot water at that event. He got a big cheer from the Red Sox-heavy crowd when he told them, "I hope to be back here soon and maybe someday not too far off I'll come back in a Red Sox uniform." When word got back to the Senators' front office, owner Calvin Griffith said, "I don't think Roy was quoted correctly, but if he did make the statement, he was speaking out of turn. Sievers is not going to be traded. He's going to be in a [Senators] uniform next season. The right offer hasn't come along."[10]

Following New Hampshire, Roy went back home to St. Louis. On January 20, the St. Louis chapter of the Baseball Writers' Association of America held its first gala dinner to honor the Association's 50th anniversary. One thousand people attended this stellar event, which named St. Louis's all-time team. Players from the Cardinals and the Browns included George Sisler, Rogers Hornsby, Frankie Frisch, Marty Marion, Kenny Williams, Terry Moore,

Johnny Brown, Stan Musial, Hank Severeid, Urban Shocker, Dizzy Dean and Red Schoendienst. Roy was honored as the Outstanding Sports Figure of St. Louis for 1957.[11]

Finally Getting His Due

Besides the significant numbers he produced during the 1957 season, Roy earned another distinction. Cookie Lavagetto told the press, while attending the World Series in October, "He's the only man on our ball club who's not for trade. We are trade-minded and every man on our club can be had except Sievers."[12]

After leading the league in home runs and RBI, with five walk-off home runs and 331 total bases, Roy finally had leverage. He also seemed to have developed some skills as a negotiator. Maybe it was the Red Sox talk or Roy just being a little cagey, but by the time spring training 1958 rolled around, Roy would finally get a salary commensurate with his abilities.

As early as October 1, 1957, Cal Griffith had wanted to discuss his salary with him. But Roy thought differently: "Yes, Griffith wanted to talk to me about my salary, but I told him I was busy getting ready to go play winter ball. I was barnstorming with the Bolling brothers. I just wanted him to stew a little."

Meanwhile, trade rumors abounded again during the long winter months, as they always do. Despite management's saying that Roy was off the table, Griffith coyly entertained a variety of offers. There was brief talk of an inter-league trade to Cincinnati, along with rumors of a massive four-player trade with the Yankees. The Senators were in the bidding for Kansas City second baseman Billy Martin, but Griffith couldn't swallow their exorbitant price: Martin for Sievers, straight up! "They're talking through their opium pipes," Griffith said.[13]

"Where I really wanted to play" said Sievers, "was in Boston. There were a lot of rumors goin' around they would trade me for Malzone and Jensen, but it'd never come about." Red Sox General Manager Joe Cronin was married to Calvin Griffith's older sister, Mildred. Griffith was never going to sell his star player, much less his biggest gate attraction since Walter Johnson, to his brother-in-law. Besides, he knew better than to incur the wrath of the star-starved nation's capital and risk the sinking of his own ship. Roy was that big.

Roy let all of those talks go by, then countered with his first offer: $40,000. "I knew they wouldn't go for it," he said. "I knew Mickey [Mantle] was makin' that much and more, with all those World Series wins. But I knew

I had to start high if I was to get what I really wanted: double my salary from '57."

Griffith said he wouldn't go above $30,000, and that was that throughout the winter. Roy told writers in St. Louis that he would stay home until his terms were met. He made several trips to Washington during the winter to visit with Griffith, but made no progress. He also returned four contracts unsigned.[14]

In the end, Roy won, holding out for $36,000. The contract he signed on February 27 made him the highest-paid Senator in the history of the franchise at that time.

The interest in playing for Boston stayed with him, however. "I got to be friends with Ted Williams later in life," he recalled. "We'd be at autograph shows all over, and we got to be friends. He always respected me as a hitter and that's a great compliment comin' from him. He used to say, 'Kid, if we'd a gotten you, we would have won some pennants.'"

Roy headed off to spring training. In the meantime, Calvin Griffith was vehemently denying rumors that he was moving the team to Minneapolis.

Carbon Copy

In April of 1958, *Sports Illustrated* saw the Senators this way:

Strong Points: The Senators have Roy Sievers, the American League's home-run and runs-batted-in champion, which takes care of left field; and that's almost it. However, strange as it might seem, Washington has real depth—in catching. Clint Courtney, Lou Berberet and Ed Fitzgerald are all good major league catchers who give Lavagetto his only real chance to maneuver. Right fielder Jim Lemon showed in 1956 that he was the power hitter to complement Sievers. He slumped last year, but he still must be considered a relatively strong point on this weak-hitting club. Rocky Bridges, for years the best second-string shortstop in the National League, came to the Senators in midseason last year and showed Washington how that position should be played. Now, if he could only hit. At third base, as usual, is that Washington institution, Eddie Yost—a good, steady, dependable ballplayer known mainly for his ability to draw walks. The best thing the team has going for it pitcher-wise is Bud Byerly, who in two straight seasons has been the team's most effective relief man and one of the league's best.

Weak Spots: They boil down to two fairly fundamental inadequacies—lack of hitting and lack of pitching. The pitching staff's earned run average was 4.85, worst in both leagues. Not one starting pitcher gave up fewer than four earned runs a game, and the whole staff could only put together 31 complete games. The four regular starters—Stobbs, Pascual, Ramos and Kemmerer—lost nearly twice as many games as they won, with Stobbs the worst offender at 8 and 20. Sad to say, virtually the same pitchers will be back this season. Despite Roy Sievers, the Senators tied for last as the worst-hitting team in the major leagues (.244). Because of him they weren't last in runs, hits and

> total bases. They were seventh. And it will be up to many of the same old hands to supply the team's batting power this year.

Lavagetto, now in his first full year as a manager, spent the spring trying to tweak the team into shape. His "pet project" was trying to turn free-swinging Faye Throneberry into a decent hitter and right fielder. Jim Lemon, despite his .285 average and 17 homers, struck out a lot and was a defensive liability. Throneberry had seen limited time on the Red Sox bench in 1957, which led to a rusty .186 average and a dim future. Lavagetto saw something in the young man and "coached him up" during the spring.

Pete Runnels was traded to the Red Sox for Norm Zauchin and Albie Pearson, leaving second base platooned with Herb Plews and Ken Aspromonte. Rocky Bridges, he of the large tobacco wad in his cheek, would have an All-Star year at shortstop. That left third base to "The Walking Man," Ed Yost.

There were, however, several bright spots on the team. "Little" Albie Pearson (5'5", 160 pounds), patrolling center field, would win "Rookie of the Year" honors. "Big" Norm Zauchin (6'5", 220 pounds) was looked upon to add a big bat to the lineup and to spell Roy at first base, when Lavagetto wanted Roy in left field. Steve Korshak was trying to take the catcher's spot away from Clint Courtney (to no avail), and Bob Malkmus was positioned to become the utility man. Ralph Lumenti, the bonus baby from Massachusetts, was being groomed to become the third man in the starting lineup, but that would not pan out. Powerful yet erratic young Harmon Killebrew, who Lavagetto hoped would supply the punch necessary in the middle of the lineup, struggled at AAA and appeared in only 13 games during the season.

The Sporting News had the Senators finishing seventh again in 1958. In fact, they would finish eighth.

Another Opening Day

Roy got off to another slow start during the pre-season, due to several circumstances. His contract wrangling with Calvin Griffith meant that he held out from going to spring training for two weeks, which set his conditioning behind schedule. Just as he was getting into pretty good shape, the injury curse struck, literally. On March 14, while talking with some of his Red Sox friends during spring training drills in Sarasota, he was hit by an errant Jackie Jensen foul ball, which put a deep bruise on his thigh, sidelining him for 13 days.[15]

When he got back at the end of March, his timing was way off, understandably. He was pressing for hits, striking out and grounding out with frequency. These problems would carry over even into Opening Day.

The Opening Day lineup looked like this:

Ed Yost	third base
Albie Pearson	center field
Roy Sievers	left field
Clint Courtney	catcher
Jim Lemon	right field
Norm Zauchin	first base
Herb Plews	second base
Rocky Bridges	shortstop
Pedro Ramos	pitcher

A throng of 26,765 hopeful Senators fans crowded into Griffith Stadium on April 14, a beautiful 72-degree day, to watch President Eisenhower throw out a really nice, high first pitch to open the 1958 season. Whitey Herzog elbowed his way through the crowd to capture the Presidential prize. That would be about the last ball he'd catch in a Senators uniform.

Since the presidency of William Howard Taft, the Senators had had the distinction of starting the regular baseball season early and having the President throw out the ceremonial "first pitch," forever giving the team the honor of being the "Nation's Team." Living up to that sobriquet would be another matter altogether. They would own another dubious title: "First in war, first in peace, and last in the American League."[16]

But on that April day in 1958, Pedro Ramos went all the way, tossing a magnificent five-hitter to lead the Senators to a 5–2 win over the Boston Red Sox. Roy went 1-for-4 on the day, but that one hit was an RBI single in the bottom of the fifth inning, scoring Ed Yost from third.

Roy finally came out of his spring doldrums on April 19, and he did so with a vengeance. Playing the Orioles at Griffith Stadium, in the bottom of the ninth, with the Senators trailing 3–2, he took a Mike Fornieles fastball deep to left center to tie the game. The Senators eventually won the contest with an Ed Fitz Gerald pinch-hit single scoring Courtney from third.[17]

Just to rub salt into the Orioles' wounds, Roy hurt them again the next day. He hit a double and a triple early in the game, helping to keep the Senators in a 5–5 tie. Then, in the bottom of the ninth, he took Murray Wall's first pitch deep into the left field beer gardens (also known as Sieverville) to win the game with his first walk-off homer of the year.[18]

Those two homers would be Roy's total output for the month of April. A pulled calf muscle on May 11 sidelined him again, limiting his May output to four. But he would rebound greatly, smacking 11 dingers in June, eight each in July and August, and five in September. In spring training, Roy told reporters he would be happy with 30 homers, 100 runs batted in, and a .300 batting average. He was close on all counts. His year-end totals would be 39 homers, 108 RBI, 299 total bases, and a .295 batting average. He would also place sixth in the MVP voting in 1958.

A High Schooler's Choice

Washington-area resident and retired Montgomery County Circuit Court Judge Bill Turner was a batboy for the Senators from 1956 through 1959, and he remembers the beginning of the 1958 season well.

> I started [being a bat boy] when I was 16, 1956 through 1959. I played baseball at Montgomery-Blair High School here in Silver Spring my sophomore year. They were only grades 10 through 12 back then. I played my sophomore year. Then, in my junior year, I made the team again.
>
> Well, starting in 1958, the Senators did pretty good for the month of April. Unfortunately, we lost to the Orioles on Opening Day, then to the Yankees for their home opener the next day. Then we came back home and took two out of three from the Orioles and it looked like we were on a roll.
>
> Then the Yankees came into DC to play two games to finish the series off after their home opener. Since the Yanks always drew so well, there were sure to need everyone on deck for that series. The first game was a Monday night game and we lost to them. But the second game was a day game, I think it was a Tuesday or Wednesday or something, so, my mom wrote me a letter to excuse me from school.
>
> Well, that day, Roy hit a home run to win the game in the bottom of the ninth inning, and I was at the plate to greet him and celebrate. Well, there was a picture taken of me shaking hands with him as he crossed the plate, and it wound up in the *Washington Post* the next day saying, "Sievers hits home run to win the game, and blah, blah."
>
> So the next day I go to school, and I go out for [baseball] practice and the coach says, "Hey, Turner, I want to see ya for a minute."
>
> So he says, "Hey, where were you yesterday?" and I said I had an excuse. My mother wrote me a letter excusing me from school for personal reasons. And he said, "I'm not concerned about your mother. I want to know where YOU were." And I said, "I had another commitment I chose to go to, and my mom okayed it and all."
>
> So he pulls out this picture on the front page of the *Post* and says, "You were down at Griffith Stadium yesterday, weren't you?" And I said, "Yes I was." So he says, "Turn in your uniform, you're off the team. I can't have players missing practice for their own … whatever." So I said sorry about that and turned in my uniform.
>
> So I went out for it [baseball] next year, and the coach says, "Okay, you can go out for it and all, but I have to have your assurance that you won't miss games or practices for other games or batboy duties, or anything at Griffith Stadium." And I said, "Okay."
>
> So that day [of tryouts] was Opening Day [of 1959] and Jim Ryan, who was another batboy, filled in for me, and he caught the first pitch from President Eisenhower. And to this day, I always tell him, "Half that ball is mine!"
>
> So, it was a result of Roy's home run that I got into all that trouble and I've told that story many, many times.[19]

International Star

Roy's star was really on the rise in 1958. He was besieged not only with requests for local television, radio and newspaper interviews, but with requests from international venues as well.

On April 24, Roy and Albie Pearson participated in the first trans-Pacific baseball interview in history. The national radio station of Japan, NHK, partnered with the U.S. Information Agency to do a series of interviews between Americans in various walks of life and their Japanese counterparts. The Japanese radio officials asked that the first program of the new series be about baseball.

The interview was filmed simultaneously in Tokyo and at Griffith Stadium before the start of a three-day Senators-Yankees series. Roy and Albie fielded questions from Masato Saito, sports director of NHK, and Sotaro Suzuki, sports columnist and part owner of the Tokyo Giants baseball team. Pearson, always quick with a quip, asked a question of the interviewers: "Since you in Japan are a day ahead of us by the clock, who won today's game to be played between the Yankees and us?"

With the ice thoroughly cracked, the two Japanese broadcasters went on to ask the men a variety of questions about where they were hitting in the lineup, where they liked to play (Roy said he preferred first base) and what size bats they used and when. Roy and Albie handled themselves with grace and aplomb in this new and history-making experience.[20]

Roy was specifically asked to appear on this broadcast because of an article by Robert Creamer, "The Art of Hitting," which appeared in the March 31, 1958, issue of *Sports Illustrated* magazine. This was the second in a series of "how to" articles entitled "Big League Secrets," featuring some of the greatest baseball players of the time. Part one featured Brooklyn Dodgers ace Sal Maglie on pitching. Part two went to Roy on hitting. Part three had Milwaukee Braves great Del Crandell on catching. Part four went to Yankees legend Gil McDougald on playing the infield, and part five had Phillies anchorman Richie Ashburn explaining the outfield and base running.

"Waiting is the secret to hitting," said Roy in the article. "It's something like skeet shooting. You react after it goes poong! There's a point in skeet shooting where you have a shot, but the longer you wait up to that point, the surer your aim is."

Roy went on, with the aid of many beautiful hand-drawn illustrations, to explain what to look for, how to stand, how to hold your hands, how to understand the strike zone (as well as the umpire's view of it!), and what size and weight bat to use, as well as providing many other pieces of sage advice.

But in simplification, his whole approach was: watch the ball, see the ball, hit the ball. "The better you are at watching the pitch as it comes to you, the longer you can wait before you swing. And it's important—waiting as long as you can before committing yourself," Creamer quoted him as saying.

Looking back on the article, Roy commented,

> My roommate, Jim Lemon, and I would talk about hitting all the time. Whenever we'd get together with other teammates or with other guys from other teams, all we'd talk about was hitting. That's all Ted [Williams] would talk about! Studying the pitcher's mannerism, watching how he let the ball go [what they call now the "release point"], what he'd throw you when in the count and so on. Ted said to watch them *all* the time.

The article went a long way toward cementing the fact that Roy had become a respected and feared hitter in the league, deserving to be mentioned in the same breath with Williams and Mantle.

Oh, Oh, Oh, It's Magic!

It wasn't in his job description, but Cookie Lavagetto had to become Mandrake the Magician to try to keep the Senators at least competitive for the season.

When Roy went down with a calf pull in May, so did almost all of the team's run production. Although Roy's home run output was still lagging a bit in May, he was getting timely hits and driving in runs without the benefit of a lot of homers. However, there was precious little run support elsewhere in the lineup. After the calf pull, with Roy out for almost three weeks, Lavagetto was forced to bring Rocky Bridges, usually a seventh- or eighth-place hitter, up to the third spot to try to create some run production. Neil Chrisley filled in for Roy in the outfield, as well as Faye Throneberry, called up from Indianapolis, to help out when Albie Pearson went down with a case of the mumps.

On the field, the situation was almost identical. Herb Plews had been positioned at third, due to the .190 performance of Ed Yost, and Ken Aspromonte took over at second; however, Aspromonte failed to produce with his bat, so Lavagetto moved Plews back to second, and reinstated Yost for better defense (at least) at third. Added to the mix, Norm Zauchin went down with a shoulder injury mid-season, causing Lavagetto to bring in light-hitting Julio Becquer at first base. In the outfield, Pearson and Lemon were adequate, but too many balls were getting through the gap. Pearson hit well, but Lemon did not, hitting singles instead of homers and striking out too many times per at-bat.[21]

Running out of rabbits to pull out of the hat, Lavagetto tried to swing a deal to get at least one healthy arm in the outfield by swapping Ed Yost for Indians slugger Rocky Colavito, but Indians General Manager Frank Lane also demanded Pedro Ramos, which would have decimated an already weak pitching staff.[22] Ramos and Pascual had been handling the bulk of the work of the pitching staff, doing good work in the middle of the year, along with Russ Kemmerer and Hal Griggs. However, lack of run support had cost them wins and given them high ERAs. Fortunately, magician Lavagetto was able to swap Eddie Cicotte's grandnephew, Al Cicotte, for Tigers reliever Vito Valentinetti, in order to shore up the relief corps of Tex Clevenger, Bud Byerly, and submariner Dick Hyde, who was having an All-Star year.

Once Roy came back, though, it was Katie bar the door. He had a June that would be the rival of "The Mick," banging out 11 round-trippers and driving in 24 runs.

For some reason, Roy had been in a drought in Boston, going homerless at Fenway since May of 1956. But this too did pass. On August 6, he took Boston's Tom Brewer deep twice for home runs number 29 and 30, then hit number 31 off Frank Sullivan the next day.

"I don't know what the problem was at Fenway," said Roy in an interview. "I loved playing there. If I coulda gone anywhere to play, it would have been Boston. That short left field was perfect for me."

More for the Record Books

Monday, June 2, 1958, would mark another milestone for Roy. With no one on in the top of the fourth inning, he pounded a Jack Harshman fast ball into the deep left field bleachers of Baltimore's Memorial Stadium to break up a 0–0 tie and start the Senators on the way to a 2–1 victory over the Orioles. It was not only the 163rd homer of his career, but also his 128th homer as a Senator, passing Goose Goslin's 127 and setting the new Senators all-time home run record.

It also seemed to be the impetus the team needed to get out of the aforementioned slump. Rocky Bridges raised his batting average to .305, Albie Pearson began hitting again, going 2-for-5 in that Baltimore game with an RBI, and big Jim Lemon found his home run swing again.

Sweetest of all, in the bottom of the sixth inning of that Orioles game, Rocky Bridges snared a wicked line drive off the bat of Brooks Robinson to start a triple play, crushing an Orioles rally and getting pitcher Hall Griggs out of a big jam. It was a feat the Senators had not accomplished since 1954.[23]

A Dream Come True

Every baseball team has diehard fans of every age, but the stars seem to shine the brightest in the eyes of young followers. Such is the case today for the young women and men who become batgirls and batboys—and such was also the case for Bill Turner, batboy for the Senators from 1956 to 1959.

"I had always wanted to be a baseball player from ever since I could remember, so it was a dream come true to me," Turner said.

> It was everything you could imagine. They were my heroes and I was standing there, shining their shoes and givin' them their bats. And my last year, I pitched batting practice for the pitchers, so I kinda felt like I was one of them. It was just a marvelous dream. The only reason I didn't do it for a year or so was I ended up going to the U of M and playin' baseball for them, and of course, they traveled, and of course, I couldn't do both, so I just had to give it up. It was just … a dream.

Asked how he ended up as a batboy, Turner said,

> Well, that's a funny story in itself. Do you know the name Moss Collins? Woodside Elementary School had a summer athletic [camp] softball and all like that, and Moss was our coach. And he worked in the concession stands [at Griffith Stadium] and I use to bug him when I was 13, 14 years old, "I wanna go down and work at the concession stands." So finally he says, "If you get a social security card, let me know." So I got a SS card and he says, "Okay, you can come down and I'll get you a job." But the concession stand he got me was underneath the stadium behind home plate, so I couldn't see the stadium, so it was like being in a basement all day. So what happened was, the bat boy then was a fella by the name of Alden Lerner, and he would come to the stand to get hot dogs for the fellas who weren't playin' or for the bullpen, and so I got to know him. So at the end of the year, they were home for their last home schedule, and Alden came, and I said, "Okay, well I guess I'll see you next year." But he says, "No, I'll be goin' away to college so I won't be doin' it next year." So I said, "Oh, who's gonna take your place?" And he says, "I don't know," and I said, "Boy, I'd love to have that job." So he says, "Come on with me, and I'll take you to the clubhouse and introduce you to Freddie Baxter," who was the clubhouse manager. And I went there and met Freddie and all, and he took my name and number and all, and he said, "Call me next March if you're interested, and when we come up from Florida [after spring training] if you're interested, it's yours." So, that's how that happened! Very serendipitously!

Turner wasn't in it for the money. He and the other batboys were paid only $2.50 per game, but they did get tips.

> Well, they weren't very high tippers in those days, but we got some tips. At the end of the year, we'd get like 20 bucks from the players, somethin' like that, but we didn't get a whole lot of tips. Occasionally, you would do something out of the ordinary and they'd certainly tip you for that, like this one time Jimmy Ryan, one of the ball boys went to go get some of the players' laundry at the dry cleaners around the corner, and he'd get some tips for that. But no, we didn't get a lot of tips back then. But it wasn't the money. I would have paid them to do it.[24]

Every kid's dream job! Jim Ryan, Bill Turner, and Bob Farmer as Senators batboys in 1958 (courtesy Bill Turner).

The Happy Harmonizers

June 6, 1958, dawned drizzly and overcast in Washington, D.C. Roy Sievers, Albie Pearson, Jim Lemon, Russ Kemmerer, and Tex Clevenger, dressed in sparkling white Senators home uniforms, assembled at nearly the crack of dawn in front of the Reflecting Pool on the National Mall. They were bleary-eyed after an extra-innings loss to the Athletics the night before, but they were not there to play ball. They were there to sing.

Along with our intrepid crooners came Howard Devron, accordionist extraordinaire and dean of the society dance bands. Devron had probably been up into the wee hours as well, playing for one of the many society soirees that he booked with regularity. Rounding out the "band" came Senators play-by-play man Bob Wolff with his ukulele.[25]

Wolff was no stranger to the limelight. He had started singing and playing his ukulele with the Duke Ambassadors Jazz Band during his undergraduate days at Duke University. More than that, he wanted to play baseball; however, in 1938, on a baseball scholarship at Duke, he broke his ankle sliding into second base. While convalescing, he started hosting a campus radio show, "Your Duke Parade," on local NBC affiliate WDNC. In an interview, Wolff related how his coach, Jack Coombs, said, "I've never seen an arm or a leg outlast a voice. If you wanna make the big leagues, keep talking."[26]

So Wolff began his broadcasting career in 1939, while still attending Duke. By 1947, he had signed on with the DuMont Network's WTTG to do play-by-play with the Senators, becoming their pioneering television voice. By 1949, he was doing Maryland University and Washington Capitols bas-

Howard Deveron (accordion), "Tex" Clevenger, Jim Lemon. Russ Kemmerer, Roy Sievers, "Angelic" Albie Pearson, and Senators broadcaster Bob Wolff warble a happy tune in the early hours of the morning of June 6, 1958, on the nationally syndicated "Today" show, hosted by Dave Garraway (photograph from the private collection of Bob Wolff).

ketball, college and pro football, and, along with radio legend Arch MacDonald, Senators radio and TV.

> I would bring my ukulele with me on the long road trips, just to break up the boredom. I'd get a bunch of guys together and just start to harmonize on popular songs of the day. Guys would come and go with the team, but the reputation and fun of the group got around, so guys would come up and ask to audition. Can you imagine now asking players to join a singing group? They'd think you were deranged or ask you how much you were going to pay!

"The Singing Senators," as they were called, had become so popular that Wolff was booking them at functions all over the metropolitan area. On this day, however, they had assembled at the Reflecting Pool to go on national television. Wolff had arranged for the group to perform live on the *Today* show on NBC affiliate WRC Channel 4. Dave Garraway, avuncular host of the show, would set up and introduce them, and they would have a full seven-minute spot on each of the three one-hour segments of the show.

"Angelic" Albie Pearson sang lead tenor and did a solo on Cole Porter's "Night and Day." Lemon and Kemmerer took some melodies, while Sievers and Wolff supplied support in the tenor section. Pitcher Clevenger held down the baritone and bass duties. Crooning such tuneful ditties as *Take Me Out to the Ball Game, Peg of My Heart, For Me and My Gal, I Want a Girl, Heart of My Heart, Carolina in the Morning,* and several more, the boys were the hit of the show.[27]

It proved to be a good omen. The boys went out and beat the Tigers on June 7 and again on June 8. "Yeah, the Singing Senators. I remember that," said Roy. "We got to be pretty good. I liked singing with the guys back then. We could sing pretty good for a bunch of ballplayers. Albie had a great voice, I tell you. We had fun. Made me happy to be in Washington."

Remembering those times, Wolff spoke of Roy in glowing terms:

> Sievers was a full baseball player in every sense of the word. I don't think I have ever met a nicer guy in baseball. As a batter—most home run hitters have that long swing, they come way back, a big full motion, and come through and hit the ball and keep the swing going through. Sievers was what you'd call a "wrist" hitter. He took a short swing, but the power [was] when he moved his wrists in the right way; short, right close to the ball, like a Joe Louis punch. That was the power that gave him home runs; short, compact, powerful swing, like a right cross to the jaw.[28]

There's No Business Like Show Business

Creative people, songwriters, playwrights, and writers love to pick up on aphorisms like the one penned by Charles Dryden with reference to the

1904 Washington Senators: "Washington—first in war, first in peace, and last in the American League." Sayings like that one are powerful fuel for the imaginative fires.

Roy Sievers came to the Washington Senators in 1954 and quickly broke the franchise home run record in his first year on the team. So is it any a wonder that, in that same year, University of Maryland graduate and longtime Senators fan John Douglass Wallop wrote the best-seller *The Year the Yankees Lost the Pennant*?

In that tale, Joe Boyd, a middle-aged real estate dealer and long-suffering Washington Senators fan, laments in front of his TV set each night: "If we just had one hitter, one long ball hitter, we could beat those damn Yankees! I'd sell my soul for a long ball hitter." No sooner has he uttered the words than a "Mr. Applegate" appears and offers to turn him into the great slugger "Joe Hardy" to play for the Senators—in return for his immortal soul.

This Faustian legend was adapted for the stage by Mr. Wallop and legendary Broadway writer George Abbott. Music was penned by Richard Adler and Jerry Ross, who wrote the 1953 hit "Rags to Riches" for a young Tony Bennett and the music to the 1954 smash Broadway hit *Pajama Game*. In May of 1955, *Damn Yankees* premiered on Broadway to sellout crowds.

In 1957, Roy Sievers set the Senators' franchise record of 42 home runs. So in 1958, George Abbott and Stanley Donen wrote and directed the film adaptation of the show for Warner Brothers pictures. The entire Broadway cast went out to Hollywood to do the filming, with one exception. Handsome matinee idol Tab Hunter was cast in the Joe Hardy role in place of Stephen Douglass.

There was only one problem: Hunter looked pathetic swinging a bat and didn't have a clue how to hit! Who better to act as a stand-in than a bona fide slugger like our own Roy Sievers?

Although the film's interior and some exterior scenes were filmed in the old minor league Wrigley Field in Los Angeles, the live action shots were of Sievers hitting at Griffith Stadium and Detroit's Tiger Stadium. Watching the film, one can't help but notice the number "2" on his back! One interesting side note: Joe Hardy was a southpaw. To make the right-handed Roy appear to swing left-handed, the film producers dressed him in a mirror-image uniform. The image was then reversed in the production phase.[29]

"Yes, that's me swinging the bat in the movie," Roy recalled. "I didn't go out to Hollywood. I met the cast one night up in New York during a road trip. They were all very nice, and I got some pictures taken with the cast. They were a lot of fun."

Roy had truly become the toast of the town. "I was hangin' around with a lot of stars at the time: Tommy Dorsey, Eddie Fisher, Milton Berle, Bob Hope. Sinatra stopped his show one time in Las Vegas to introduce me from the audience."

"I met Rita Hayworth at this function in New York one time. Boy! She was a looker!" he said with a gleam in his eye.

Roy, the Slugging Senator

In 1958, Roy would become instrumental in reviving a great national entertainment.

The National Congressional Baseball Game had been an annual charity fundraising game in Washington since its inception in 1909 by Representative John Tener of Pennsylvania. Tener, a former professional ballplayer, tapped into the nation's growing obsession with organized baseball to start this very successful contest. The Democrats ruled the game for the first six years. The game became such a success that ultimately it was broadcast on the radio, starting in 1928. It continued, with interruptions during the Depression and World War II, until Speaker of the House Sam Rayburn finally ended it in 1958, citing injuries, physical strain, and the interruption of Senate business.

Not wanting to see it die, Charlie Brotman tried to revive it. Brotman was the public address announcer for the Senators, as well as the announcer for all of the Presidential Inaugural parades. Using his connections with Congressmen, he tried to drum up interest in staging the game on his own, but could not reach a "quorum" of participants. So he decided instead to stage a home run hitting contest between Mickey Mantle and his New York congressman and Roy Sievers and his congressman from Missouri. The contest was a tremendous success, with Mickey beating out Roy by one homer.

When asked about the hitting contest, Roy replied, "Yea, Charlie Brotman come up to me and asked if I would like to be in a hittin' contest with Mickey. Hell, I'd been in a hittin' contest with him since I come to the Senators in '54. I said sure, and we had some fun at the park. I didn't know it was gonna turn into a big thing. We was just havin' some fun before one of our games."

After that event, Brotman had all the Congressional participants he could want. The new Speaker of the House, John McCormack, with help from Brotman and a new Capitol Hill newspaper, *Roll Call*, revived the game in 1962.[30] To date, the Republicans hold a narrow margin of victory, 41 to 40, over the Democrats.

One Last Insult

With the 1958 season in the record books, Roy could look back proudly, having hit 39 home runs with 108 RBI, and batting .295. It was nearly a carbon copy of 1957. But even with all of those great numbers, Calvin Griffith wanted

Sievers, the "swinging" stunt double for Tab Hunter in the movie version of "Damn Yankees," shows off his Joe Hardy–like form for another appreciative hometown crowd (photograph from the 1959 Senators yearbook).

Sievers to take a ten percent pay cut, saying he did not lead the league in any offensive categories.

Griffith's salary wrangling with Sievers was part and parcel of his tight-fisted operating style. Bill Turner, the erstwhile Senators batboy, was affected by it too.

> In the summer, when the other teams come in, especially New York, Boston, I noticed their bat boys came with them. So I [asked them], "Oh, so you guys travel with the team when school's out?" And they said, "Yeah, the team brings us with them on a trip, about a three stop trip every year." So I went to Freddy Baxter [the clubhouse manager] and asked, "Can I go on a trip with [the team]?" So he says I'd have to clear it with the front office. So I asked, "Can you do that for me?" and he says, "No, you can go up there and do it yourself." So I went up there and had a meeting. It wasn't with Calvin, it was somebody in the office, and I said, "Do you think you could ask Mr. Griffith if I could go on a trip like the other bat boys?" and he said, "Okay, I'll let you know."
>
> So he comes back and says, "Turner, we're going to Baltimore over the weekend. If you can get there, you can be the bat boy." So I had to drive to Baltimore to be the bat boy; they wouldn't take me on the trip. They wouldn't pay for my fare, which was typical of Griffith management back then.[31]

Recalling his wrangling over salary, Roy said,

> Players got along with the owners pretty well back then. Of course, we were our own agents and it was tough battling those guys. Two of the toughest guys in the world to deal with were [former Browns owner] Bill DeWitt and Calvin Griffith with Washington. They were two of the toughest owners to battle for money. Connie Mack was like that as well. Luckily, I didn't do too bad with them. But I should have done better."

Roy held out of spring training once again, finally settling for $35,000 in March of 1959.

The Zeitgeist

Nineteenth and early twentieth century baseball was the purview of a "spikes high, win at all costs" mentality that permeated both leagues for decades. This was a game for tough men. Get a gash from someone slicing into you with his spikes? No problem: get some tobacco juice and dirt, spread it on the wound, go on and finish the inning.

It was just a game to most of the everyday players, and the owners saw it the same way. The "stars" of the day made between $2000 and $4000 a year and were considered "millionaires" of their times. The rank and file players worked for considerably less, struggling to make ends meet and sometimes working part-time jobs even during the regular season. The club owners were aware of this, and salaries were never quite commensurate with the abilities of the players. Games were played in bare-bones wooden parks with few creature comforts, but providing high profits for the owners.

Although the rowdiness was cleaned up somewhat with the hiring of Judge Kenesaw Mountain Landis to be the Commissioner after the 1919 Black Sox scandal, the "Ty Cobbs" of the league never disappeared. They often went on to become managers.

Clark Griffith, original owner of the Senators, was a product of 19th-century baseball. Born in the Missouri territory in 1869, he grew up, albeit sickly, with four older siblings. He learned about baseball from the soldiers who had returned from the Civil War and started pitching for a local Hoopeston, IL, team at age 17, earning ten dollars in 1886.

Griffith began playing in the American Association in 1891, first for the St. Louis Browns and then for the Boston Reds. In 1893, he was signed to play for Cap Anson's Chicago National League club, staying there for eight years and becoming a true star.

In 1900, he began his foray into baseball management and politics. He was instrumental in the development of the Players Protective Association, an organization ostensibly established to protect ball players' rights, health, and negotiations with club owners. Although it was not successful, it became a catalyst for the establishment of the American League when the owners of the National League turned down the players' petition for a raise in pay. With this ammunition, Griffith had the power to recruit some of the biggest National League stars to help establish the new league in 1901.[32]

Griffith knew that the money was made in baseball through ownership, and the way to ownership, at that time, was through management. Charles Comiskey signed Griffith to manage and be the star pitcher for the new Chicago White Sox in 1901, where he won 24 games and led the team to the pennant. In 1903, he left the White Sox to manage a new team, the New York Highlanders. He pitched and managed there until he retired from playing in 1907, then resigned in 1908. He went on to manage the Cincinnati Reds from 1909 to 1911.

But Griffith ultimately wanted to be an owner, and he would do whatever was necessary to achieve that goal. When Washington Senators manager Jim McAleer made a deal to become president of the Boston Red Sox in 1911, it left a vacancy in DC. Even though the franchise had never had a winning season (sound familiar?), Griffith wanted to be an owner and wanted back into the American League. When his old pals Charles Comiskey and Ban Johnson wouldn't help him out with a loan to buy the club, he literally "mortgaged the ranch" owned by himself and his brother to purchase a ten percent share in the team. He signed on to be their manager in the spring of 1912. He managed the club successfully until 1920, when he raised the funds necessary to own 80 percent of its stock outright. He built the first and only World Series-winning team in Washington history in 1924. The team went on to win the pennant again in 1925 and one last time in 1933, and then were not seen in the first division for a long, long time.[33]

Clark Griffith's relationships with his players, and Calvin Griffith's as well, were governed by a combination of owner parsimony and baseball contract rules. Regarding the former, Bob Wolff remembered:

> Miserly could certainly be the word used, as far as putting money into the ball club. Mr. Griffith [senior] himself lived in a very small home. I don't know where Calvin lived, I never visited his home. But I do know, the ball club existed on, really, on how many hot dogs they sold, how many peanuts they sold. He had all the members of the family working on the refreshment stands, to help with the finances. I guess they had to borrow the money to put the ballpark up. There was so little income coming in. There was no TV income when he began, radio was very small, and Washington, unfortunately, had very few businesses. It was a government town. They could only afford one or two ballplayers who could play well, and the other guys were really just fill-ins.
>
> So when they got the offer to go to Minnesota, they promised them a big TV and radio contract, a new stadium, they promised them all these different things. It was new money into the ball club. He really had no choice. They were criticized for not building the team better because they didn't have the money.[34]

With regard to baseball contracts, control was completely in the hands of the owners because of the reserve clause, which prevented players from exercising any free agency with regard to the teams they played with. Established in an agreement between the National League and the American Association in the 1880s,

> The reserve clause was a clause in player contracts that bound a player to a single team for a long period, even if the individual contracts he signed nominally covered only one season. For most of baseball history, the term of reserve was held to be essentially perpetual, so that a player had no freedom to change teams unless he was given his unconditional release.... Players were forced to accept a system built around the reserve clause. Until the amateur draft was instituted in 1966, amateur players were free to negotiate with any team interested in signing them. For most players, that was the last time in their careers that they had any control over where they played. Once signed to a professional contract, players could be re-assigned, traded, sold, or released at the team's whim. The only negotiating leverage that most players had was to *hold out* at contract time, refusing to play unless their conditions were met.[35]

The reserve clause and many other player issues were routinely challenged almost every decade through attempts to unionize the players. The most serious of these occurred in 1946, when Robert Murphy organized the American Baseball Guild. Murphy, a lawyer and former examiner for the National Labor Relations Board, saw the threat of the Mexican Baseball League as an opportunity for arbitration. Mexican businessman Jorge Pasquel and his brothers used approximately $50 million of their own money to establish the League and then used their wealth to entice professional players from "north of the border" to jump. Many did, including Dodgers catcher Mickey Owen and pitcher Sal Maglie, Giants outfielder Danny Gardella, and Freddie Martin and Max Lanier, pitchers with the St. Louis Cardinals. The major complaints were the horribly low post–War salaries, contracts, severance pay, and poor working conditions.

The Yankees, Dodgers, and Giants filed for a restraining order to stop the Pasquels from raiding their teams; however, in so doing, they brought a lot of undue attention to the reserve clause and its ten-day severance provision. The attorney for the Pasquels argued that Major League Baseball was an illegal monopoly and painted the players' contracts as a form of indentured servitude.

New York State Supreme Court Chief Justice Julius Miller found in favor of the New York teams, but in so doing, he asked many pointed questions concerning the players' contracts. He based his decision upon the sanctity of the contract, not the equity.

These legal wranglings frightened the team owners into acceding to a new $5,500 salary minimum, expense money for training camp and road trips, severance pay, and other contractual adjustments. But Murphy and the players shied away from attacking the reserve clause. Years later, when he'd become active as a player representative, future Hall of Famer Ralph Kiner said the abolition of the clause remained unthinkable. "We never, *never* thought we had a chance of getting rid of it."[36]

So it was this environment into which Roy Sievers was thrust and where he had to play. It was a veritable "put up or shut up" existence. Calvin Griffith fought his players tooth and nail to keep their salaries low in the wake of such luminaries as DiMaggio, Mantle, and Mays, who were steadily pushing the salary boundaries higher and higher.

When asked about the reserve clause, Roy responded:

> I had hurt my shoulder and wasn't sure if I could play no more. When I got traded to Washington, I was just happy to be playing anywhere. There was nothing you could do about it. If you wanted to play ball, the owners had all the power. It was only the big stars like Yogi, Mickey, Whitey, Ted or Willie who had the power to say, "I'd rather sit than sign." The only thing you could do was to play as best you could and try to fight the owners for more money each year.

Life at Home

Once the last out of the last game of the season was made, Roy would look forward to getting back home to Joan and the kids. Life at 7 Forest Home Court was relatively idyllic for the Sievers family. Moline Acres was nestled in the quiet (in those days) northwest suburbs of St. Louis. Roy's son Robin remembers it like this:

> We lived at Forest Home Court until we made the big move to the "country" north on Bellefontaine Avenue. We didn't see [Dad] a lot. He would be gone most of the year and then he would be barnstorming in the winter. We would get to see him in the summertime. We moved a couple of times during the summer, up to Chicago when he was playin' there. We'd all go up there for a couple of months. We did that when he went to Philadelphia as well. Mom would just pack us all up and drive us back and forth.
>
> I was playin' ball a lot so we just stayed here [in St. Louis] all the time. Mom actually taught me how to play ball since dad wasn't around too much. Financially, we didn't realize we were a little bit better off than most people. I would think, back in '57, '58,

Roy with his wife Joan, son Rob and daughter Shawn in their suburban St. Louis home (AP photograph/St. Louis Post Dispatch).

> '59, Dad was makin' good money for the times. He didn't always make that much. Startin' out, Dad had to work a lot of jobs in the off season, layin' carpet and such. And a lot of barnstorming. We were just livin' in a normal neighborhood. It really wasn't anything special. Dad was just a ballplayer and that was his job. We did what we had to do and we didn't feel like we were missin' much.

Both Rob and Shawn agreed that they liked to see their Dad play as much as they could. "I used to love to go to grandpa's house," said Rob. "He didn't have a TV, didn't like 'em. But there he'd be, sittin' in the living room right next to the big Philco radio, listenin' to a ball game every day."

> I remember seein' Dad play a lot of times, especially when he was with Philadelphia, he'd come through here to play the Cardinals. And of course with the White Sox. They had a great television network back then. They called their games on TV so we saw him a lot. I remember those shorts! [Veeck] had them wearin' shorts all the time. And that exploding scoreboard. Everything was just crazy up there. Mom hated the spotlight, and bein' here in St. Louis was good for her. St. Louis was a National League town, and since Dad was playin' up in Washington and then in Chicago, she didn't have any kind of "star status" like the Cardinals' wives had. She was just a regular kinda gal and liked it like that.

Wistfully, Rob said, "We missed him a lot, but you do what ya gotta do."[37]

9

The Times, They Are A-Changin'

The winter of 1958 saw Roy Sievers once again picking up extra money on the barnstorming circuit, but this time it had a decidedly Southern flair.

Roy joined the Bobby Avila All Stars along with his roommate Jim Lemon, Billy O'Dell and Gus Triandos of the Orioles, Jim Bunning, Paul Foytack and Frank Bolling of the Tigers; Cal McLish of the Indians; and Pete Runnels of the Red Sox. Avila, veteran second baseman for the Indians, actually owned a pretty good AA-designated ball club in Mexico City and was considered a hometown hero.

Pitted against the Avila All Stars was a group of the same name led by none other than the great Willie Mays. His collection of luminaries included Elston Howard, Al Smith, George Crowe, Ernie Banks, Harry "Suitcase" Simpson, Jim Pendleton, Gene Baker, Brooks Lawrence, Connie Johnson, Wes Covington, and Frank Barnes. Starting in Monterey on October 14, they followed the warm winter sun to Mexico City, Poza Rica, Puebla, Veracruz, and Merida.[1]

However, in Mexico City things got a little hotter.

In 1958, relations between the United States and Latin America were at an all-time low. The Latin American countries complained that the U.S. was too intent on the Cold War and anti-communism and turned a blind eye to the economic and political needs of Latin Americans. In short, they needed bread, not bullets. They criticized the Americans for supporting many dictators simply because they claimed to be anti-communist. Case in point: the U.S. awarded the Legion of Merit to Venezuelan dictator Marcos Pérez Jiménez in 1954. Jiménez was overthrown by a military coup in January 1958.[2]

In the spring of 1958, President Eisenhower sent Vice President Nixon on a goodwill tour of Latin America, ostensibly to show U.S. support for the region. In Caracas, Nixon's motorcade was stoned, surrounded, and attacked by demonstrators. Nixon barely escaped with his life, and Eisenhower was forced to send a naval squadron to the Caribbean to intervene to save Nixon if necessary. Nixon escaped, but the event served as a poignant wake-up call about the tense relations in Latin America.[3]

Robert C. Hill, the U.S. Ambassador to Mexico, noticed that the boys would be playing in Mexico City and invited Sievers, Mays, and Avila to attend the American part of the International Film Festival. *Sports Illustrated* reported thusly:

> The U.S. Ambassador to Mexico had a rather subtle diplomatic chore to assign to just the right group of men and was casting about to find them. Who filled the bill? Why, three big league ballplayers, naturally.
>
> The problem was that the U.S. part of Mexico's International Film Festival was going badly. From a balcony of the National Auditorium, where the festival was held, a Communist claque hissed and whistled not only at American films, but at American flags as well. Others in the huge auditorium [capacity: 13,000] were taking up the hissing, and the result was an anti–U.S. demonstration.
>
> All this changed, though, when *The Defiant Ones* was shown, the third U.S. offering in the eight-nation festival. It is a moving plea for racial tolerance, and it brought frequent bursts of applause from the Mexican audience. When it ended, Ambassador Robert C. Hill and his pretty wife went from their ambassadorial box to the stage. With them were the three ballplayers to whom the Ambassador had turned for help: Roy Sievers of the Washington Senators, Bobby Avila of the Cleveland Indians, and Willie Mays of the San Francisco Giants.
>
> Avila, a native of Mexico, spends his winters there and enjoys the status of a national hero. Sievers and Mays happened to be in Mexico playing winter baseball. They had watched the movie as guests of Ambassador and Mrs. Hill. On the stage, only Avila made a little speech, in Spanish. The other two just stood there: Willie Mays, a Negro boy from Westfield, Ala., and Roy Sievers, a white boy from St. Louis, side by side with Bobby Avila, who grew up in Veracruz, Mexico; and all three of them stars in big league baseball. Up in the balcony the Communist claque hissed and whistled. But it couldn't make itself heard because there was too much applause.[4]

Larger Than Life

The tour turned into both an international and a financial success for all involved; however, it forced Roy's wife Joan to do double duty for him. Stuck in Mexico for most of October and early November, Roy was unable to attend the myriad speaking and awards events to which he was invited. The YMCA Industrial Athletic Association of St. Louis presented their Outstanding Sportsmanship Award to him on November 5, and Joan was called on to accept on his behalf. Robert Rollins, the association president, presented the award to Roy "because he is the type of a man he is and not just because he's a great player."[5]

Such testimonials to Roy's character were frequent then and are recurring features in the recollections of those who saw him in action. Bill Turner, the Senators' batboy in the late 1950s, shared these memories:

> Who was my favorite player? I know this is gonna sound pre-recorded or something, but Roy Sievers, no question about it. Roy was the type of guy who would go out of his way to come in and pat you on the backside, or on the head and say, "Whadda ya doin' today," or, "Hey, why don't you get busy, you loafer," you know, just make you feel you were part of the team, you know? Most of the players were all good guys, but there were a couple who were like, "You're the bat boy, get outta my way," and like that, but not Roy.
>
> When we were on the on-deck circle, [Roy would] take his bat and sorta tap me on the back, and he'd look at me and say, "Turner, look at that girl in the first row over there. You oughtta try and date her, she's really good lookin.'" And he would point out girls that he thought I oughtta go to, to try and get a date. Cuz he'd say, "You got a date tonight?" and I would sheepishly say, "No, no." He was sort of fatherly like that, but it made me feel like I was one of the guys.
>
> In fact, Roy—not like today's players who you want an autograph or something ya gotta pay 'em five dollars or somethin'—Roy, when the game was over and he went to the parking lot to get his car, he would stand there and sign autographs until the last person was there. And there were a couple of times he had plans with his family after the game, and he would say, "Turner, I can't stand out there for 15 or 20 minutes today," and he'd give me the keys to his car and say, "Go get my car and drive it around back, cuz I gotta go today." So he was definitely my favorite. He was just a good guy.[6]

Phil Wood, noted Washington area sports broadcaster and host of the popular post-game talk show *Nats Talk Live*, speaks of Roy in near-mythic terms.

> Roy Sievers was the first baseball player who ever signed an autograph for me. It would have been 1959, I'm eight years old and we had seats pretty much adjacent to the Senators dugout. I stopped off to buy a baseball; it wasn't an official ball but it was a decent baseball. There was a chain of drugstores in DC called Drug Fair. I bought a baseball at Drug Fair on the Sunday morning before we drove to the park. Roy came out and he basically walked right over to the stands, 'cause there were fans already lined up. He went out of his way to make sure he signed everything he could. And he seemed to be so much larger than life to me. Wearing a major league uniform was the equivalent of wearing a Superman suit. It had that kind of aura to it. Roy was a bona fide hero to all of us. When he was traded to the White Sox, it was like a body blow when I heard he'd been traded.[7]

More of the Same

As 1959 dawned, Roy was holding out once again at the start of spring training over money disputes, and *Sports Illustrated* once again provided its dire predictions for the Senators. Pay special attention to the first two sentences:

The only attraction that keeps that small group of fans wandering back to Griffith Stadium and retains the franchise in Washington is the batting prowess of Roy Sievers. The team's one-man offensive show, Sievers hit one-third of the Senators' home runs (39) and knocked in 108 runs to rank third-best in both categories in the American League. Otherwise, the sole pretense of power Washington can boast of with a straight face comes from two 6-foot 5-inch swingers, Right Fielder Jim Lemon (26 homers) and First Baseman Norm Zauchin. Standing a full foot shorter in the batter's box, tiny Albie Pearson stroked enough singles and doubles to win the league's Rookie of the Year award; because of him, the Senators have an outfielder who can run as well as hit. Scrappy Clint Courtney, who doesn't let the Washington lethargy affect him too much, gives the Senators a solid major league catcher who hits an occasional long ball. The nicest thing to happen in Washington since Dolley Madison was the development of Submarine Pitcher Dick Hyde into the top reliever in baseball. He wasn't too sharp this spring, but last year he won 10 games and saved 19 others to account for just about half the Senators' wins. On top of that, he had a remarkable 1.75 ERA. The long-relief man for the team, Tex Clevenger, appeared in the most games in the league (55) and won nine of them. Pedro Ramos and Camilo Pascual, the Senators' only starting class pitchers, are both able young men—so able, in fact, that the Yankees have expressed interest in both of them.

Weak Spots

They still pay off in baseball on hitting, pitching, fielding and a few other talents like those. The Senators don't have much of any of them. Once again, they finished last in both leagues in pitching and batting, and nothing Washington did over the winter and spring seems likely to change that. New additions Reno Bertoia and Ron Samford have lifetime major league batting averages of .239 and .206 respectively. Infielders Ken Aspromonte and Jose Valdivielso can stop a ball but not hit one. Reserve outfielders Faye Throneberry and Jim Delsing don't scare many pitchers when they walk up to the plate. Jim Lemon hits home runs but he strikes out far too often, and batted only .246 last year. And so on down the line. Once you get past Ramos and Pascual, the list of starting pitchers fades into negligibility. Russ Kemmerer is considered the third man, but he lost 15 games and allowed 4.62 earned runs a game last season. Beyond him there's some hope, but mostly an aching void. Sievers and Lemon are not good outfielders, to phrase it gently. Too many balls that should have been stopped have been skipping through the infield for years. Herb Plews plays second base because he can hit, which is a sad commentary on the hitting skills of the other infielders.

The Outlook

Manager Cookie Lavagetto knows he is not going to set the world on fire, or even singe it, with these Senators. If there's a surer prospect than the Yankees finishing first it's the Senators finishing last.[8]

Cookie Lavagetto spent that spring prestidigitating once again. He had told Calvin Griffith in late October 1958 that he would be putting Roy on first base permanently in 1959 and that Griffith needed to find him a left fielder. Lavagetto had been less than impressed with the hitting output of Norm Zauchin and Julio Becquer, who had shared first base duties in 1958.[9]

Lavagetto decided to move Jim Lemon to left to cover Roy's old territory, and Albie Pearson over to right, where he preferred to play. He initially intended to give rookie Dan Dobbek a good look-see in center field. Dobbek had impressed both Lavagetto and Chuck Dressen in spring camp in 1957, but then had to report to the military and missed the whole season. However, the Dobbek plan soon went by the boards, as rookie phenom Bob Allison so impressed Lavagetto with his arm that the manager shifted Pearson back to center and put Allison in right.[10]

Gone to the Tigers were "Steady" Eddie Yost and Rocky Bridges. Hoping that young Harmon Killebrew had been seasoned enough in AAA ball the previous season, Lavagetto gave him a long look at third base. The manager was desperate for more power in the lineup, and Killebrew had proven he could hit the long ball.

Lavagetto put the handsome Reno Bertoia at second base and minor league veteran Ron Samford at shortstop, then swapped them around during the spring, along with Jose Valdivielso, hoping to find a combination that worked with both bat and glove.

"Scrap Iron" Clint Courtney reported to training camp battered and bruised. He had rolled his half-ton truck down an embankment on his Louisiana farm, throwing himself out the windshield in the process. He would be platooned with another bespectacled backstop, Steve Korshack, as well as Ed Fitz Gerald and former Browns and Tigers catcher J. W. Porter. Lavagetto also gave Porter a look at left field.

The usual suspects in the pitching corps all returned: Pascual, Ramos, Griggs, Kemmerer, Fisher, Hyde, Abernathy, Romonosky, and others. Chuck Stobbs, one-time Senators ace who had been sent to St. Louis, got a new pair of glasses and convinced Calvin Griffith to give him a shot with a superb "what have you got to lose" proposition.[11]

A healthy Sievers would belie his usual slow spring start, smacking five home runs and leading the team with a .377 batting average during the exhibition season. With the departure of Eddie Yost to Detroit, Roy was rewarded by being named team captain.[12]

And Away We Go

April 9, 1959, came up cloudy and dry, yet turned an unseasonably hot 87 degrees by game time, as 28,000-plus Senators fans watched Vice President Richard Nixon chuck a long first pitch almost to the third base bag, leaving the Orioles and Senators players scrambling for the Presidential souvenir. Pitcher Pedro Ramos elbowed his way into the presidential box to shake hands with the Vice President "for good luck." It worked.[13]

Ramos was masterful, allowing only two runs on seven hits. The Senators were more than up to the task, plating nine runs on 14 hits. Norm Zauchin, who caught fire during the spring, had convinced manager Lavagetto he was the first baseman to beat, so Lavagetto had moved Roy Sievers to left field for the home opener. Roy singled in Reno Bertoia for the first run in the bottom of the first. Harmon Killebrew started his Hall of Fame journey by taking Jack Harshman deep in the fourth inning, and Bertoia added another long ball in the fourth. Ramos actually took a shutout into the ninth, but gave up a double to Bob Boyd and then a homer to Gus Triandos. The Senators prevailed, 9–2, even though they fell victim to a rare triple play, the first of its kind in an Opening Day game.[14]

All in all, it was a propitious start for our intrepid Senators. But you know how the saying goes.

Pain and Powerball

If ever there was a roller coaster year for Roy, it was 1959. Just when he thought he was going up, an injury would send him back down to start over again. In mid-April, while lunging for an outside pitch in Baltimore, he wrenched his back and was sidelined for nearly a week. Then, coming back in Detroit in early May, he went all-out for an Al Kaline long ball and crashed into the chain link fence in Tiger Stadium. He recalled it vividly: "I was playin' Detroit in '59. I went back for a ball in left field and hit the fence and heard my shoulder go snap! And I thought, 'Oh no! I've done it again.' Put me on the bench again."

This injury sidelined him for nearly three weeks. One good thing did come from it, though: Lavagetto put him at first base for the rest of the season to save his ailing arm. This was still a positive for the club, since Norm Zauchin had fallen into a protracted slump.[15] On July 19, Kansas City's Jerry Lumpe spiked Roy on a routine groundout at first base. This one put him on the bench for five days. Roy remembered: "That one was pretty bad. I had to have stitches. Doctor said if it had been an inch lower it would have cut my Achilles tendon. I could have been out of baseball for life."

All these injuries would drastically deplete Roy's home run total for the year. He had only a single homer each in April and May, but came back with five in June and nine in July. Slumping badly, he had only a single homer in August, usually his most productive month. He rallied in September and hit four long balls to end the year. All told, Roy lost one-quarter of his season to injuries.

Kansas City Athletics Jerry Lumpe spikes Roy on a routine groundout in a July 19, 1959, game. Roy was sidelined for a week with stitches in his heel (© 1959, Richard Darcey/*The Washington Post*, courtesy Phil Wood).

But not to worry. A phenomenon was occurring in the nation's capital. By the end of May, 22-year-old Harmon Killebrew was leading the league with 18 home runs. Rookie center fielder and former University of Kansas fullback Bobby Allison had accounted for nine long balls, and veteran slugger Jim Lemon had taken AL pitchers deep 12 times. With a healthy Sievers contributing five dingers in June, the quartet was no longer "The Singing Senators" but became "The Fearsome Foursome." One Washington scribe also dubbed them "the new SALK shots" after Dr. Jonas Salk, who invented the polio serum. SALK stood for Sievers, Allison, Lemon and Killebrew.[16]

The four big lumberjacks became a real shot in the arm (all pun intended) for the championship-starved fans in Washington. The papers abounded with talk of a new home run Murderers' Row to rival the 1927 Yankees (158), the 1930 Cubs (171), the 1937 Tigers (150) and the 1956 Yankees (190). Hopes ran high for a first-division finish, and some fans were camping out for World Series tickets.

By the end of the season, Killebrew tied the Indians' Rocky Colavito for the home run crown with 42 homers, Lemon posted 33 dingers, Allison contributed 30 and Roy hit 21. They would nearly lead the league in homers, falling only four short to the Cleveland Indians, 167 to 163.

However...

Unfortunately, all these big hitters could not a team make. When Roy slumped, so did the rest of the team. Roy was the type of "little engine who could" player who picked up steam as he went along, as evidenced by his usually strong output in the summer months. But when he got hurt, it would take him that much longer to get back into the swing of things. Less noticed than his prodigious home run output was his ability to drive in runs, the timely singles and doubles that could move runners in or along, but that ability was just as important to such success as the Senators had.

The team's problems basically boiled down to two facts:

- Aside from the Fearsome Foursome, nobody on the team was hitting.
- Even with all the homers, the Fearsome Foursome still didn't drive in many runs.

The home run totals looked like this:

	HR	*RBI*	*Hits*	*Solo HR*	*RBI HR*	*Average*
Killebrew	42	105	13	19	23	.242
Lemon	33	100	148	17	16	.279
Allison	30	85	149	21	9	.261
Sievers	21	49	93	15	6	.242
Totals	**126**	**339**	**532**	**72**	**54**	

The team totals for the Senators and the Orioles looked like this:

	HR	*RBI*	*Hits*	*Runs*	*Average*	*W/L*
Senators	163	580	1,205	614	.237	63–91 (8th)
Orioles	109	514	1,240	551	.238	74–80 (6th)

The Senators out-slugged everyone in the American League except the Indians, but managed an anemic 1,205 hits and a pathetic .237 team batting

The 1958 Senators team photograph. A smiling Roy Sievers is in the middle row, fourth from the left (courtesy Bill Turner).

average, the worst in the league. They outpaced the floundering Orioles in almost every category, yet still kept a death grip on last place. Courtney, Pearson, and Zauchin, big run producers and hitters from 1958, all had a bad year. The lone bright spot was second baseman Ken Aspromonte, who chimed in with 82 hits for the year. Low output league-wide, but he led all the other hitters on the team outside of the Big Four.

Bob Allison had a career year and won the AL "Rookie of the Year" Award, the second in a row for the Senators and the first time a last-place team won that title back to back. Camilo Pascual won 17 games, led the league in shutouts with six, and placed second in the league with a 2.63 ERA. Harmon Killebrew tied for the league's home run lead with 42 homers. Jim Lemon hit 33 home runs and did NOT strike out 100 times or more, as he had done in the past.

But overall, the weak pitching, weak interior hitting, and sloppy defense led to another lackluster last-place season.[17]

Friends in High Places

Despite his up-and-down season, Roy still had one true and ardent admirer: Vice President Richard Nixon.

In July 1959, Nixon was sent to Moscow by President Eisenhower to open the American National Exhibition at Sokolniki Park. The exhibition was part of a cultural exchange program, an effort to promote understanding between the two countries. Prime Minister Nikita Khrushchev seized the opportunity to rail against the U.S. Congress's recent resolution condemning the Soviet Union's "control over captive peoples of Eastern Europe." In the "kitchen debates" (so named because they occurred primarily in the kitchen of the model American home that was on display), Nixon and Khrushchev then engaged in a Cold War back-and-forth, gleefully filmed and recorded by the media. In the end, both men backed off, probably realizing too late that their voices had been raised a tad higher than appropriate.[18]

It just so happened that the Senators got themselves into a protracted slump right about the same time Nixon went to Russia. Starting on July 19, the team lost 22 out of 23 games, not breaking out of the slump until August 12.

Nixon was probably one of the most knowledgeable baseball fans to occupy the White House. He kept up on the players' stats religiously, especially Roy's. When he heard about the slump, he put a plan into action. "Yeah, Nixon said he called the White House when he was comin' back from overseas," Roy said in an interview. "And said 'I want Lemon, Killebrew, Allison, and Sievers out to the airport.' We were all there waitin' for him to land."

A large group of people turned out at Andrews Air Force Base in suburban Maryland to cheer home the conquering hero, Mr. Sievers being among the throng. Roy was one of the first people that Mr. Nixon spied in the crowd, and he broke ranks from established arrival protocols to personally go over and talk to the Fearsome Foursome.

> Yeah, Nixon come over to us and says, "What the hell is wrong with you guys!?" And I says, "I don't know, Mr. Nixon, we're just not hittin' too good and our pitchin's not so good either." Then he says, "I'll tell you what, I'll be out there tomorrow night." Usually when he come out to a game we would win, but we lost that night and a few more after that. But he invited me over to the White House for a lunch. Never forget that. Boy that was somethin'!

Roy waxed philosophic in an August interview with Shirley Povich, dean of the Washington sports writers:

> Slumps are something you can't fight. The more you worry, the tighter you get. I'm not going to let down, but it looks as if I'm going to have to chalk up this year as a bad

one. I've been in slumps before, but it seems the hawks got me this year. I haven't been able to do anything right. But I feel fine now and I'm sure I can come back.[19]

Calvin Griffith was charitable to the big slugger. "He's always trying, and he's a fine team man. Besides, he's done a lot for the youngsters like Harmon Killebrew and Bob Allison." Griffith maintained that he didn't intend to repeat the mistake he had made with Pete Runnels—trading off a player after a bad year.[20]

However, it seemed that Griffith was talking out of both sides of his mouth, as he was wont to do.

The Trading Game

In March of 1959, in the midst of a lot of trade rumors, Griffith had held firm on Roy:

I would not trade Sievers or any of my top three pitchers ... for second-line material.... If I took several second-flighters in a package deal for Sievers, like the White Sox offered me, I wouldn't be as well off as I am with just Sievers. At least I know that he's one of the great sluggers in the league. He's an attraction. He means more to us than having three or four mediocre players.... The way things stand right now, I'd say that Sievers is going to remain with the Senators, because we're not going to give cream for skimmed milk.[21]

In June of 1959, Bill Veeck, who had become part-owner of the White Sox in March and who had nurtured and mentored the young Roy Sievers in 1949, desperately wanted his bat in the White Sox's pennant contending lineup. He proposed a deal that reportedly would send outfielders Al Smith and "Jungle" Jim Rivera, pitcher Ray Moore, one of two catchers (Johnny Romano or Earl Battey), and one of two infielders (Billy Goodman or Earl "Torgy" Torgeson), plus $250,000 in cash, for Sievers, catcher J. W. Porter, and a second-line pitcher.

"The monetary value of players and cash for Sievers alone was estimated at around $400,000, with the total offer for three Washington players figured at $500,000," scribe Edgar Munzel noted. After hours on the phone, right before the 1:00 AM trading deadline, Griffith inexplicably turned Veeck down.[22] Veeck went out and traded for outfielder Minnie Miñoso and third baseman Gene Freese. But that was in June.

In the "what have you done for me lately" world of Calvin Griffith, Roy Sievers had become damaged goods. The term used by the media was "expendable." His injury-fueled slump of a year was the catalyst that allowed Griffith to burn all bonds that might have held him to Sievers. Deemed "untouchable" in 1957, by the end of the 1959 season Roy and Jim Lemon and Pedro Ramos had become chum for the trade waters.

At the 1959 winter meetings in Florida, the club owners voted to open up trading across the leagues. Tired of the "same old warmed over deals" offered by all the American League clubs, Griffith started talking with the National League's Dodgers, Phillies, Cubs, and Pirates. Griffith was adamant that he wanted front-line players for his big hitters, Sievers and Lemon.[23]

Buzzie Bavasi, general manager of the new Los Angeles Dodgers, offered utility man Don Zimmer, pitcher Danny McDevitt, and rookie outfielder Ron Fairly for Sievers, Russ Kemmerer and Reno Bertoia. Griffith said he wanted Bob Lillis instead of Zimmer, and things went very cold from there.[24]

Casey Stengel, a whimsical double-talker of Herculean proportions, mused to the sports writers:

> I could win the pennant in 1960 if I could make deals for Sievers and Frank Lary, the Detroit pitcher, and just keep 'em on the bench. Sievers likes to punish our pitchers and Lary makes a living out of baffling my hitters. I figure that getting them out of circulation would give me enough to win!

Stengel offered $250,000, second baseman Andy Carey, and a shortstop named Fritzie Brickell for Roy's services. "Second line" players, as Griffith explained it. He was adamant that he wasn't going to trade Sievers or his big arms, Pascual, Ramos, or Hyde, for "scrubs." He wanted All-Star Gil McDougald included in any deal he made with the Yankees. General Manager George Weiss said no.[25]

Not As Long This Time

Roy didn't barnstorm in the winter of 1959, choosing instead to stay home with Joan and the kids and working on getting physically better. He spent several months running, exercising and playing handball with fellow St. Louisans Stan Musial, Red Schoendienst, Norm Siebern, and trainer extraordinaire Frank Bauman.

Cal Griffith knew he would be having big salary discussions before spring camp opened in February. Allison and Killebrew had each been signed for a paltry $7,500 at the beginning of 1959. Both had had tremendous seasons and surely wouldn't be signing for anything near that figure for the 1960 campaign. In addition, 32-year-old veteran Jim Lemon had cut down his strikeouts a bit and had his best year to date.

During February, Roy, Bob Allison, and Jim Lemon were all holding out for better money. In an interview with the *St. Louis Post Dispatch*, Sievers said, "I think I was the last to sign the past four years, and it's beginning to look like I'll be last again this time."[26]

But Roy knew his bad year in 1959 didn't give him much leverage, and with all of the trade rumors running around, he had to act quickly. Surprising all the scribes, he reported on time to the 1960 spring training camp in Orlando and signed his contract for $33,000, a cut of $2,000 from his 1959 salary.

Roy reported to camp willing and eager to start anew. Always a big draw with the fans, he decided to try his hand at sports broadcasting and was hired by WLOF-AM radio in Orlando to do a nightly five-minute sports talk show.[27]

Time to Move On

It was no secret that Calvin Griffith was unhappy with Washington as a baseball town, despite his protestations to the contrary. However, the situation was more his fault than not. He relied on Joe Cambria, his Cuban scout, to find him cheap ballplayers, and with a few exceptions that's what he got. The Senators' farm system was being sold piecemeal and lacked any talent to speak of. Griffith's own monumental mismanagement of player trades and deals was legendary. Weak hitting, fielding, and pitching led to lackluster teams, despite Roy Sievers's heroic bat. All of this led to dwindling revenues and a disappointed fan base. Add to this a dank, cavernous stadium in a depressed neighborhood, devoid of adequate parking, and one can see why, when other cities came calling, Griffith would respond.

Ball clubs moving to different cities was unheard of in the first half of the 20th century, but nothing is more permanent than change. The Boston Braves, one of the oldest franchises in the history of the game (originally the Boston Red Stockings in 1871) opened the floodgates in 1953 with their move to Milwaukee. The St. Louis Browns moved to Baltimore in 1954, and the Athletics followed suit, going from Philadelphia to Kansas City in 1955.

Precedent had been set.

Minnesota was desperate for a major league baseball team and had been working hard for many years to entice one to come to the state. As early as 1954, the New York Giants were considering a move to Metropolitan Stadium in Bloomington, Minnesota, home of their primary farm team, the Minneapolis Millers; however, when the Brooklyn Dodgers went West at the end of the 1957 season, San Francisco successfully courted and won the Giants, also in 1957.

Minneapolis set its sights on the Cleveland Indians, who refused to budge from the banks of the Cuyahoga River. So Minneapolis and Houston, Texas, began their assault on the Senators.

Frick and Frack

Griffith began the war of words when he openly announced that if Minnesota made an offer, he would listen to it. "The door is not closed." he said. "I would study the offer on its merits."[28]

Baseball Commissioner Ford Frick expressed vehement opposition, calling the idea of moving the ball club "silly."

As Washington sportswriter Shirley Povich reported,

> "Frick doesn't have a vote," Griffith said. "We don't have to pay any attention to him."
>
> "If Griffith can't operate successfully in Washington, a fine baseball town, how can we assume he can operate well in Minneapolis after the novelty there wears off?" asked Frick. He also said he did not consider Washington a trouble spot, and added that organized baseball's prestige would suffer without a team in the nation's capital.
>
> Frick also pointed out that the Washington franchise is not a distress case where a club owner is saddled with heavy losses. "The Washington club always shows a profit even when it finishes in eighth place. Simply because a club owner wants to make more money than he is making is no cause to move a franchise."[29]

Further opposition to the move came from H. Gabriel Murphy, a longtime friend of the "Old Fox," Clark Griffith. Murphy had bought a 40 percent share of the team from John Jachym in 1950. He had been openly critical of Calvin Griffith's mismanagement of the team during the 1956 All-Star Game and strongly opposed any movement of the franchise.

Murphy filed suit in the District of Columbia court to block the team from leaving. When the judge ruled against him, he filed with the U.S. Court of Appeals, where he was also rejected. Murphy then filed an appeal with the Supreme Court, and also filed a petition with Chief Justice Earl Warren for an injunction that would stop the club "from concluding any action on the transfer of the franchise until the Supreme Court has reviewed my petition." Warren declined to hear the case, and Griffith's attorneys countered that Murphy should be required to "cover [the injunction] with a $5,000,000 bond for possible damages.[30]

Attention in High Places

It seems safe to assume that there could be no possible way to move a major league baseball team, or any sports franchise for that matter, out of

Washington, D.C., without politics coming into play. Opposition to the Senators' move was extremely strong, and the American League owners feared that politicians would take umbrage at this displacement.

They were right. Rand Dixon, chief counsel of the Senate Anti-Trust and Anti-Monopoly Subcommittee, said moving the team "would disturb a lot of people in Congress."

Congress had investigated Organized Baseball in its dealings in interstate commerce as early as 1888. After the American and National Leagues emerged in 1901, baseball's antitrust exemption and the reserve clause would be the focus of numerous lawsuits and Congressional hearings for the next 70 years. In the 1950s, several players brought lawsuits against organized baseball over the reserve clause. This attracted the attention of Congress, which held hearings on the possible need for legislation regarding baseball's eligibility for exemption from antitrust requirements. In particular, baseball matters were of interest to Representative Emanuel Celler (D-NY), chair of the House Subcommittee on the Study of Monopoly Power, and to Senator Estes Kefauver (D-TN).[31]

In 1958, after Dodgers owner Walter O'Malley and Giants owner Horace Stoneham collaborated to move their teams to the West Coast, Congressman Celler introduced a bill that would bring baseball under antitrust laws. Meanwhile, in the Senate, Senator Kefauver said that he would "closely monitor" all the actions with respect to the formation of a new league.[32] The famous "Kefauver Hearings" began in the summer of 1958, bringing to Washington some of the greatest names in the game, including Casey Stengel, Mickey Mantle, and Jackie Robinson, to testify as to the validity of baseball's monopolistic hold on its players and on the cities which they occupied. In the winter of 1959, Kefauver reported out a bill that would strip baseball of its antitrust exemption.

This environment gave Griffith leverage, as sportswriter Dave Brady observed:

> Even if Griffith's request to transfer is turned down by the American League, there is the possibility that he might take his case to civil courts on the grounds that no one has a right to prevent a business moving anywhere it sees fit. Thus Griffith would be putting Organized Baseball in a monopolistic light. This might be enough to frighten the owners into approving Griffith's request because baseball always has been indeed wary about going to the courts where it might risk its favored position under the antitrust laws insofar as the reserve clause is concerned.[33]

Meanwhile, Branch Rickey, somewhat at loose ends after resigning as general manager of the Pittsburgh team, forced the antitrust issue by moving to form the rival Continental League. The AL and NL responded with expansion plans that included keeping a team in Washington. As the Clark Griffith blog explains it,

> Expansion was a reaction to Branch Rickey's efforts to create the Continental League, a third major league. There is nothing more alarming to an established major league in any sport than the creation of a competitor. Rival leagues are either absorbed or crushed. Here the decision was to crush the new league by expanding to its major cities, Minneapolis-St. Paul, Houston, New York and California. A new franchise was to be placed in Washington to avoid antitrust legislation that would take away the antitrust exemption created by the Supreme Court in the Baltimore Federal League case in 1921. The act of crushing competitors is an antitrust violation and had a new team had not been placed in Washington, there was real fear of Congressional action repealing the antitrust exemption as Congress had been focused on the antitrust exemption prior to this action.[34]

In the midst of all this confusion, a former Ohio Senator, George E. Bender, made a bid to buy the Senators from Griffith for $7,000,000 in order to keep the team in the nation's capital. "Instead of transferring the franchise to Minneapolis, I hope that Griffith will consider my offer," said Bender. "This is a good baseball town and deserves a big league team. My money is neither Washington nor Cleveland money, but it's real money and it's available right now to make a deal."[35]

That offer was rejected.

All of this transpired in the winter months of 1959–1960. Griffith trod lightly, dodging and double-talking to gain time, yet ultimately keeping the team in Washington for the 1960 season. On June 28, 1960, Kefauver's bill was narrowly defeated by four votes. Breathing a sigh of relief, all the baseball owners knew they could not confront the new Continental League without risking more wrath from Congress. Branch Rickey recognized this as well; consequently, on August 1, he withdrew the Continental League's bid for recognition as a third major league after assurances from the other owners that expansion would occur.[36]

On October 26, 1960, the American League owners approved the expansion of the league to ten teams. The National League had done so nine days earlier, so it was more or less *a fait accompli*. Calvin Griffith had the green light; he began his move to Minneapolis-St. Paul and rechristened the Washington Senators as the Minnesota Twins.[37]

Where Is Roy in All This?

In February of 1960, Roy went down to spring training in Orlando with every intention of righting his ship, but injury struck again. After slapping a double against Detroit's Frank Lary on March 13, he took a fast ball to his left elbow from Detroit rookie pitcher Phil Regan, which sidelined him again for a week. Neither he nor Jim Lemon nor Bob Allison could seem to find their long-ball swing. But manager Lavagetto wasn't too concerned: "It usually take those big hitters a little extra time to start to produce in the spring," he said. "They'll have their timing back when the season opens."

Sam Mele is truly one of the last of the "grand old men" of baseball. Originally he signed with the Red Sox, but had to defer because of wartime service from 1943 to 1946. As Roy did in the Army, Sam spent his Navy service playing ball against the likes of Joe DiMaggio and Phil Rizzuto. After mustering out, he made the Red Sox parent club in 1947, where none other than Ted Williams took a liking to him and helped him transition to the big leagues.

Mele played with Boston for three years, then played for the Senators from 1949 to 1952. After Washington, he had stints with the White Sox, the Orioles, and the Cincinnati Reds, and he ended his playing career with the Indians. He began his coaching career with the Senators in 1959 and 1960. He moved with the team to Minnesota in 1961 and become the manager in mid-year when Cookie Lavagetto was fired. He would go on to take the Twins to their first-ever World Series in 1965.

In a phone interview from his home in Quincy, Massachusetts, Sam Mele spoke about Roy with great admiration:

> He was simply the best, simply fantastic, he was just fantastic. That's really the only word I can think of about the guy. Fantastic hitter, a pretty good fielder, ran alright and had some power. He was great to coach, no problem. He did everything you wanted him to do, no questions asked, and he gave you all he had. And he was so easy to get along with; teammates, opposition, umpires, everybody! He was just the best. He did a lot to help out the younger players like [Harmon] Killebrew and Bobby Allison in 1959. He was just great to get along with.[38]

Bob Allison told Herb Heft that he "adopted" Sievers as his mentor in 1959:

> Roy was great to me this season. He had me move closer to the plate so I could reach the pitches I was previously missing on the outside corner. He also taught me not to lunge. "Don't be impatient," he said. "The ball will come to you. Wait for it." He and Cookie both convinced me not to swing for the fences. I found they were correct. Every once in awhile I did get the urge to go for all the marbles. Never when I took the urge did I hit a homer.[39]

Heavy Trade Talks

Calvin Griffith made Roy the subject of trade talks all year long. Teams like Kansas City and Detroit made competitive offers, but Griffith refused to budge. He was looking for the deal that would bring the team what it needed, and both Griffith and Lavagetto were desperate for a catcher and a second baseman.[40]

Veteran catcher Clint Courtney was injury-prone, and Hal Naragon was rusty from too much bench time. Former George Washington University football star Steve Korcheck was only adequate behind the plate, and his anemic .159 batting average made him more of a liability than a threat.

Handsome third baseman Reno Bertoia was slick with the glove and the ladies. Zoilo "Zorro" Versalles looked like a ballet dancer at shortstop, and first baseman Julio Becquer completed the Cuban Triumvirate. All of them played like Mays and hit like Williams.... Esther Williams! Other than "The Fearsome Foursome," there were no reliable hitters in the lineup. Versalles, at age 19, was deemed unreliable and was eventually sent down to the minors for more "seasoning."

Veeck ... Again!

The Chicago White Sox surprised everyone by winning the American League pennant in 1959. The "Go-Go Sox" won by emphasizing pitching, speed and defense over power. They were last in the league in home runs but led the league in stolen bases, fielding percentage, and team ERA. They featured the extraordinary double play combination of two future Hall of Famers, Luis Aparicio and Nelson Fox. Catcher Sherman Lollar led the team with only 22 home runs; however, the rest of the team made up for it in timely hitting (Loller had 134 hits for the season, Fox 191, Aparicio 157, Bubba Phillips 100, Al Smith 112, and Jim Landis 140). Aparicio led the league with 56 stolen bases, a feat he accomplished ten times during his 18-year career.[41]

That year the LA Dodgers won their first National League pennant since moving from Brooklyn by beating a vastly stronger Milwaukee Braves team in a best-of-three playoff series. In the World Series, the White Sox battled bravely against the great Dodgers arms of Don Drysdale, Sandy Koufax, Johnny Podres, and Larry Sherry, but ultimately succumbed, four games to two. Big-hitting first baseman Ted Kluszewski pounded out three home runs and catcher Sherm Lollar contributed one.

Owner Bill Veeck decided not to stand on his laurels for 1960. He wanted some home run punch to support the slap-hitting Go-Go Sox. He knew that pennants were good, but the fans loved the long ball.

And so it was that on April 4, 1960, Veeck, after months of wrangling with Calvin Griffith, mortgaged the team's future. Roy Sievers was traded to the Chicago White Sox for catcher Earl Battey and big-hitting Don Mincher, who had yet to play his first major league game, and $150,000 in cash. (Remember that Griffith could have had nearly twice as much money and players had he taken Veeck's offer in June of 1959.)[42]

The sidewinder to this story would be revealed later in the year. In its September 14 issue, *The Sporting News* reported the rumor that Veeck had made the Sievers deal subject to Griffith's promise not to sell Senators ace pitcher Camilo Pascual to the Yankees. One week later, the paper ran a letter from Herb Heft that reported the following:

> Mr. Griffith said: "That story is completely false. When Bill Veeck and I discussed the Sievers trade, I asked for Earl Battey and Sammy Esposito as the players we wanted in the exchange. He would not let us have Esposito. We talked some more and the players we agreed to receive were Battey and Don Mincher. It's as simple as that. Any story about Bill Veeck's extracting a promise from me not to sell Pascual in connection with [the Sievers] deal has no foundation whatsoever. I never had any intention of selling Pascual to the Yankees or anyone else. Remember, before I made the Sievers deal with Chicago, I had already rejected a half-million dollar offer for Pascual by Gabe Paul of the Cincinnati ball club."[43]

"[Chicago manager] Al Lopez was like my god uncle, we were so close," said Maury Povich in an interview. "I think he did that [trade] just to thumb his nose at Calvin."[44]

Off to the Windy City

"I was a little surprised by the trade," said Roy. "The fans in Washington treated me real good and so did Mr. Griffith. I was sad to leave but I was happy to be back with [Bill] Veeck. Chicago had just won the pennant, and I thought, 'Here's my chance to play with a good first division club.' I felt we could have won the World Series that year."

But Roy would have trouble fitting into the Sox lineup. White Sox manager Al Lopez publicly stated that he didn't know what he was going to do with Sievers and privately said he thought Veeck gave up too much to get him. Lopez was high on his own big hitter, Ted Kluszewski, and positioned him at first base; however, he conceded that Sievers could move in, if or when "Big Klu" should falter. He also suggested the same should anything befall left fielder Minnie Miñoso or right fielder Al Smith. Lopez thought that the competition of having two men at first base would "keep them on their toes."

The media was abuzz about the White Sox' chances of winning the AL pennant again in 1960. Lopez was extremely optimistic as well, as he stated

A smiling Roy Sievers poses in his brand-new Chicago White Sox uniform in March of 1960 (AP photograph).

to the press: "Sievers will be a great insurance policy for us. He can spell Ted Kluszewski at first, Minnie Miñoso in left, and when he's not doing that, he can pinch hit."[45]

Lopez had made it clear: Roy was to be a utility player. He was relegated to the bench for the first time since starting with the Senators in 1954.

Same Struggles

Platooning with Kluszewski for righty-lefty match-ups and doing some pinch-hitting, Roy languished. But Lopez had problems with which he had to deal. Kluszewski started off on fire, then cooled quickly. When Klu didn't hit, Lopez put Roy in. Roy looked like his old self, hitting his first and second home runs in a White Sox uniform against his old Washington teammates Russ Kemmerer and Jim Kaat during the May 5–7 series. However, Roy began to slump after that. Lopez benched him again and put Klu back in. Klu responded at first, but quickly cooled off again. So Lopez countered by pulling Klu and platooning Roy with Earl Torgeson.[46]

Nature would finally prevail. Kluszewski, who had herniated a disc in his back after a clubhouse altercation in 1956, pulled his back out badly in early June. Lopez relented and put Roy at first base for the duration.

Roy was very much in the mold of all of the big power hitters of his era. It took a while of playing steadily to get the swing and the timing just right. At the end of May, he was hitting an anemic .182 with only three home runs. By June 15, he had only upped his average to .220. He was familiar with all the AL pitchers; he was just off his game. Once he got into the regular lineup, he caught fire.

From June 23 through July 18, Roy went on a tear, turning in a 21-game hitting streak, the longest in both majors that year. He had a career-best month on July, punishing Baltimore and Washington pitchers in particular. He hit 12 homers, had 30 RBI, and batted over .400 for the month. By August he had raised his total batting average from a puny .182 to a robust .322 and had taken over third place in the hotly contested AL batting race.[47]

Roy paced the Chisox to a 1½-game lead at the end of July and was a frontrunner for the 1960 MVP Award. His mid-season performance prompted manager Al Lopez to opine: "I blame myself for not playing Roy Sievers every day from the time we got him. But he wasn't hitting much early in the season and I alternated Roy with Ted Kluszewski. What I didn't realize was that Sievers must play every day to keep his timing."[48]

When asked about his preference of playing position, Roy said, "I prefer to play first base. It's easier on the arm. I figure I can prolong my big league career playing at first, but I don't know about that outfield. When I play, I have to play hard. Maybe one throw will hurt the arm again. I wouldn't want to risk it. Of course, I'll play wherever they want me, but I figure on sticking around for a few more years."[49]

Although the Sox cooled off in August and September, finishing third in the standings, Roy made a most fluid transition and for the first time in his career played on a team with a winning record. Looking back on that season, Roy said, "We had some great hitters in 1960; Klu, and Landis, Miñoso, Gene Freese, Al Smith. We coulda done better but I was happy to play for a winner for once."

Despite playing in only 127 games that year, Roy batted .295, drove in 93 runs, and lit up Bill Veeck's new exploding scoreboard in Comiskey Park with 28 round-trippers.

Yackity Yak, Don't Talk Back

Roy had built a reputation on being a 100 percent team player. He was never thrown out of a game or talked back to an umpire in his career. However, in Chicago, for the only time in his career, Roy would lose his patience with a manager. As he tells the story:

> Al Lopez was a good manager. He didn't say much to ya, but he was fair with everyone. One day, I was out in left field and made an error, and we lost the ballgame. So, when I come back to the dugout and sit down on the bench, Lopez says something to me and I said something back. I got angry and said, "Mr. Lopez, do you think I go out to the outfield to make an error and lose ballgames? I wanna win like everybody else." So, we're walkin' back through the runway and Nelly [Fox] is next to me and he says, "You said the wrong thing!" I said, "Why?" He says, "Watch and see." Lopez benched me for a week. One week! Because I talked back to him. Never did it again.

Owner Bill Veeck was ebullient with his praise for Roy. "He's a wonderful team man and a great fellow. I guess I'm funny about ball players. Sievers was always one of my favorites because he has class in addition to everything else. I've been trying to get him for a long time and I think he's well worth the price we had to pay for him."[50]

On the Comeback Trail

With his quiet determination, Roy was intent on showing everyone in the majors that his 1959 season was a fluke, a season besieged by injury. Happy to be with a first division club, Roy punished the other teams in the league with his bat. The Orioles, in particular, became bird seed in his hands. Roy hit .354 and drove in 18 runs against them, leading the league in those categories.[51]

With his timely hitting and run production, Roy was further determined to prove Al Lopez wrong. Lopez's statement that "the Sox had paid too much for Sievers" became a tasty morsel for him to eat, which he did with gusto. Lopez said, "The man who scores runs is as important or more important than the man who drives them in. A man can't knock in runs if there is no one in scoring position, unless he homers." He observed that Sievers "has been at bat only 400 times and yet he lead the club in scoring runs. Just compare that record with some of the others."[52]

By the end of the season, Roy did show just how valuable he was to the White Sox. The comparison looks like this[53]:

Player	*Games*	*AB*	*Hits*	*Runs*	*RBI*	*HR*	*TB*	*Avg*
Sherm Lollar	129	421	106	43	46	7	150	.252
Roy Sievers	127	444	131	87	93	28	237	.295
Nellie Fox	150	605	175	85	59	12	225	.289
Luis Aparicio	153	600	166	86	61	2	206	.277
Gene Freese	127	455	124	60	79	17	219	.273
Minnie Miñoso	154	591	184	89	105	20	284	.311
Jim Landis	148	494	125	89	49	10	192	.253
Al Smith	142	536	169	80	72	12	242	.315

If one looks carefully at the above statistics, it is both remarkable and undeniable just how important Roy was to the team. Remarkable in that because he was platooned for the first part of the season and didn't begin playing steadily until June, Roy was tied with Gene Freese for fewest games played (127) and was seventh on the team in at-bats (444). Now comes the undeniable. Although he was fifth on the team in hits, he was third in runs scored (with 87 to the 89 each notched by Miñoso and Landis), and he scored more runs than Fox, Aparicio, and Smith, all of whom had significantly more at-bats than he did. Add to this that he led the team in home runs (28) and RBI (93) and was third in batting average (.295), behind Smith (.315) and Miñoso (.311—Minnie Minoso had an All-Star year and led the league in hits with 184). On top of that, Roy was third on the team in total bases with 237 (Miñoso had 284 and Smith had 242).

So, with all this run production, why was it that the Sox finished third in the American League in 1960? "It was pitching that prevented us from taking the flag [in '60]," Roy maintained. "I think [Cal] McLish and [Juan] Pizarro [traded to the Sox in 1961] will give us enough of a lift to make the difference [this season].[54]

Suffice it to say, Roy silenced his detractors with a solid year at the plate and endeared himself to the South Side faithful, who were very happy indeed that he was hitting his tape measure homers in Comiskey Park instead of Griffith Stadium. Roy looked forward to another good year in the sun.

10

The Best Is Yet to Come

One very good thing developed out of Roy Sievers' trade to Chicago; it brought him a little closer to home.

> The kids could only come see me for about two weeks during the summer, after school let out. It was hard on them and on me, not being able to be around them during the season. When I got traded to the White Sox, it was a little closer for Joan to drive the kids up to see me play. I liked playin' in Kansas City too because I had a brother who lived near there as well.

Roy's daughter Shawn recalled a childhood story:

> It was hard on us as kids, not being able to see Dad for a long time. We were always told by Momma that when we went to go see Dad play, that no matter what, he couldn't come home. He couldn't come home until the season was over or if someone was dyin.'
>
> When I was little, I was playin' on a swing set by school and I fell off and hurt myself pretty bad. I hurt my kidney and had to be hospitalized. Daddy was notified about it and flew home to see me. I was sleepin' and didn't know Daddy was there. When I woke up, I saw Daddy and I started to cry and scream, "I'm dying, I'm dying!" Momma calmed me down and asked me why did I think that and I said, "Because Daddy's here and he can only come here if someone's dying!"[1]

Damage Control

The Sox ended the 1960 season 87–67, for a third-place finish in the American League. Skipper Al Lopez, the majors' winningest manager with a .610 percentage, waxed philosophic about the year:

> Our main trouble this year was that the pitching staff never was coordinated. In the spring, the starters were bad and the relief men were doing a fine job; the last half of the season, when the starters finely got rolling, the bull pen sagged. In July, I thought we were on the way to the pennant when the team began clicking as a unit with Roy Sievers as the big man on offense. But then Sievers slowed down and we stopped winning.[2]

Owner Bill Veeck was just as apologetic as Lopez:

> Why did we fail? The biggest reason was pitching. That's evident from the statistics. We led the league in hitting and fielding but not in pitching.... This step down in pitching is reflected in the one-run decisions we've lost. Last year we won 30 and lost 15, but this season we dipped to 21 wins and 22 losses.

Always the optimist, Veeck was quick to point out the many positives on the year:

> One of the bright spots certainly was Baumann. Others were Minnie Miñoso, who had one of the greatest seasons of his career; Al Smith, who was in the fight for the batting title most of the way; Roy Sievers, who picked the club up and lifted it back into the race in June, July, and August; and Aparicio, who improved at the plate while being as good as ever in the field.[3]

Despite a terrible 0-for-23 slump at the end of the season, Roy had another tremendously productive year. Playing in only 127 games, he hit for a .295 average and tallied 131 hits, 28 home runs and 93 RBI. Of his 28 home runs, 15 were solo shots and 13 were with men on base.

He totally dominated the Orioles in 1960, hitting .354 and driving in 18 runs against Birds pitching. He didn't make the All-Star team in 1960, but he did receive good consideration for the MVP Award again.

Most importantly, he continued to do what he did best: drive in runs.

Money Ball?

This fact did not go unnoticed by manager Al Lopez. In several media statements, Lopez may have presaged the coming of the "money ball" era. When asked by a reporter, "What single quality would you rather see in a ball player on your team—in other words, what makes one player more valuable than another if there isn't a marked difference in ability?" Lopez didn't hesitate for a minute.

> I'll take the fellow who can score the most runs. I know the tendency is to go for the guy who hits the long ball. He's the one who commands the biggest salary. There is no question that this is important, but runs are the things that win ball games and I'll take the guy who scores them.
>
> Take our ball club. You can't take anything away from guys like Roy Sievers and Ted Kluszewski who hit fourth for us. But if Luis Aparicio, Nellie Fox and say Minnie Miñoso or Jim Landis are going good up there in the first three positions, Sievers and Kluszewski can knock in many a run during the season just by hitting a ground ball or a fly ball to the outfield. That's because those other guys get on base, run the bases well and get themselves in scoring position.... You don't win in this game unless you can cross home plate.[4]

The 1960 top ten AL leaders in runs scored were a veritable amalgam of first-division players:

Mantle:	119
Maris:	98
Miñoso:	89
Landis:	89
Sievers:	87
Aparicio:	86
Fox:	85
Francona:	84
Killebrew:	84
Lemon:	81

Only Miñoso, Sievers, Fox, and Francona were in the top ten in batting average, while only Mantle, Maris, Sievers, and Lemon were in the top ten in RBI.[5]

Easy Winter

Roy stayed off of the barnstorming circuit during the fall of 1960, choosing to stay closer to home. In late October, however, he took a quick trip to Houston. Hungry for an expansion team, 4,582 fans lined up at Busch Stadium in Houston to watch the Solly Hemus National League All Stars beat the Pete Runnels American League All Stars, 3–2. The annual benefit game of the Houston Professional Baseball Players Association was played to support Boys Harbor of La Porte, TX.

Roy and several other members of both teams participated in a free clinic at the stadium the day before the game, attended the Rice-Texas football game, and were guests at a banquet held in their honor. All of the players donated their time and talents to this worthy cause.[6]

And Away We Go

Roy relaxed during the winter after his excellent season with the Sox. His friend Bob Burnes, reporter with the *St. Louis Globe-Democrat*, asked if he had seen or discussed a contract for the upcoming season yet. When Roy responded that he had not, Bob asked if he expected any difficulty. Roy shook his head and said: "Not with Bill Veeck. He's always been my best friend in baseball. I'm not the least bit worried. We'll get together without trouble."[7]

The big fun happened in January of 1961. On a typically cold and windy January 23, Roy attended the annual Major League Sporting Goods Convention at the Morrison Hotel in downtown Chicago. Roy had signed with the Rawlings Company of suburban St. Louis to endorse his line of baseball gloves, the RSP Personal Model outfielder's glove and "The Claw" model T-105 first baseman's mitt.

Newspaper accounts say that he and Veeck talked together for a little while in the hotel's lobby during the afternoon. No one knows what was said. However, later that evening, Veeck was the main after-dinner speaker at the convention, and began to relate how things had changed in baseball. That's when the Marx Brothers routine started, as Veeck said:

> You know, when I was with the Browns all I had to do was wave a $100 bill before an athlete and he'd be happy to come to terms. Roy Sievers was with me then. He knows.
>
> But things are different now. I talked to Roy about his contract before the meeting, but that $100 bill won't work now. However, right now I'd offer Roy $2,000 more than the last figure I proposed to him.

Without missing a beat, Roy jumped up from his chair and shouted, "I'll take it!"[8]

"That's an absolutely true story" said Roy in an interview. "Veeck set the whole thing up. He said, 'I'll give him $2,000 more than last year,' and I jumped up and said, 'I'll take it.' Veeck always had a flair for the dramatic."

Roy, who had signed for $35,000 the year before, signed his 1961 contract that night for $37,000.

Of interest at the convention that year, Dewey Soriano, president of the Pacific Coast League, made a proposal to adopt a "pinch hitter" rule for the pitcher, an early version of the designated hitter. Roy and Bill Veeck were definitely in opposition.

"I don't believe it would help the game," Roy said. "We've played the game like this for years. Why change? The fans seem to like it the way it is. And besides, the pitchers love to hit. They're always bragging more about the hit they got than they ever do about their pitching."[9]

Roy went home and immediately set out to get in good shape for the season. Working out at the St. Louis University gym with Bob Bauman, he quickly got down to his 204 pound playing weight. "I'm in great shape," he told reporters. "By the time I get to our spring camp, I ought to be able to go at full speed."[10]

Roy predicted he would hit at least 30 home runs and drive in more than 100 runs for the Sox in 1961.

Another Good Year in the Sun

Roy came down to the Sox's spring training camp loaded for bear. Ailing Ted Kluszewski would be taken by the California Angels in the expansion draft, leaving first base as Roy's domain for the season. In great playing shape at the start, Roy proceeded to pound opposing pitchers all through the month of March. Then he really caught fire.

Opening Day of 1961 saw the White Sox pitted against Roy's old team, the Washington Senators, although, with the departure of the majority of his old teammates to Minnesota in 1960, one would have to call this the "new" Washington Senators. Managed by former Senators All-Star batting champ Mickey Vernon, the new Senators were a conglomeration of aged veterans like Gene Woodling, Dale Long, Bobby Shantz, and Mike Garcia, along with some never-heard-of-before names like Dutch Dotterer, Coot Veal, Joe Hicks, and Chester Boak.

On another "balmy," 53-degree, drizzly DC day, 26,725 diehards came out to watch President John F. Kennedy chuck a mighty heave over the third base bag to inaugurate the new season. The presidential toss was caught by White Sox outfielder "Jungle Jim" Rivera. Traditionally, he who catches the ball takes it up to the President for an autograph. According to *Chicago Tribune* reporter David Condon years later, Rivera looked at the autographed ball and demanded, "What kind of garbage college is that Harvard, where they don't even teach you to write? What kind of garbage writing is this? Do you think I can go into any [bar] in Chicago's South Side and really say the President of the United States signed this baseball for me? I'd be run off! Take this thing back and give me something besides your garbage autograph."

Laughing, the young president agreed to sign the ball more legibly. "You know," Rivera said, "you're all right."[11]

Future Hall of Famer Early Wynn got touched up in the Senators' half of the first inning, giving up singles to Coot Veal (who?) and Marty Keough. Gene Woodling tripled them home, and the Senators took an early 2–0 lead. Roy came up in the top of the second inning and promptly reminded his old team why they shouldn't have traded him. He turned on the first Dick Donovan fastball he saw and drove it 420 feet into the center field stands.

The game would seesaw back and forth until it knotted up at 3–3 in the seventh inning. In the top of the eighth, Minnie Miñoso would "take one for the team," promptly steal second, then advance to third when Senators catcher Pete Dailey tossed the ball into center field on the throw down from home. Roy's sacrifice fly to left field scored Minnie from third with the go-ahead run, and that's how the day ended: our man Roy coming through in the clutch.[12]

I've Heard That Song Before

Try as they might, the White Sox pitching staff could not get consistent in the first half of the season. By the end of May, they had slumped to a 16–27 record. However, our Mr. Sievers would have none of it. Roy was in terrific form right off the bat. By the end of April, he was killing the ball at a .319 pace, having collected 15 hits, including three homers, one triple and two doubles for a total of 28 bases, plus he was leading the team in run production with ten RBI and 11 runs scored. All of this and he had struck out only four times in 13 games. Roy was off to the same kind of epic start he had in his career year of 1957.

Roy hit three homers in April, seven in May, and eight more in June, including a June 3 walk-off dinger off his old friend, New York Yankees pitcher Art Ditmar, whom he took deep 11 times in his career.

In particular, Roy went on a tear against the Indians. In a Wednesday doubleheader, he scored six runs on five hits combined to lead the Sox to a sweep. In the bottom of the fourth inning of the first game, he became the fifth player in White Sox history to smack a grand slam home run as a pinch hitter, taking Johnny Antonelli deep and helping the Sox to a 15–3 shellacking of the Indians.[13]

Then injury struck again.

On June 23, on a humid Chicago night, with the wind blowing off the lake, Roy fielded a grounder down the first base line and fell down on the dewy grass as he wheeled and tried to cut back to the bag. He tried to break his fall with his elbow and jammed his right shoulder.

Yes, that shoulder.

White Sox team physician Dr. Joseph Coyle said the injury was muscular, thankfully. Roy's injury-prone right shoulder was becoming the stuff of legend.

Roy had 18 homers and 45 RBI at the time of the injury, which sidelined him for nearly a week. He returned as a pinch-hitter in the ninth inning of the June 28 Tigers game and promptly spanked pitcher Don Mossi for a two-run home run in a terrible, 12–5 White Sox loss.[14]

Roy's prediction of 30 homers and 100 RBI at the beginning of the season came very close to coming true. He had another stellar year: 145 hits, 76 runs, 27 home runs, 92 RBI, 61 walks, 62 strikeouts, and a .295 batting average that matched his average in 1960. He didn't even come close to the league lead in the home run category. This was 1961, the year Roger Maris would break Babe Ruth's fabled single season home run mark with 61 homers, while Mickey Mantle would place second with 54 and Harmon Killebrew, Orlando

Cepeda and Jim Gentile would tie for third with 46. Teammate Al Smith edged Roy out as team home run leader with 28. Once again, the injury bug took valuable at-bats away from him.

Trade Bait Again

To say the 1961 White Sox were heavy with veteran players would be an understatement. They had five position players 33 years old or older, and 13 players on the active roster in their 30s or 40s. Early Wynn led the Geritol crowd at age 41, followed by Gerry Staley at 40, Jim Rivera at 39, Earl Torgeson and Turk Lown at 37, Warren Hacker and Sherman Lollar at 36, Billy Goodman, Cal McLish and Minnie Miñoso at 35, Roy Sievers at 34, and Nellie Fox and Al Smith at 33. (One couldn't be too sure about Miñoso, though. He and ex-Senators pitcher Connie Marrero had "questionable" Cuban birth certificates.)[15]

The Sox had by far the oldest team in baseball in 1961, yet they led the American League in batting and stolen bases for the second year in a row, thanks in large part Luis Aparicio's league-leading 53 thefts. Even Roy swiped one base in 1961! The team finished fourth in the league with an 86–76 record and was never really in contention throughout the year. Al Lopez figured, we've tried adding power instead of speed; time to go back to speed over power.

The winter trade meetings began on September 21. Roy was still a potent power threat, and many a team expressed interest in his bat. The Red Sox's executive vice president, Dick O'Connell, and manager Mike Higgins had several meetings with the White Sox brass, trying to weasel Sievers away from the Pale Hose. The Red Sox had wanted Sievers for a long time, having tried to get him away from Calvin Griffith several times while Roy was with the Senators. Roy had always hoped to play in Fenway Park, where he could slay the Green Monster with many a double or a dinger.[16]

End of an Era

There is little doubt that White Sox owner Bill Veeck was the game's greatest innovator, if not its greatest showman. He was a pioneer in baseball finances. He was magnanimous to his players, something unheard-of in the Golden Age of baseball. And his first love was always the fans. Here is Warren Corbett's description of Veeck's first season with the White Sox:

He gave away orchids on Mother's Day. In the same game, the "lucky chair" prize was 36 live lobsters. Other fans received 1,000 cans of beer, 1,000 pies, 1,000 bottles of root beer, 1,000 cupcakes, and 100 free restaurant dinners. "You give a radio or a TV set—so what?" he explained to *Sports Illustrated*. "What does that do for the imagination? Nothing. If I give him 50,000 nuts and bolts ... that gives everybody something to talk about." He also staged free days for cab drivers and bartenders, believing they were valuable public-relations boosters for the club. After fans booed left fielder Al Smith, Veeck let everyone named Smith (or Smythe or Schmidt) in free as Al's guests. Comiskey Park attendance reached a franchise-record 1,423,144, but it fell just short of the Chicago record set by Veeck's father's Cubs in 1929.

In 1960, Veeck introduced his most lasting innovations. He put players' names on the backs of their road uniforms (names were added to home uniforms the next year) and built an exploding scoreboard to celebrate the home team's home runs. "It shrieks, wiggles, burps, whines and twinkles," *The Sporting News* marveled. "Fireworks explode beneath the scoreboard while tape recordings give out virtually every sound imaginable ... a cavalry charge, machine-gun fire, two trains crashing head-on, subway screeching, jet bombers, and a woman screaming, 'Fireman, save my child.'" The cacophony delighted fans and infuriated opponents. Cleveland outfielder Jimmy Piersall threw a baseball at the board. Casey Stengel orchestrated a puckish response: After Mickey Mantle hit a homer, Stengel and the Yankees paraded in front of the visitors' dugout waving sparklers. Most other teams eventually added names to their uniforms and sound-and-light shows to their scoreboards.[17]

But by 1960, Veeck's heavy smoking had caught up with him. He would go into coughing fits that sometimes made him pass out. In April of 1961, doctors at the Mayo Clinic evaluated him and prescribed retirement. Veeck sold his share of the team to Arthur and John Allyn, two of his partners.

Off We Go—To the City of Brotherly Love

Desperate for good pitching, the two new partners agreed with manager Lopez's assessment of the team dynamic, and Sievers was traded to the Philadelphia Phillies for pitcher Johnny Buzhardt and infielder Charlie Smith. The Phils had been in the market all winter for another big power hitter to bolster the interior of their lineup, which featured Pancho Herrera as their lone long-ball swatter. Phillies General Manager John Quinn was looking to shake up the team's chemistry and was in desperate need of some sort of attraction to shore up the sickly gate at Connie Mack Stadium. The Phils needed some pop in the batting order.

"I was surprised [at the trade]," said Roy in an interview with Allen Lewis, award-winning sportswriter for the *Philadelphia Inquirer*. "I had heard rumors that I would go, but sort of expected the Cards or Red Sox to get me. But that's the way baseball goes. At first, I was disappointed at leaving a first division club for a last-place one, but after thinking it over, I'm not. I've been on last-place clubs before, but I have always given 100 per cent out on that field, and I certainly will for the Phillies."

Roy was pleased by the trade. Though he confessed to Lewis that he could not play a full schedule any longer, he asserted, "I should have at least three more years in which I can play 125–130 games a season." He was looking forward to depositing a few dingers into the left field seats at Connie Mack Stadium. "It's a good park to hit in for a right handed pull hitter like me. Right field isn't easy, but I don't hit out there much. I used to be a straightaway hitter, but for the last six or seven years, I've been mostly a pull hitter. Cookie Lavagetto helped me by getting me to move up on the plate and that helped me to pull more."

Roy did express some misgivings about National League pitching, though.

Roy (left) is traded to Philadelphia for pitcher Johnny Buzhardt and third baseman Charlie Smith, November 1961 (AP photograph, used by permission).

> I've faced the National League pitchers only in exhibition games in spring training, and it will take a little while to know how they pitch me and the difference in the strike zone. I understand they call more low pitches in the National than they do in the American League, but they give you the high pitches, so it all evens out. Then, too, the pitchers in the NL don't know me.[18]

Roy was going to have to pull the ball ... a lot. Most of the National League parks were built like Yellowstone, and ancient Connie Mack Stadium was one of them. It was a comfortable 334 feet down the left field line but 447 feet to straightaway center. Forbes Field in Pittsburgh was 457 feet to straightaway center, and the mammoth Polo Grounds in San Francisco, home of Willie Mays' spectacular "catch" in the 1954 World Series, was 480.

Roy, at 35 years old, went to the Phillies and became a senior statesman on a young, hungry club that would prove to be a contender. He was the only regular position player over the age of 27, and was instantly respected for his strength and leadership.

The Little General

Gene Mauch was born to be a fighter. Gene Tunney, "The Fighting Marine," was his father's favorite boxer, and his father vowed he was going to name his son after a winner. And so he did on November 18, 1925.

Mauch was a product of the rough-and-tumble, post-war National League. He played parts of nine seasons from 1944 to 1957 with the Brooklyn Dodgers, Pittsburgh Pirates, Chicago Cubs, Boston Braves, St. Louis Cardinals, and Boston Red Sox. In 304 games and 737 at-bats, Mauch hit .239, with five home runs and 62 RBI, striking out 82 times.[19]

He started managing minor league ball in 1953, but admitted he was too young for the position at the time. He successfully managed the Red Sox's Triple-A affiliate Minneapolis Millers to the Junior World Series in 1958. He initially declined an offer to join the Phillies' coaching staff in 1960, saying he wanted to focus on management. But when veteran manager Eddie Sawyer resigned after the first game of the 1960 season, Mauch was offered and accepted the position.[20]

Gene Mauch hated to lose. Period. And losing would set off his biggest weakness: his irascible temper. A losing game would mean hours of raging, sulking, and constant re-evaluation of what could have been done to win the game. He was both hated and feared by most umpires, with whom he would argue constantly. He was not above cajoling and sometimes mixing it up with opposing players or even his own. Buffet tables were not safe from his fits of anger. He made Ty Cobb look like a kindergarten teacher.

This classic story is retold often. Mets catcher Jerry Grote reached into the Phillies' third-base dugout at Connie Mack Stadium to catch a foul pop. MLB rules at the time stated that a player might reach into an opposing team's dugout only at his own peril. Mauch, knowing an enemy player was fair game under such circumstances, chopped Grote across the arms as he reached for the ball. Baseball rule no. 7:11 was changed that off-season.[21]

Mauch's second-biggest weakness was his poor sense of public relations. In an age where television had begun to grow and expand nationwide, Mauch was almost completely bereft of basic public relations skills. He was excoriated in the press for having the temerity to imply that he would have platooned Yankees legend Lou Gehrig, citing his defensive weaknesses.[22]

Taking over for Eddie Sawyer in 1960, Mauch inherited a Phillies team filled with youngsters, minor leaguers, and several remnants of the 1950 "Whiz Kids" team. The 1960 team played to a disappointing 59–95, last-place finish. Mauch's second year as manager would be downright dismal, with the team going 47–107 and finishing dead last in the National League in attendance with only 590,039 masochists attending the games that year. The Phils became infamous for losing 23 games straight, the second-longest losing streak in baseball history. Shortstop Ruben Amaro, Sr., recalled, "We went out there and played our asses off, but we were just overmatched. We were so young. It was like a kindergarten team playing a fourth grade team."[23]

But 1962 would be the turnaround year for the Phillies. They would go 81–80 thanks in large part to the home run production of young players who were given up on too soon by their former clubs, players like Johnny Callison (26), Tony Gonzalez (20), Don Demeter (29) ... and Roy Sievers (21). Mauch, a disciple of the "small ball" school, used bunts, the hit-and-run, sacrifice flies, and stealing bases, as well as the timely homer, to fullest advantage. The Associated Press writers' pool named Mauch the 1962 "Manager of the Year."[24]

Same Song, Different Town

Hungry for another long ball swatter, the Philadelphia scribes waxed poetic about Roy Sievers during spring training 1962. Sandy Grady of the *Philadelphia Evening Bulletin* used a great musical metaphor for Roy's "sweet swing":

> When Mr. Sievers strides into the batting cages here, the .250 hitters are magnetized. They stare with unabashed awe at Mr. Sievers, as though he were Sophia Loren in a bikini. The .250 hitters ogle Roy Sievers' bat, flashing with lithe, sudden grace, the way jazz guys sit around a joint to hear Miles Davis [play his] horn.

Grady asked Roy how his hitting had changed, and Roy responded,

> Oh, the last two-three years I've become a better hitter. Strangely enough, the operation on my shoulder helped me. I had always been a straightaway hitter, but after the doc cut me I started pulling the ball. Cookie Lavagetto moved me closer to the plate, too. The pitchers were killing me with the outside stuff, and as I was telling Don Demeter, the toughest thing to learn is to lay off the bad, high pitch. You get smarter."[25]

But as we have seen, Roy had another chronic problem besides his shoulder: his slow starts. Once again platooning at first base, he struggled mightily at the plate early in 1962. It took him until midway through May to get his first extra-base hit, and by June 13 he was batting only an anemic .190 with just five home runs. But as he always did, Roy caught fire in mid-season. He became the Phillies' most effective hitter after June 13, smacking 16 round-trippers, driving in 59 runs, and batting .297.

Sievers would have only one "walk-off" homer that year, so to speak. On September 7, he hit a homer for the go-ahead run in the top of the tenth inning against Claude Raymond of the Braves at County Stadium. Phils pitcher John Baldchun shut down the Braves in the bottom of the inning to hang on to the victory.

Roy ended the year having played in only 144 games, but with a total of 21 long balls, 80 RBI, 125 hits, 61 runs, and a very respectable .262 average. Surprisingly, he did better hitting right-handed pitchers than left-handers, batting .286 against righties as opposed to .222 against southpaws.[26]

Gene Mauch remained optimistic about Sievers going into the offseason. "Roy is the type of hitter who relies a great deal on his knowledge of the pitchers, what they throw and where they throw pitches in different situations. I think the fact that he did so much better the last few months than he did the first couple indicates that he will have made the adjustment and be ready to take up where he left off [in 1962.]"[27]

Roy's home run production was a little low in comparison to earlier years, but he continued to produce timely hits and get on base frequently. Sixteen of his 21 homers were hit in his home park, showing that he liked the approachable left field fence. His homers were also productive, 12 being solo shots and nine hit with runners on base.

Another good year, as he had predicted.

A Whole New Year

Roy knew he had had a so-so year in 1962, so there would be no drama with holding out for a big pay raise. Having signed for $35,000 in 1962, Roy signed his 1963 contract early for $33,000 and reported to spring training with renewed hope and vigor.

John Quinn and Gene Mauch spent the winter months shoring up the Phillies, making smart trades for young rising stars. It was almost unheard-of during that long winter, but the Phillies went into camp with their starting lineup almost ready to go. Roy was slated to play first; speedy Cuban Tony Taylor would be at second; and Don Hoak would be at third. The outfield, filled with sluggers, would be Don Demeter in left, Tony Gonzalez in center, and Johnny Callison in right. Clay Dalrymple was set as catcher.

That left Bobby Wine and Ruben Amaro to battle it out for the starting shortstop spot. Mauch was hopeful that veteran Earl Averill would be the answer to their backup catching and pinch-hitting prayers. The pitching staff would be led by Art Mahaffey, with Cal McLish, Chris Short, Dennis Bennett, and Ray Culp rounding out the hill-toppers. Quinn and Mauch also saw to it that they acquired youth and speed to go along with the seniors on the team. Of the entire 35-man roster, 12 players were over 30 years old. The most senior among them was McLish at 37, followed by Sievers at 36; Don Hoak, Jim Lemon, Bob Oldis, and relievers Johnny Klippstein and Billy Klaus at 35; and Ryne Duren at 34.

Roy got off to another slow start in the March spring training games. Although confident and sure-handed at the bag, he was having some trouble at the plate, getting only three hits in 33 at-bats and a lowly .091 batting average.

Then the injury animal bit again.

Maybe it was because Roy had touched him up for a grand slam in June of 1962, but the Reds' Jim Maloney went inside a little too close during a March game and drilled Roy with a fastball to the ribs. Roy had trouble catching his breath, but refused to be taken out of the game until the eighth inning.

"It hurt at the time," Roy told Allen Lewis, "but once I caught my breath it was not too bad and I had a couple of good rips late in the game."

> Then, that night, it gave me a lot of pain. I had trouble getting into bed and, when I laid down, I heard something snap. Maybe it was snapping back into place. I called Doc [Trainer Joe Liscio] and he gave me a sleeping pill. In the morning, I went to see Dr. [Vernon] Hagan.
>
> The first two X-rays didn't show anything, but finally he decided to take another and found the fracture of the tenth rib. I have to wear this elastic bandage for at least

> a week, and he said I couldn't swing a bat for from two to three weeks, although he said I could run within a week.
>
> I hadn't been getting any hits, but physically I was in the best shape in seven years. I think I would have been all right. I was seeing the ball clearly and it was just a matter of getting my timing. I don't know how long it will take me when I do get back.[28]

Roy did not start the season, missing his first Opening Day game since the start of his professional career. Mauch decided to alternate Don Demeter and Frank Torre at first base. Once Roy got back, he played well but was definitely showing signs of slowing down. He played in 138 games total, 126 at first base. He got hot mid-season, hitting at a .356 pace during a 16-game stretch in which the Phils won 13 out of 16, the last seven in a row. But his streak of nine consecutive seasons of 20 or more home runs was snapped. He finished the season with 19 homers, 82 RBI, and 108 hits, while scoring only 46 runs. His .240 batting average was his lowest since his jinx-ridden season of 1952. However, he had two more RBI than he did in 1962 (when he hit .262), and that was only one behind team leader Don Demeter.

He also had one more glorious moment during the 1963 season, one that couldn't have been more beset with drama.

On a hot, humid July 19 at Connie Mack Stadium, New York Mets pitcher Roger Craig, trying to end his 13-game losing streak, thought trading jerseys with his teammate and close friend, Tracy Stallard, would bring him some luck.

It didn't.

Pitching his heart out and scattering only three hits over eight innings, Craig took a 1–0 lead to the Phillies' bottom of the ninth. Johnny Callison popped up for the first out of the inning. Tony Gonzalez smacked a 1–0 fastball against the scoreboard, and it bounced back between two Mets outfielders for a triple.

The stage was set. Up stepped Sievers.

Roy hit Craig's first pitch onto the left field roof for his ninth homer (and his only walk-off) of the season—the 300th of his career. With that belt, Roy became the 23rd player in baseball history to hit 300 home runs.

"I remember my first," Roy told Allen Lewis. "It was off Freddie Hutchinson when he was with the Tigers in a game at St. Louis. I remember my first grand slam. It was off Bobby Shantz and we scored ten runs in the inning. And I won't forget this one. I was just trying to hit a fly ball and get the run home, but as soon as I hit it, I knew it had a chance."[29]

Craig sat motionless and resolute in the Mets' locker room. He answered the same question asked by several reporters with the same resignation as a prisoner sentenced to life without parole. "No, I didn't think about the losing streak in the ninth inning. I made a bad pitch, that's all. It was my fault. I wanted to get it low so he wouldn't hit a fly ball and score the tying run. I threw it hard but I threw it high."

Always the gentleman, Roy was sympathetic about Craig's plight: "I know how he feels. I've been through things like that. With me, I start striding too fast. I go into a slump—a long one—and I just can't do anything right. It's one of those things that happen in baseball—one of those tough things."[30]

The forever smiling Sievers shows off his crisp, white Phillies uniform, saying "I'll keep wearin' the monkey suit until they tell me not to" (National Baseball Hall of Fame Library, Cooperstown, New York).

Two days later, Roy would take Roger Craig's friend and teammate, Tracy Stallard, deep for his 301st home run, moving into 21st place on the all-time home run list. Then, to add insult to injury, Roy came up again against Craig in the nightcap of an August 20 twin bill, again with Craig holding a 1–0 lead in the bottom of the ninth, and Roy took him deep again to tie the game, which the Phillies would win in the 12th.

In his retirement, Craig would say those were the two toughest losses of his career.

The Volcano Erupts

Gene Mauch hated to lose—especially late in the year, when it could really mean something. Case in point:

September 22 saw the Phillies visiting the expansion Houston Colt .45s. The Phillies' Chris Short would battle Houston's Hal Brown for eight tough innings, scattering 13 hits between them. Houston manager Harry Craft called on reliever Turk Farrell to hold the fort before the Colts could have their last at-bats.

No late-inning heroics for our man Roy, though. Farrell struck out Sievers and Don Hoak, and Clay Dalrymple grounded out meekly to the first baseman to send the game into the home ninth.

Right fielder John Weekly singled off Short to start the inning. First baseman Carl Warwick got the bunt sign from manager Craft and reached first when Short forced Weekly at second. Short walked left fielder Jim Wynn, putting Warwick at second. Third baseman Bob Aspromonte, always tough in the clutch, singled Warwick home to tie the game.

Mauch had seen enough and brought in Johnny Klippstein to try to take the game into extra innings. Craft sent up Rusty Staub to pinch-hit for catcher John Bateman. Staub grounded out to first unassisted, but pushed Wynn and Aspromonte forward on the bases.

Up to the plate came Joe Morgan, a rookie just up from the farms in Durham, North Carolina. Morgan had pinch-run for pinch-hitter Johnny Temple in the bottom of the eighth and stayed on to play second base, a position he would play regularly throughout his 21-year Hall of Fame career, mostly with the "Big Red Machine" of the Cincinnati Reds.

Morgan took Klippstein's 2–0 fastball into right field, scoring Wynn from third and winning the game. It was more than Mauch could stand. The win would have meant the Phillies taking fourth place and earning a share in the World Series money, something everyone had worked hard for all season.

Norm Gerdeman was a former minor league second baseman who never made it up to the show. His love of the game was so strong, though, that he kept in the game by becoming the clubhouse man for the Colt .45s. He and his wife, Evelyn, took great pride in setting a delicious buffet for the visiting teams on the last night of a series.

After the final out, Mauch walked into the clubhouse after everyone else was in the room.

> For ten minutes or so, Mauch paced up and down, back and forth, beside the buffet in the center of the room.... Every time Mauch walked by, he would reach over, grab a handful of food, and throw it.... Slices of watermelon and cantaloupe went flying around the room. He overturned the container of ribs and chicken the Gerdemans had prepared with such loving care. A pan of barbecue sauce, among other items, went splashing into the lockers of Wes Covington and Tony Gonzalez, and all but covered their street clothes.
>
> Mauch was silent during most of his food-tossing spree, although once he addressed his players in general and told them they were a bunch of "Little Leaguers." ... After the manager retired to his office in the corner of the clubhouse, one of the players cracked, "Boy, the food sure goes fast around here."

As was his way, Mauch would cool down, apologize for his behavior and, on this occasion, buy Covington and Gonzalez new suits.[31]

Not Over Yet

Despite such antics, overall the Phillies had an excellent year in 1963, going 87–75 for a very respectable fourth-place finish behind the Dodgers, Cardinals, and Giants. The team showed they were solid throughout the lineup and were ready to get into contention next year.

Roy might have slowed down a step, but his bat was still as lethal as ever. When he didn't start at first base, he was usually used as a pinch-hitter. And he still seemed to love late-inning heroics. Of his 19 homers that year, eight came in the late innings. Roy continued to drive in runs as well. Eleven of his long balls scored either two or three runs, while seven were solo shots. His "grand" night came on May 6, when he took Cincy's Bill Henry deep and cleared the bases with the big salami. Roy's 19 long shots placed him third on the team behind Johnny Callison (26) and Don Demeter (22). Productive as always, his 82 RBI were second only to Demeter's 83.

There was still some gas in the tank—but 1963 would turn out to be Roy's last season as an everyday player.

11

Coming Home

> If the Phillies opponents thought they were tough this season, then they better beware in 1964, says pitcher Johnny Podres of the Dodgers. "Those Phillies are no longer the coming club," said Podres, "They've arrived."
>
> Many of the Phillies players think they can win the pennant this year. "I hope I'm back with 'em," said infielder Ruben Amaro. "I was with this club when it was a bunch of rinky-dinks. And I want to be with them when they go all the way. And it might be sooner than you think."[1]

The Phillies had every reason to believe that 1964 would be their year. They had fought hard under their feisty manager, clawing their way up from the cellars of 1957 through 1961, to become legitimate contenders in 1963.

Sports Illustrated seemed to think along those lines as well:

> Dead last in 1961, seventh in 1962 and fourth last year, the Phils have become the National League team on the move. The right side of the infield is just about what the right side of an infield should be, with power (Roy Sievers) at first and speed (Tony Taylor) at second. Sievers, one of the few players left who ever wore the uniform of the St. Louis Browns, had 82 RBIs last year while hitting for his lowest average (.240) in 10 major league seasons. Sievers will be backed up by John Herrnstein, a left-handed batter who hit 45 homers in two International League seasons and knocked in 156 runs.
>
> Outlook: There is strong pitching here, better than average hitting and speed, plus some problems in the outfield that may be solved by a late trade. This season could bring the start of a winning tradition to Philadelphia.[2]

Goodbye to the Man

Before the new season began, however, Roy Sievers had some celebrating to do. On October 20, 1963, he joined 1,500 adoring fans, teammates, umpires, sportswriters, family, and baseball brass at the beautiful Chase-Park Plaza Hotel in downtown St. Louis to bid a fond baseball farewell at the retirement dinner for Stan "The Man" Musial. Roy, a longtime friend and workout partner of Musial, was honored to sit at the head table with Hall of Famers Jimmie Foxx, Bob Feller, and Joe Cronin, along with stars Willie Mays, Yogi Berra, Ernie Banks, Red Schoendienst, Joe Cunningham, Birdie Tebbetts, and Wally Moon.

Missouri Senator Stuart Symington, a close friend of Musial, attended along with Mayor Raymond Tucker, as well as Commissioner Ford Frick and National League President Warren Giles. Players, managers and executives from almost every team in both leagues lined up to be in attendance.[3]

"That was a big night," said Roy. "It couldn't have happened to a nicer fella and a great, great ball player. To this day, I think he's one of the most underrated ball players to ever play the game. What he did for the Cardinals for all those years was just amazin.'"

Musial was showered with gifts and praise, as toastmaster and former teammate Joe Garagiola once again kept the evening humorous. "Mr. Cub," Ernie Banks, brought down the house when he read this "telegram": "Congratulations on your clever and wise decision. We wish you great happiness in your retirement. Signed: NAACP [long pause] the National Association for the Advancement of Cubs Pitching."

"The Man" of the American League, Mickey Mantle, unable to attend after having surgery on his ailing knees, sent heartfelt congratulations. And Joe Garagiola brought down the house by reading a declamatory note from "a friend": "After slaughtering my pitching staff for several years, Casey Stengel appreciates your retirement. Signed, Casey Stengel."

Proceeds from the $50-a-plate dinner went to fund a statue of Musial which was erected at the new riverfront Stadium in June of 1970.[4]

With the departure of Musial, Roy Sievers moved into elite company among active players. He placed in the top ten in eight of 15 major offensive categories, which included games played, doubles, homers, total bases, extra base hits, extra bases, RBI, and walks. Roy's name would be mentioned with the likes of Mantle, Mays, Snider, Aaron, and Mathews, to name but a few.[5]

Shaping Up for the Season

Roy may have had it in the back of his mind that this season might be his "last hurrah," so he decided to get going early. He went down to the Cardinals' early training camp in St. Petersburg, Florida, in January of 1964 to work out at the famous Eberhardt camp under the direction of St. Louis University physical education director Dr. Walter Eberhardt. Eberhardt's intense, seven-day workouts of stretches, calisthenics, aerobic conditioning, and running had been instrumental in decreasing the number of spring training injuries in the Cardinals' camp. Roy, along with Cardinals Joe Cunningham, Norm Siebern, Don Blasingame, Ken Boyer, Del Rice, and Stan Musial, found these workouts to be of tremendous advantage. He seconded the words of Cunningham, who said, "Since I started working out under Doc in the winters, I've found spring training two or three times easier than it used to be."[6]

The "Squirrel," who was the senior man on the field after the retirement of Stan Musial, occupied a place of honor behind the on-field instructor. He kept the workouts light and funny with his barbs and jabs and general foolishness on the field. "Look at [Cardinals outfielder] Charlie James and [first baseman] Bill White working hard NOW!" he quipped.[7]

New Faces of '64

Gene Mauch felt he had a real contender this year, so it was no surprise when the roster turnover for 1964 was considerably lower than in previous seasons.

Pitching, the biggest factor in major league baseball, was always foremost on Mauch's mind. To ease this worry, the Phillies acquired the services of Detroit Tigers veteran, All-Star Jim Bunning, and his battery mate, Gus Triandos. Bunning, who had won 118 games for the Tigers from 1955 through 1963, would become one of a handful of pitchers to win 100 games in both leagues. He was looked upon to be the ace of a staff which included regulars Jack Baldschun, Johnny Klippstein, Art Mahaffey, Cal McLish, Chris Short, and Rick Wise, among others.[8]

All of the "usual suspects" from the previous year returned to camp in 1964; however, the big news was hard-hitting, swift-of-foot Richie Allen. Allen, who had led the International League with 33 home runs in 1963, was invited to report to training camp early, along with rookie first basemen John Herrnstein and Costen Shockley. Allen was looked upon to become the everyday third sacker, while Herrnstein would likely be platooned with Sievers at first base and in the outfield.

Mauch was still searching for a right-handed-hitting outfielder to augment the punch of his southpaw swingers, Johnny Callison, Wes Covington, and Tony Gonzalez. He was hopeful that rookies Danny Cater or veteran Vic Power would fill that bill.

Dimming Lights

Roy Sievers (age 37) and teammate Cal McLish (38) would have the distinction of becoming the "elder statesmen" on a team of youngsters hungry for a chance at the NL gonfalon. Both signed their respective contracts early in February and worked hard on conditioning themselves before spring training camp officially started. McLish, who had been hampered by a shoulder problem in 1963, pitched to a respectable 3.26 ERA that year, going 11–5 in 1962 and 13–11 in 1963.

Despite his slumps, Roy had had productive years in both 1962 (21 HR, 80 RBI, .262 average) and 1963 (19 HR, 82 RBI, .240 average.) "I think I got another good season left," he told the *Philadelphia Evening Bulletin*. "I'll keep wearin' the monkey suit until they tell me I'm not doin' the job."

Roy was more than honest about his lack of production in 1963 and was enthusiastic about being platooned with John Herrnstein or Costen Shockley. "I got tired. Why lie about it. I'm not as young as I used to be. I'll be in and out of the lineup and should get all the rest I need."[9]

Another Good Start

Roy hit well during spring training, getting two hits, including a double, in the Phils' exhibition opener against the Colts on March 14 and proving that the extra conditioning paid off. Touching up pitchers in both leagues, Roy still provided long-ball punch and timely hitting throughout the spring. He got two hits against the Mets on March 16, two against the Senators on March 19, and a homer off the Pirates on the 29th.

Roy also participated in the rude awakening of Mets rookie pitcher Steve Dillon on March 25. In one nightmarish inning, Dillon gave up three walks, singles to Danny Cater and Sievers, and a double to Alex Johnson. He gave up only three runs but lost the game, 10–0.

But it wasn't all work and no play for Roy. On March 31, Roy, an enthusiastic bowler since his high school days, joined with teammates Art Mahaffey, Jim Bunning, Dennis Bennett, Cal McLish, Johnny Klippstein, and Ruben Amaro, along with representatives from all American and National League teams, to participate in the third annual Major League Baseball Bowling Tournament in Tampa, Florida. Featuring two of the nation's top bowlers, Dick Weber and Tommy Tuttle, the tournament was broadcast nationally on the NBC Sports Special, which aired on April 4. Each player won a share of the prize money, and a good time was had by all.[10]

One more year in the sun. The veteran Sievers reports to Senators' spring training in 1965, determined to show them he's still got the old pop in the bat (National Baseball Hall of Fame Library, Cooperstown, New York).

In With a Bang

Gene Mauch sounded like vintage "Stengelese" when he told Allen Lewis of the *Philadelphia Evening Bulletin*, "I think we're capable of winning 95 [games] and how high that will take us I don't know. Of course, if you're good enough to win 95, you can't tell what might happen."[11]

Mauch had reason to be hopeful. The pitching staff was shaping up nicely, his youngsters were hitting at an improved clip, and Roy, named "Most Impressive Veteran" by *The Sporting News,* was already hitting his mid-season stride.[12] Having had such a good spring, manager Mauch couldn't help but start Roy at first base on Opening Day of 1964. On a balmy, 61-degree April 14, 21,016 diehard Phillie Phanatics filed into Connie Mack Stadium to watch their hometown Quakers take on the New York Mets.

Roy, ever the hero, got the party started. After Johnny Callison and Richie Allen walked, he smacked an Al Jackson fastball into the deep left field stands to give the Phils a lead they wouldn't relinquish in the 5–3 victory.[13]

Less than a week later, Roy, Richie Allen, and Art Mahaffey took advantage of the out-blowing winds of Lake Michigan as all three blasted homers off the Cubs in the top of the fifth inning. The Cubs answered in the bottom half with homers of their own by Lou Brock and Billy Williams, marking only the eighth time in MLB history that two clubs had hit five home runs in one inning.[14]

However, all was not quiet on the home front. After 15 years of baseball widowhood, Joan wanted Roy to retire. She felt the pressure was getting too much for him. Roy, of course, was more upbeat about it. "It's too soon to quit," said Roy. "Besides, where could I make the money I make in baseball and still have fun?"[15]

More Hot Fun in the Summertime

Here's a classic case of "boys will be boys." May 10 saw the Phillies playing the Cincinnati Reds in a home game. The Phils' bullpen was located in the right field corner of the stadium. National League bullpens were traditionally not enclosed by a fence. Roy got into a Joe Nuxhall slider and took it deep down the right field line. The ball landed fair and hopped into the Phillies' bullpen, and the relievers decided to play a little "hide the ball." Right fielder Frank Robinson told the reporters: "There were about six or seven Phils in the bullpen and none would move. I was looking around for the ball on the ground, but I finally found it on the bullpen bench, lodged in the corner where the bench joins the wall of the stadium. I had to push Ryne Duren out of the way before I saw it."[16]

By then, Roy was chugging as fast as his 37-year-old legs could carry him. By the time Robinson got to the ball, he was rounding third and heading home for his first-ever inside-the-park home run.

But that day, youth would outweigh skill. Robinson fired a bullet to first baseman Deron Johnson, who in turn fired a perfect strike to catcher John Edwards to nail our intrepid hero at the plate. The Reds went on to prevail, 3–0. As Roy remembered it:

> Yeah, I hit the ball down the first base line, and I see the first base coach wavin' me around yellin' "C'mon, c'mon!" So I headed for second and I see the third base coach wavin' me and yellin' "C'mon, c'mon!" and by then Robinson finds the ball and relays it into the infield and they get me out by one foot! I mean, I thought I was safe, but the umpire calls me out. And I never lived that down, neither! I thought I had it.

Change Is Coming

Roy was having a great start to the season, hitting both American and National League pitchers alike. With the retirement of Stan Musial in 1963, Roy moved into the top 10 out of 15 hitting categories: games, at-bats, runs, doubles, home runs, total bases, extra base hits, extra bases, RBI and bases on balls.

And then it happened. As always, an injury.

Maybe it was the inside-the-park try against the Reds, maybe it was just age catching up with him, but a few days after the May 10 game, Roy suffered a severely strained calf pull in his right leg. The pull was bad enough to cause hemorrhaging at the ankle, and Roy was unable to put weight on it for over a week. The injury hampered his mobility for the entire month of June. John Herrnstein and Danny Cater were called in to cover for him at first base, and Roy was relegated to the bench for mostly pinch-hitting duties. He tried valiantly to bounce back, only to re-aggravate the leg injury in July.

And so it was that on July 16, Roy was sold to the Washington Senators for $20,000 on a 30-day conditional basis. The Phillies also put aging veteran Cal McLish on waivers. McLish, hampered by a shoulder injury, was having a difficult time coming back into the rotation. The team called up pitcher John Boozer and first baseman Costen Shockley from their Arkansas farm team in the Pacific Coast League.[17]

Roy knew he was going back to Washington; his wife told him so. As he explained it, "I called Jo one night, and she said she had a funny dream that I was going back to Washington. I told her it was only a dream. The next day, the Phillies told me I had been sold to Washington."[18]

The trade was just another of the many "what ifs" in Sievers' life.

The "Phabulous Phold"

No sooner had Roy left than the Philly scribes began to second-guess Mauch and the trade:

> The Phils certainly are taking a new approach to a pennant drive—releasing the veterans and bringing up the kids. They let go of Cal McLish and Roy Sievers. Most clubs spend exorbitant prices in August for a pinch-hitter like Sievers, who might give them the long ball to break up just one or two games. That can make the difference for the million-dollar jackpot. A pennant drive is no time to be cutting down the payroll.[19]

The 1964 Phillies team was a dream to behold that year. After jumping out to an early lead in the standings, they wowed their fans with timely hitting, great pitching, and stellar fielding. Bobby Wine had won the Gold Glove Award at shortstop in 1963, and Rubén Amaro would win it in 1964. On Father's Day, June 14, perennial All-Star Jim Bunning threw the first National League perfect game in 84 years, also the first since Don Larsen's perfecto in the 1956 World Series. Johnny Callison had one of his greatest years in the majors, hitting 31 home runs with 104 RBI, and a .274 average. The icing on the cake would be his walk-off home run for the National League victory in the 1964 All-Star Game. Added to all of that was "Rookie of the Year" sensation Richie Allen, the quintessential five-tool player, who would tear up the NL to the tune of 29 home runs, 38 doubles, 13 triples, a .318 batting average and a league-leading 125 RBI.

A team of destiny ... almost.

In those days, the math was a bit easier to figure out, and the stakes were considerably higher. Without any playoffs, just the World Series, it was a simple case of win-and-you're-in. With 12 games left in the 1964 regular season, the Phillies held a 6½-game lead in the National League. But over the last week and a half of the season, the team went into a complete freefall, losing ten consecutive games in seemingly every manner possible. Gene Mauch misused his starters, Jim Bunning and Chris Short, in some instances pitching them on two days' rest. The Phillies kept losing and the Cardinals kept winning, eventually beating out the Reds and the Phillies to win the NL pennant and then beating the Yankees in the 1964 World Series. The Phillies and Reds tied for second, one game behind the Cardinals, and the "Phabulous Phold" went down in baseball legend.

It was not until 16 years later, when the team won the pennant and the World Series, that many felt the Phillies' curse was gone. Chico Ruiz's steal of home plate on September 21, 1964, which began the ten-game losing streak, was equated with the Red Sox's "Curse of the Bambino." Even after 1980, in seasons when the Phillies faltered for no explicable reason, their shortcomings were blamed on the curse of Chico Ruiz.[20]

Frank Thomas, former All-Star who played first base for the 1964 Phillies, remembers:

> I can't believe the team went into such a free fall. It seemed like there was nothing we could do to stop it. If Roy had been with the team, I'm sure he would have helped the club. He was a better hitter than people give him credit for, 'cause he played on last place teams. Roy was a great guy, down to earth and solid. He doesn't get the recognition he should get from the Hall of Fame.[21]

Back Home Again in Ol' DC

Roy returned to the Senators, only to find there was a sack full of first-sackers. Dick Phillips, acquired from the Giants in 1963, was the starting first baseman, and Joe Cunningham, acquired from the White Sox in exchange for Bill Skowron, was the backup.

Ever the optimist, Roy looked upon the trade as a positive.

> I think it's a good break for me coming back to Washington. Gene Mauch told me I would be with the Phillies as long as he was. Gene is still there, but I'm gone. I'm not blaming him or anybody. John Quinn [Phillies general manager] is a fine man and treated me well.
>
> I had an idea I'd be released by the Phillies. Gene told me at 37, my age, it was tough to place me. Another thing was my salary. A lot of clubs wouldn't take it on.[22]

Roy came back to DC and was immediately benched by team physician Dr. George Resta in order to mend that ailing leg. He joined Don Zimmer (groin pull), Jim King (appendicitis), Ed Brinkman (twisted ankle), and Jim Duckworth (heat exhaustion) at the end of the bench that, according to Bob Addie, looked like a ward in a TV hospital drama.[23]

Roy, in his last formal photograph with the Senators before being released in April of 1965 (National Baseball Hall of Fame Library, Cooperstown, New York).

Roy spent the rest of the season platooning and pinch-hitting. He still managed to find some pop in the old bat, hitting four long balls in 58 at-bats.

One in particular came off his old friend, Camilo Pascual of the Minnesota Twins.

Always quick with a quip or a joke, Roy pulled one on his old friend, Stan Musial. Musial, on a trip to DC to work on his job as a consultant to the President's Council on Physical Fitness, stopped by the Nats' locker room. Roy, getting wind of it, started to pantomime Musial's famous "corkscrew" batting stance, feet together, crouched over, and wiggling his hips. As the laughter subsided, Musial just said, "Hmmm, that stance will never make it. Tell that guy to forget baseball!"

On a road trip to Boston, Roy heard that his mentor, Ted Williams, was laid up at the New England Baptist Hospital. Sneaking in to visit him, Roy recalled:

> Ted was watching a baseball game on TV, and he concentrated just as hard as he did when he was playing ball. We had a real nice talk and he seemed pleased to see me. Personally, I think Williams is the greatest hitter I ever saw. When I was in a slump, the first one I went to was Ted. He used to straighten me out. I know when I was with Washington the first time, I used to go to Ted and then go out and beat Boston because Ted straightened me out."[24]

With a .172 batting average by the end of the season, Roy was put on waivers.

One Last Time

Roy was invited to spring training in 1965 by his home team, the World Champion St. Louis Cardinals. But he once again showed the great character that had been his lifelong trademark: he signed with the last-place Senators instead. "I felt I owed it to George Selkirk to go to Florida as a free agent with the Senators," he told sportswriter Neal Russo. "They picked me up when the Phillies let me go last year. They knew I had a bum leg at the time, but they still paid $25,000 to get me."[25]

Roy was re-signed by the Senators in the spring of 1965. He went down to camp in Pompano Beach, Florida, with renewed hope for one last year in the sun. Manager Gil Hodges gave him a thorough look-see and liked what he saw. However, Roy was the low man on the totem pole, and there was another logjam of six first basemen at camp. As Roy remembered it later, "Hodges told me I wasn't gonna play regular. I was too old and too banged up to play day to day. He said he was gonna pinch hit me and use me against left handers. That was fine with me, just so's I'm playin.'"

Roy continued to get hits and a few home runs during the exhibition season. But after just 12 regular season games and 21 at-bats, he was granted his unconditional release in May. With the unconditional release, Roy was free to find employment elsewhere. However, after unsuccessful tryouts with both the Cardinals and the White Sox, he knew it was time to hang them up. His 17-year career as a major league player was over.

The Senators acquired the services of the mammoth Frank Howard from the Los Angeles Dodgers in the spring of 1965. At 6 foot, 7 inches and 225 pounds, the 1960 "Rookie of the Year" would become the "new" Roy Sievers, putting tape measure home runs into the upper decks of the D.C. Stadium in southeast DC. Howard had played against Roy from 1962 through 1964 when Roy was with the Phillies, and in some spring training and exhibition games.

Howard was effusive with his praise:

> I only knew Roy as a Senator for just a few months in the beginning of '65 'cause he got released shortly after the season started. I knew him from playin' some exhibition games when he was with the Phillies in '63 and I was with the Dodgers. I got to know him a little bit during spring training, but I got to know him very well after I finished playing.
>
> Roy Sievers was a pro's pro. He epitomizes what professional baseball is. He had great work habits, great pre-game preparation based upon who was pitching that night. He really studies the game. Harmon [Killebrew] told me [Roy] and Jim Lemon really helped him a lot, as far as game preparation and working a pitcher.
>
> Roy was an outstanding breaking ball hitter, as well as the fast ball. He had a great swing for Fenway Park and Tiger Stadium. In 1959, they had Roy, and big Jim Lemon and Killebrew and Bobby Allison [on the Senators]. If those guys were playin' in Fenway, they coulda hit a hundred and forty home runs!
>
> For whatever reason, there never have been that many right hand hitters with that picturesque, mechanically sound swing. I told Roy [at an autograph show] the three guys, I thought, had that mechanically sound swing from the right side of the plate were Mark McGwire, Dick Stuart and Roy. Roy just smiled at me and said, "Ya know, Ted Williams told me I had the letter perfect swing."[26]

Putting It All to Good Use

Roy might have lost a step, but he probably could have made up for it with a career in bowling, of all things. He had always been a good athlete and excelled at many physical sports. He was an excellent golfer, played basketball and handball regularly, and loved to bowl. And he won trophies there as well.

In the spring of 1965, Roy was invited to be a last-minute replacement for Don Zimmer at the Major League Baseball/Bowling Championship. The event, hosted by Roy's pal Joe Garagiola, was broadcast on national television on NBC's "Sports in Action" program. Roy was the spark plug in the American

League's victory over the National League, 137–134. Roy also won the Sporting News Trophy for high single game with a roll of 235.[27]

But Roy wasn't through with baseball just yet.

In 1966, Roy found his way back home—almost—to the team for which he originally played, the St. Louis Browns. He accepted an invitation from Bill DeWitt, friend and one-time Browns General Manager, to join former teammates Don Heffner and Ray Shore and become the batting coach for the Cincinnati Reds. Roy joined Dave Bristol, Mel Harder, and Whitey Wietelmann to form the biggest coaching staff the Reds had ever had. Wearing his crisp new Reds uniform and sporting a stopwatch, Roy quipped to the press, "I've finally arrived!"[28]

Roy worked hard for his pal Don Heffner, but the Reds finished in seventh place that season, and his contract was not renewed for the following year.

Sievers was then offered a managerial position in the Orioles organization to pilot the AA Elmira Pioneers in the Eastern League. Before he began with Elmira, however, he was asked by Wes Westrum, the new manager of the New York Mets, to come down to St. Petersburg and work with one of their new young hitters, Ron Swoboda.

Swoboda, a product of Baltimore's Sparrows Point High School and the University of Maryland, bore an uncanny likeness to the young Roy Sievers. Like Sievers, he had a promising rookie year in 1965, belting 19 home runs, 91 hits, and 15 doubles for a .228 batting average. Then, just like Roy, he slumped in his second year. The NL pitchers figured him out, allowing him only 76 hits, eight home runs and nine doubles for a weak .222 average.[29]

Casey Stengel, Swoboda's first manager, was noted for saying, "He will be great, super, even wonderful. Now, if he can only learn to catch a fly ball."[30] Swoboda's lack of prowess in the outfield notwithstanding, he had the potential of becoming a true long-ball threat in the Mets' lineup. "Professor" Sievers was called in to work with the youngster.

"He has some of the same problems I had when I first come up with the Browns in 1949," Roy told sportswriter Jack Lang. "[He] has trouble laying off the high, tight pitch and all the pitchers know it. They feed him that one up around the shoulders and he goes for it. Suddenly, he's in a hole. Then he starts pressing and they've got him."

Lang wrote that Roy was trying to get Swoboda to understand that many times a high pitch is a ball. "I'm trying to get him to be more determined at the plate," said Roy. "He's got to be more aggressive. I'm not trying to do a thing to his stance or his swing. They did that to me my second year, tried to get me to go to right field more often. I went from a .306 hitter to .238."[31]

Out to the East

The Pioneers played their games at Elmira Park, a stadium Roy had not seen since his minor league days. Roy had played one month at Elmira before he was sent to Springfield in the Three-I League. Returning to the park as a manager, Roy looked at its left field fence and said, "That wall doesn't look so high now, but in 1948 it looked 100 feet high."[32]

Roy skippered the Elmira team to a second-place finish in the Eastern League in 1967, with a respectable 74–65 record. In one game in particular, he showed what would be his biggest asset as a manager: patience. With the Pioneers playing the Reading Phillies on May 2, 1967, Roy watched as rookie pitcher Jerry Johnson was roughed up for two runs before retiring his first batter in the top of the first inning. In the second, he let Johnson bat with two men on base, and Johnson promptly struck out. Roy let Johnson labor through the game. In the seventh inning, with a runner in scoring position, Roy chose to let his pitcher bat again. Roy's patience was rewarded when the youngster singled in the winning run of the game.[33] "Yeah, I remember that kid," said Roy in an interview. "I had a lot of managers show me a lot of patience, especially when I hurt my shoulder so bad. I figured I should give the kid the chance to earn his way onto the ball club. He turned out to be all right."

After his season at Elmira was over, Roy was asked to help out at the fall instructional league camp in Sarasota, Florida. Roy, along with minor league managers Clyde McCullough, Pete Pavlick, and Bill Virdon, went down south under the direction of Bob Scheffing, the Mets' Player Personnel Director. Roy got to work with Nolan Ryan, Jerry Koosman, Duffy Dyer, Kenny Singleton, and Paul Lindblad, among others, all of whom went on to outstanding big league careers.[34]

Last Hurrah

After his winter ball assignment, Roy was reassigned to the Memphis Blues in the Class AA Texas League in 1968. The Blues had developed a bad habit of losing one-run ballgames, dropping 27 games by a run in 1967. Roy led them to a respectable, albeit losing, season of 67–69.

In 1969 and 1970, Roy was hired by long-time Senators friend Whitey Herzog to pilot the Burlington Bees, an Oakland Athletics' farm team in the Class A Midwest League; however, after two losing seasons, Roy was let go. Herzog explained why:

> I was the Director of Player Development [with the Mets] and we were the first team to use the Tele-Key service. Typically, the managers would write up a written report

> after each game and normally I'd get ahold of it two or three days later. Now, after they'd finish their game at night, they'd get on the Tele-Key service in the clubhouse and they'd call the game in. [The Record-O-Phone by Robosonics was one of the very first remote answering machine systems in the U.S. One could call into that phone service and leave voice messages. The person on the other end had a Tele-Key, a whistle-like tone generator, which would activate the answering machine.][35]
>
> If there was an injury or something they would want me to call 'em the next day and see what's goin' on. So I remember the Memphis [*sic*] Bees were playing in El Paso and for about three days I hadn't heard from Roy. So I called him up after they had completed their series down there and said, "Roy, what's goin' on?" So he started talkin' to me about goin' over to Mexico last night and havin' a few Tequilas or somethin,' I don't know, he wasn't much of a drinker. So I says, "What did you [the team] do last night?" and he says "Let me get the paper." And I said, "WHAT?? You don't know if your team won or lost?!" I said, "Roy, I don't think you're made out to be a manager." I really didn't think he enjoyed it, so I let him go and I brought in Roy McMillan to manage the team for the rest of the season.[36]

"Whitey had to fire me," Roy said. "He said I just didn't have 'the eye' to be a manager. And he was right."

Proud Papa

In 1970, there was another Sievers name starting to garner attention in the media. Roy's son, Robin, was signed by the Sarasota Cardinals of the Florida International Gulf Coast rookie league. Robin had been a star athlete at Hazelwood High School in the northwestern suburbs of St. Louis, lettering in football, basketball and baseball.

Rob was a six foot, 170-pound, left-handed-hitting third baseman who could flash the leather at the hot corner. He had the distinction of starting the first triple play ever recorded at Lang Field in FIL history. After six games with the Cardinals, Rob was promoted to the Lewiston (ID) Broncs, the Single-A affiliate in the Northwest League. Smashing three home runs there, he was transferred to the Midwest League's Cedar Rapids (IA) Cardinals in 1971. Rob would wind up his career with the Orangeburg Cardinals in the Western Carolina League in 1973.

Rob remembers:

> I hit about three or four homers in Idaho and a few more when I got to Florida. Unfortunately, I got drafted in the Army and it sort of ruined my career. It was also unfortunate I signed with the Cardinals, 'cause they really didn't have a good organization for promotin' people. Joe Medwick, of all people, was my batting coach, and he was ancient by then. I was a pull hitter and they tried to make me a slap hitter to left field but I couldn't run too good. I wasn't very fast. It really wasn't the right thing for me. I thought I was good enough and everyone else thought I was good enough but I never really made it.[37]

As his dad says, "Robin was a good ballplayer. He was a third baseman and he could hit. He'd a been a good ballplayer had he been scouted."

Moving On and Making the Circuit

Roy came back to St. Louis, much to the delight of his wife, Joan, and the kids, Shawn and Robin. He went to work for Yellow Freight Systems as a foreman at the delivery house in St. Louis. After 18 years, he was unceremoniously fired one month before he would have been fully vested for a pension. "Yes, after they let me go I was really mad," he remembered. "But I told Joan, 'Well, I guess it's time for me to retire.'"

Roy retired to suburban St. Louis and spent his time with his children, Shawn and Rob, and with Joan until her untimely passing in 2006.

Roy became a darling on the autograph show circuit and at many Old Timers Games, especially in the St. Louis and Washington, D.C., areas. Bing Devine, General Manager for the St. Louis Cardinals during the late 1950s and early 1960s, had authentic St. Louis Browns replica uniforms made for a Cardinals-Browns reunion. Bill Madden described the uniform thusly: "Although it's a replica, you could hardly tell the difference from the real thing—and as most collectors will tell you, an old Brownies' uniform is among the rarest of gems today."

Roy has since turned down lucrative offers for that uniform on the collectibles market. He told Madden, "I liked it so much, I asked Bing if I could buy it and take it home with me. He said, 'Take it, it's yours.' It's nice to know collectors think so much if it, but the fact is, so do I. This uniform is something I'll keep for the rest of my life."[38]

Always the competitor, Roy hit two singles for the American League All Stars in the 1989 Old Timers Classic at Pilot Field in Buffalo, NY.

In 1996, Roy joined with former Senators greats Frank Howard, Ed Yost, Jim Lemon, and Mickey Vernon, along with Dodgers veterans Cal Abrams, Joe Pignatano, Tommy Holmes, Cal McLish, and Bobby Morgan, as featured guests at a Senators-Dodgers reunion for the First Annual Leukemia Society's Sports Humanitarian of the Year Award, given to the Dodgers' great Hall of Fame manager, Tommy Lasorda.[39]

Over the years, Roy and his good friend and local businessman Frank Bosqui have attended many golf outings and charity tournaments throughout the Midwest. Roy was a featured guest at many St. Louis Browns and Washington Senators reunions, and is still in demand as a speaker and at autograph shows. He has a lot of fond memories.

Author Paul Scimonelli shares a happy moment with his boyhood idol in the kitchen of Roy's suburban home in St. Louis in October 2014 (author collection).

> I used to do a lot of autograph shows, but not so much anymore. But I did get to know Ted Williams and Joe DiMaggio during the last years of their lives. I was down in Florida one year doing a card show, and Ted was gonna be there. I sat down next to him and started talkin' to him and all those people were lined up. I had about 20 photos of him and I asked him, "Ted, if you got some time, can I slide these photos in while you're signin' for everybody?" He said, "Gimme 'em," and he signed them all right there. Boy, those people were pissed!
>
> I got to sit with DiMaggio in a hotel in Florida one winter. He had his two little nieces or somethin' with him and he brought them up and we talked with them. We just talked a lot about baseball back when we was playin,' and he says to me, "Gosh it's good to talk to you. You were a great hitter." And I says to him, "YOU were a good hitter. I watched you all the time!" That was really somethin' comin' from Joe.

When asked which park or stadium was his favorite to hit in, he humorously replied, "All of 'em!" But upon further reflection, he said, "Tiger Stadium in Detroit. It had a great background. All the seats were green and you could see the ball real good. The lights were good and you could really see real well in there. I hit a lot of homers in that park."

Sixteen, to be exact.

Reflections and Testaments

Thinking back on his career, Roy mused,

> The toughest pitcher I ever faced was Bob Feller. Threw 100 miles an hour. That ball would be up on you in a hurry. I got to talk to him in his home town in Iowa, and he says to me, "You were a great hitter." I says to him, "You were a great pitcher. If I had to face you every damn day, it would have been a long career!"
>
> Allie Reynolds was also real tough. Came inside a lot. They all were tough, all those pitchers back then were tough. Nobody wanted to give up a home run if they could get away with it. Dizzy Trout had a great fastball-curve ball. Hal Newhouser had a great combo. Camilo Pascual had a great curve ball. I saw a lot of breaking balls.

Thinking back on baseball in those days, Bob Wolff reflected,

> These were real friends. They weren't ballplayers that I interviewed. They were all personal friends. We got to have lunch together, travel together. There was a camaraderie there that you don't see anymore. Roy was one of the guys I was closest to on the team. Some people cared and some people don't. He always cared.

On playing in a major market, Wolff posited,

> Where one plays is of great significance. And I covered this. You play in New York, well, it's all over all the papers, all the big TV shows, all the networks, all the advertisers, the sponsors. If you do well, you're exhorted all the time. You do poorly, you're just killed! You'll get more publicity if you're doing poorly than if you're doing well. The press in New York makes heroes and discards them very quickly.[40]

Roy earned the respect of all of the great hitters of the time. His son Rob tells this story:

> After Mickey [Mantle] died, we went up to [his memorial] golf tournament up near his home in Joplin. We were invited to go to Mickey's house, it was right there on the golf course, but I never got to go. But I was talkin' to Mickey's kids and they all said the only other [ballplayer's] picture Mickey had in his house was Dad's. It was right there on the mantelpiece.[41]

When asked what his greatest moment in baseball was, Roy's response was poetic:

> My favorite moment in baseball was just puttin' on a major league uniform for 18 years. It was just super to me, either National or American League. I don't regret one minute I spent in baseball. I just wished I could have played longer.

Roy was considered for the National Baseball Hall of Fame in 1971 and 1972. He is currently #117 on the all-time home run list.

He is still waiting for the call from the Hall.

Epilogue

As noted in Chapter 4, baseball author, historian, and sabermetrician Bill James wrote extensively about Roy Sievers, along with Joe Adcock, Vic Wertz, and Ted Kluszewski, in a March 2014 online article entitled "Four Sluggers." The four men shared remarkably similar career statistics; all became first basemen who were misplaced at the beginning of their careers at positions for which they were not suited; and all suffered either career-ending or career-defining injuries.

In his final summation of the four, James asks the most salient and prescient question: What if?

> There are people who will argue that [Sievers] should be in the Hall of Fame, *despite the four-year infarction in the middle of his career.* Sievers was the rookie of the year in 1949, hit 42 homers in 1957, 39 homers in 1958—and he wasn't any .250 hitter; he was a .290 hitter. He hit .295 or better four times as a regular. You give him back those four years that started with a foolish, mid-game decision to see if he could play third base, I think he's an obvious Hall of Famer.

Roy Sievers' career is almost totally defined by what ifs, a series of decisions and events that may have kept him from reaching his full potential as a ballplayer and an almost guaranteed member of baseball's Hall of Fame.

What if Roy had not hurt his shoulder? With his shoulder intact, Roy easily could have averaged 20 to 40 home runs and between 80 to 100 RBI for each of those four lost seasons. Do the math and he has Hall of Fame numbers, even playing for second-division teams.

What if Roy and his father had decided to sign with the Cardinals instead of the Browns? Yes, second-division clubs were easier as an entrée into the majors, but in the musical world, the saying goes, "If you play with amateurs, you sound like an amateur." One only gets better by playing with players who are better, in baseball as in music. Just being on a first-division club, like the 1949 Cardinals, would have given Roy the aura of being in a winner's camp. Even if he couldn't dethrone Enos Slaughter or Stan Musial, he would probably have had the opportunity to be traded to another first-division club, thus increasing his chances of playing for a winner.

What if Calvin Griffith had not been a tight-fisted racist who horribly mismanaged the Senators? Well, that certainly is a question for the ages. Roy had outstanding offers from contending teams like the Yankees, the Red Sox, and the White Sox which would have, or in some cases should have, put him on a pennant-winning team; consequently, he would have received more consideration from future Hall of Fame voters. Instead, Griffith kept Roy a virtual slave due to the adamantine reserve clause, refusing to trade him until he felt he was no longer effective (once again due to injury). Had Griffith traded Roy to Chicago in June of 1959, during the Sox's pennant run, there is no question he could have propelled the Sox to a championship.

What if Roy had not continued to get hurt? Injuries are always a part of the game due to the competitive nature of the participants, and Roy was no exception. All of the major trades throughout his career were predicated upon injuries that robbed him of production. It took another three decades for baseball owners to get rid of what I call the "Wally Pipp" syndrome: a player gets hurt—replace or get rid of him. Damaged goods. A healthy Sievers could have continued to put up important numbers and extended his career by another three years.

Had Roy not been playing on second division teams, would he have won the 1957 Most Valuable Player award? Since the inception of all of the various MVP awards, there has been an inordinate amount of weight placed upon winning the World Series or being in the 1st Division, rather than a player's true contribution to his team when it comes to MVP voting, as these statistics will bear out.

The indication "4 out of 8" and all the other designations means 4 out of the 8 MVP's from that time period were from World Series winners or from the World Series loser or another 1st division club.

- 1911–1914: The Chalmers Award, 4 out of 8 (50%)
- 1922–1929: League Awards, 8 out of 13 (61% rounded)
- 1931–2016: BBWAA Awards, 77 out of 85 (90% rounded)
- 1922–2016: a span of 93 years (no WS in 1994), 88 out of the 182 MVP players came from non-World Series teams (48% rounded). This statistic reflects a major paradigm shift which occurred between 1992 and 2016, when only 6 players received the award who played on World Series winning or losing teams.
- 1939 to 1963: The years many consider the be the "Golden Age" of baseball and certainly of Yankee dominance 37 out of 50–74%

- 1949 to 1965: Roy's playing years—22 out of 34 (65% rounded)
- In the entire history of baseball, only five players from losing teams have won the MVP award: Ernie Banks twice (1958–59 Cubs), Andre Dawson (1987 Cubs), Alex Rodriguez (2003 Rangers), and Cal Ripken Jr. (1991 Orioles).

What if Roy had played in more friendly confines? Yes, they pulled in the left field fences for him in 1956, from 408 to 388 and then to 350 feet, but Griffith Stadium was still cavernous in comparison to all of the other American League ballparks during the 1950s. Roy was a dead pull right-handed hitter. The majority of his home runs went to left or left-center field. Herewith a comparison:

Stadium	*Left Field Line*	*Home Runs*	*Team*
Griffith	388	91	Senators
Comiskey Park	362	26	White Sox
Connie Mack Stadium	334	38	Phillies
Fenway Park	310	25	Red Sox
Yankee Stadium	318	21	Yankees
Kansas City	350	20	Athletics
Tiger Stadium	340	16	Tigers
Memorial Stadium	330	15	Orioles
Municipal	322	12	Indians

The majority of Roy's playing career was in Washington, so it is obvious that the majority of his homers would be in Griffith Stadium (388-foot left field line). He hit 50.5% (91) homers at home and 49.5% (89) away. But how productive he was elsewhere. In just two years with the White Sox, he hit 26 of his 55 home runs, (47%) in Comiskey Park (362-foot left field line) and 29 homers (52%) away. Playing part time for the Phillies from '62 through half of '64, he hit 38 of his 44 homers, (86%) in old Connie Mack stadium (334-foot left field line). The bottom line is this: Roy hit 168 home runs (52.8%) at home stadiums and 150 homers (47.2%) in away stadiums. He definitely liked the "friendly confines" of stadiums other than Griffith.

And as my uncle Nathan would say to me: "If 'if and but' were candy and nuts, Oh! what a party we'd have!"

The Belief

Herewith my personal conclusion as to why Roy became the beloved sports figure he is: There is that inexplicable, innate "thing" with which the very few are blessed. I like to call it transcendence. One only has to look at old home movies of a five-year-old Michael Jackson, dancing and singing in the family living room in Gary, Indiana, to see that the child had "it," that undeniable "something" to which only a few are blessed.

Roy Sievers had "it," and it was recognized by all who saw him. His brothers all said that no one had to teach Roy anything, he just naturally walked to the plate and hit the ball. Richard Ben Cramer, in his biography of Joe DiMaggio, alludes to exactly the same thing. DiMaggio was more self-deprecating, though. When asked by a young rookie, Lawrence Berra, about hitting, he said, "There is absolutely no skill involved. You just go up to the plate and hit the ball!"

Those of you who have tried to use a round stick to hit a round object that is going 90 miles an hour know this to be a false statement. The modern players interviewed on radio and television will all allude to the science of hitting, how they practice, working on technique and footwork, videotaping their practice sessions, going over and over each swing until the mechanics are perfect each and every time they swing. Today's technological advances can slow-motion all of the above-mentioned factors so the minutia can be analyzed and fixed, if necessary.

None of this existed in the mid-twentieth century, and yet the annals of baseball history are filled with the names of Cobb, Ruth, Gehrig, DiMaggio, Musial, Mize, Williams, Mantle, Mays, Aaron, Snider, and many more. All possessed that innateness, that special gift of "it" that allowed them to become the players they were.

DiMaggio was called the best *natural* hitter since Shoeless Joe Jackson. Ted Williams applied a more scientific approach. Roy Sievers confided in me that he didn't do a thing with his swing until he got to the major leagues, and only then did he begin his study of opposing pitchers and hitters. It was a gift.

Along with this naturalness came his Midwesterner's charm. That totally ineffable, pleasant demeanor was Roy's gift as well, and all who knew him believed in it. And they all would do anything to help him achieve his greatness. His high school coaches all saw it, scouts Wally Shannon and Lou Magoula saw it, owners Jack Fournier, Bill DeWitt, Bill Veeck, Clark Griffith, all saw it. All of them believed.

And then the devastating, near crippling injuries and a "miraculous" surgery. Dr. Bennett believed. Bill Veeck and Bucky Harris believed; Cookie Lavagetto, Al Lopez, Gene Mauch, all believed. And all of Roy's teammates believed.

And if you know anything about Ted Williams, you will know he is not a man of faint praise. Williams was direct, combative, and acerbic, a public relations nightmare in Boston. However, when the greatest hitter in baseball says "he's got the sweetest right handed swing in baseball," one must listen and believe.

Through all of my interviews with over a dozen teammates, there was never a single untoward utterance about Roy Sievers. He was never ejected from a game for unsportsman like behavior, never had an argument with an umpire. Senator's manager Chuck Dressen wished Roy *would* have gotten angry a little more, and taken it out on the opposing pitchers! But the respect he garnered from owners, managers, and teammates was heartfelt and true because Roy treated everyone with respect.

Roy Sievers, with his affable Midwestern charm and prodigious hitting prowess, singlehandedly saved the Washington Senators franchise from folding in the 1950s. The miserly Griffiths had turned the team into a dumping ground for "what if" rookies, journeymen players and aging veterans, but the fans kept showing up to see Roy, despite the fact that there was little incentive to do so. It wouldn't be until 1965, when the expansion Senators purchased Frank Howard that the team would have another gate attraction as big as Roy. In the '50s, without Roy as the single biggest draw since Walter Johnson, the team would have folded or moved as early as 1958. In my estimation, the current Washington Nationals owe their existence to Roy Sievers.

In the "Four Sluggers" article, Bill James opined:

> There are very few players in major league history who have done what Roy Sievers did. After having a terrific season as a rookie in 1949, Sievers battled for four full seasons with a tsunami of failure, injuries and frustration—and came out of it on top. Find another player who did that. You can probably find one, but you'll realize that it's not easy to find one.

When asked if Roy had a good reputation around the league, Whitey Herzog responded:

> Oh, yeah. He was a really, really good clutch hitter. He didn't swing at bad pitches and he knew he was a low ball hitter. He was just amazing how disciplined a hitter he was. And he was just a great athlete. Even after he couldn't throw, he became a more than competent first baseman. I thought he was an above average defensive first baseman. He was a hell of a ball player, a hell of an athlete.

Baseball cards and those little green plastic soldiers were the toys of young boys. But seeing the smiling face of Roy Sievers on a 1957 Topps baseball card and actually meeting him at Picture Day was another thing altogether. The hero worship gets transferred from the card to the actual person. For the first time, you experience adult emotions you have never felt in your adolescence. You feel the frustration of a strike out and the elation of a homer. You think you can actually feel what your hero is feeling, and by this transference of adoration, you pass from adolescence to adulthood.

At the annual St. Louis Browns Fan Club luncheon in 2016, his fans showed there was no time limit on adoration. With tears welling in his eyes, 87-year-old retired surgeon Dr. Hugh "Skip" Bergman told me in an interview:

> Roy Sievers was my hero. I saw Roy play in his rookie year, 1949. I had just graduated high school, so I was about 18 at the time. He was a bit older, about 5 or 6 years older than me. [When he came up] he was very tall and muscular and handsome, they called him the Beaumont Bomber 'cause he went to Beaumont high school, but I went to McBride HS in north St. Louis. I didn't play anything, but my dad and all my brothers were all big Brownie fans. We used to go to the Browns games all the time. During the summer, we'd see at least two games every week, sometimes more depending. My dad was a doctor, so we'd go whenever he could. Roy was just enjoyable to watch, brought a little life to the team. He was just a St. Louis boy from north St. Louis where we lived and he just sort of caught my fancy. He was terrific!

My husky hero of the Golden Age of baseball, Roy Sievers, died peacefully in his home in Spanish Lake, Missouri, on Monday, April 3, 2017. His children Shawn and Rob were with him. He was 90 years old. Either by coincidence or preordination, it was The Washington Nationals and Baltimore Orioles Opening Day. I had the honor to shake his massive bear paw-like hand, those hands that could get through the strike zone in the blink of an eye. The strong Germanic stature was bent with age, but the eyes still twinkled when you would talk to him about the years he spent with the likes of DiMaggio, Mantle, Berra and Williams. He was, as always, humbled and bemused that they, like so many others, held him as one of the best hitters in baseball.

He was a gift.

Appendix

Achievements, Awards and Highlights

Achievements

- Four-time AL All-Star (1956, 1957, 1959, & 1961)
- AL Total Bases Leader (331–1957)
- AL Home Runs Leader (42–1957)
- AL RBI Leader (114–1957)
- 20 Home Run Seasons: 9 (1954–1962)
- 30 Home Run Seasons: 2 (1957 & 1958)
- 40 Home Run Seasons: 1 (1957)
- 100 RBI Seasons: 4 (1954, 1955, 1957, & 1958)

Awards and Honors

- Hall of Fame Voting:
    - 1971 BBWAA 4 (1.1%)
    - 1972 BBWAA 3 (.8%)
- *The Sporting News* 1949 American League Rookie of the Year (first one)
- BBWAA 1949 American League Rookie of the Year (first one)
- Inducted into the Missouri Sports Hall of Fame, 1992
- Honored in the "Circle of Fame" at a Washington Redskins football game, 1996
- Inducted into the St. Louis Sports Hall of Fame, 2011
- Named to the All–Senators team and invited to the opening celebration of the Washington Nationals NL expansion baseball team, 2005

Highlights

- Set season and career records in home runs for the Senators: 1954 (24), 1955 (25), 1956 (29), 1957 (42), 180 total in 3,547 at-bats
- 1957, hit home runs in six straight games to tie an American League mark

held by Ken Williams and Lou Gehrig. The major league record is eight, set by Dale Long in the National League (1956), and matched in the AL by Don Mattingly (1987) and Ken Griffey, Jr. (1993).

- One of only four players to hit pinch-hit grand slam home runs in both major leagues—the other three are Glenallen Hill, Jimmie Foxx, and Kurt Bevacqua.
- Hitting Streaks: 21 games (1960); 19 games (1961)
- Nine walk-off home runs in his career. Only Babe Ruth (12); Jimmie Foxx (12); Stan Musial (12); Mickey Mantle (12); Frank Robinson (12); David Ortiz (11); and Tony Perez (11) have had more.
- July 27–August 3, 1957, eight consecutive home runs for his team. This has been surpassed by only Babe Ruth (14); Goose Goslin (10); and Vic Wertz (9).
- Led Central Association in games (125), hits (159), runs (121), home runs (34) and RBI (141), 1947.
- Led Three-I League outfielders in assists (22), 1948.
- Led American League in sacrifice flies (11), 1954.
- Led American League in home runs (42), total bases (331), extra-base hits (70), and RBI(114), 1957.
- Led American League in intentional walks (8), 1960.

Home Runs by Park		***Home Runs Against Team***	
Griffith Stadium	91	Phi/KC Athletics	46
Comiskey Park	46	White Sox	39
Shibe Park	38	Tigers	38
Fenway Park	25	Red Sox	38
Yankee Stadium	21	Yankees	32
Municipal Stadium	20	Orioles	29
Tiger Stadium	16	Indians	26
Sportsman's/Busch	16	Senators/Twins	18
Memorial Stadium	15	SF Giants	10
Cleveland Stadium	12	Mets	8
Wrigley Field (LA)	3	Reds	6
County Stadium	3	Senators (expansion)	5
Crosley Field	2	Braves	5
Shea Stadium	2	Cardinals	4
Candlestick Park	24	Astros	4
Polo Grounds	1	LA Dodgers	4
Metropolitan Stadium	1	LA Angels	3
Dodger Stadium	1	Pirates	2
Wrigley Field (Chi)	1	Cubs	1

Homers vs. Right Handed Pitchers	229
Homers vs. Left Handed Pitchers	89
Homers at Home Team Field	150
Homers at Away Team Field	168

Roy Sievers Lifetime Statistics

Year	*Age*	*Team*	*G*	*AB*	*R*	*H*	*2B*	*3B*	*HR*	*GRSL*	*RBI*	*BB*	*IBB*	*SO*	*SH*	*SF*	*HBP*	*GIDP*	*AVG*	*OBP*	*SLG*
1949	23	*Browns*	*140*	471	84	144	28	1	16	1	91	70	1	75	2	—	2	15	.306	.398	.471
1950	24	*Browns*	*113*	370	46	88	20	4	10	1	57	34	1	42	2	—	2	11	.238	.305	.395
1951	25	*Browns*	*31*	89	10	20	2	1	1	0	11	9	0	21	0	—	1	4	.225	.303	.303
1952	26	*Browns*	*11*	30	3	6	3	0	0	0	5	1	0	4	1	—	0	1	.200	.226	.300
1953	27	*Browns*	*92*	285	37	77	15	0	8	0	35	32	0	47	6	—	0	9	.270	.344	.407
1954	28	*Senators*	*145*	514	75	119	26	6	24	1	102	80	9	77	2	11	2	17	.232	.331	.446
1955	29	*Senators*	*144*	509	74	138	20	8	25	1	106	73	3	66	0	5	4	17	.271	.364	.489
1956	30	*Senators*	*152*	550	92	139	27	2	29	0	95	100	10	88	0	4	5	12	.253	.370	.467
1957	31	*Senators*	*152*	572	99	172	23	5	42	2	114	76	11	55	0	2	7	9	.301	.388	.579
1958	32	*Senators*	*148*	550	85	162	18	1	39	0	108	53	2	63	0	7	4	13	.295	.357	.544
1959	33	*Senators*	*115*	385	55	93	19	0	21	0	49	53	6	62	0	4	2	10	.242	.333	.455
1960	34	*White Sox*	*127*	444	87	131	22	0	28	0	93	74	8	69	0	4	3	13	.295	.396	.534
1961	35	*White Sox*	*141*	492	76	145	26	6	27	2	92	61	4	62	0	4	6	11	.295	.377	.537
1962	36	*Phillies*	*144*	477	61	125	19	5	21	1	80	56	3	80	0	3	7	8	.262	.346	.455
1963	37	*Phillies*	*138*	450	46	108	19	2	19	1	82	43	5	72	2	9	5	6	.240	.308	.418
1964	38	*Phillies*	*49*	120	7	22	3	1	4	0	16	13	1	20	0	2	1	6	.183	.265	.325
1964	38	*Senators*	*33*	58	5	10	1	0	4	0	11	9	2	14	0	0	0	1	.172	.284	.397
1965	39	*Senators*	*12*	21	3	4	1	0	0	0	0	4	0	3	0	0	0	1	.190	.320	.238

Career	*G*	*AB*	*R*	*H*	*2B*	*3B*	*HR*	*GRSL*	*RBI*	*BB*	*IBB*	*SO*	*SH*	*SF*	*HBP*	*GIDP*	*AVG*	*OBP*	*SLG*
17 Years	1,887	6,387	945	1,703	292	42	318	10	1,147	841	66	920	15	55	51	164	.267	.354	.475

Chapter Notes

Introduction

1. Bill James, *The New Bill James Historical Baseball Abstract* (New York: The Free Press, 2010).
2. Author telephone interview with Frank Howard, 3 April 2015.
3. Author telephone interview with Frank Thomas, 8 June 2015.
4. Author interview with Roy Sievers, approximately January 1989, at the Atlantic City Sports Card and Autograph Show. Also, *The Sporting News* quoted Casey Stengel as saying Sievers "has the sweetest right-handed swing in the league" (Oscar K. Ruhl, "Sievers Could Be Nats' First HR Champ," 21 August 1957, 3–4).

Chapter 1

1. This quote and all quotes from Roy Sievers throughout the book, unless otherwise noted, are drawn from a series of telephone interviews conducted from 2014 through 2016 by the author.
2. "Peopling St. Louis: the Immigration Experience," retrieved from https://www.stlouis-mo.gov/government/departments/planning/cultural-resources/preservation-plan/Part-I-Peopling-St-Louis.cfm.
3. "Population of St. Louis City & County, and Missouri 1820–2010: Saint Louis Population Figures from the U.S. Census Bureau," retrieved from http://www.genealogybranches.com/stlouispopulation.html.
4. "A Brief History of St. Louis," retrieved from https://www.stlouis-mo.gov/visit-play/stlouis-history.cfm.
5. "Constructing the Fair." retrieved from http://mohistory.org/exhibits/Fair/WF/HTML/About/; "The 1904 St. Louis World's Fair: An Overview," retrieved from http://webpages.charter.net/mtruax/1904wf/home.html; and "A Brief History of St. Louis." Retrieved from https://www.stlouis-mo.gov/visit-play/stlouis-history.cfm.
6. "History of St. Louis Neighborhoods: Downtown," retrieved from https://www.stlouis-mo.gov/archive/neighborhood-histories-norbury-wayman/cbd/architecture7.htm.
7. Author interview with Roy and William Sievers, 12 September 2014, and historical records from the St. Louis Genealogical Society.
8. Author interview with Bill Sievers, 14 October 2014.
9. "History of Corkball," retrieved from http://sportsmanscorkball.com/history-of-cork ball/.
10. "Stickball: The Basics of the Game," retrieved from http://www.streetplay.com/stick ball/introduction.shtml.
11. Chris O'Leary, "Indian Ball Official Rules," retrieved from http://www.chrisoleary.com/projects/Baseball/Coaching/Documents/IndianBall_OfficialRules.pdf, 2006.
12. Fred Buck, *Street Games: Memories of a St. Louis Childhood, the Fifties and Sixties* (Bloomington, IN: Author House, 2004).
13. Author telephone interview with Bill Sievers, 14 October 2014.
14. Author telephone interview with Roy Sievers.
15. F. C. Lane, "Joseph Tinker the Shortstop Manager and His Remarkable Career," *Baseball Magazine* 11, no. 3 (July 1913): 42–55.
16. David Q. Voigt, "America's Game: A Brief History of Baseball." *The Encyclopedia of Baseball* 8th ed. (New York: Macmillan, 1990).
17. Lou Schwartz, "Sportscasting Firsts 1920–Present," retrieved from http://www.americans-portscastersonline.com/sportscastingfirsts.html.
18. Author interview with Bill Sievers, 14 October 2014.

Chapter 2

1. Information retrieved from www.stlouis-mo.gov/archives/historyofstlouisneighborhoods.
2. "Petition to Name School After Dr. Wm. Beaumont." *Journal of the Missouri State Medical Association* 19 (12): 518–519, retrieved from https://babel.hathitrust.org/cgi/pt?id=uva.3470147790;view=1up;seq=526.
3. Dan Dillon, *So, Where'd You Go to High School: The Baby Boomer Years* (St. Louis, MO: Virginia Publishing, 2005).
4. Brett McMillan, "Baseball Success Starts with Honesty for Lee Thomas," November 9, 2012, retrieved from https://brettmcmillan.wordpress.com/2012/11/09/baseball-success-starts-with-honesty-for-lee-thomas/.
5. "Why Are Basketball Players Called Cagers?" retrieved from http://www.answers.com/Q/Why_are_basketball_players_called_cagers?#slide=8.
6. "History of American Legion Baseball," retrieved from http://www.legion.org/baseball/history.
7. "History of American Legion Baseball," retrieved from http://www.legion.org/baseball/history
8. Vern Tietjen, "Browns Pick a Home-Grown Peach in Sievers," *The Sporting News*, 1 June 1949, 7.
9. Author telephone interview with William Sievers, 14 October 2014.

Chapter 3

1. J. G. Taylor Spink, "Newcombe, Sievers Win Rookie Titles," *The Sporting News*, 26 October 1949, 5–6.
2. Ray Gillespie, "Brownies Now on Buying End—Hunt Pitchers," *The Sporting News*, 1 September 1948, 12.
3. Spink, "Newcombe, Sievers."
4. "1949 St. Louis Browns," retrieved from http://www.baseball-reference.com/teams/SLB/1949-schedule-scores.shtml.
5. Ray Gillespie, "Browns Hail Sievers as 'Rookie of Year'," *The Sporting News*, 5 October 1949, 16.
6. Author telephone interview with Bobby Shantz, 28 October 2014.
7. "1949 St. Louis Browns," retrieved from http://www.baseball-reference.com/teams/SLB/1949-schedule-scores.shtml.
8. "Daniel's Dope: Sievers Clinching Rookie Laurels," *New York World Telegram and Sun*, 3 September 1949.
9. Spink, "Newcombe, Sievers."
10. Spink, "Newcombe, Sievers."
11. Bill Paddock, "Roy and Don Add Writers' Awards as No. 1 Rookies," *The Sporting News*, 7 December 1949, 18.
12. Author telephone interview with Ned Garver, 18 March 2015.
13. Art Morrow, "A's to Spend and Spend for Mack's Golden Jubilee," *The Sporting News*, 26 October 1949, 20.
14. Gillespie, "Browns Hail Sievers."

Chapter 4

1. "Barnstorm," retrieved from http://www.merriam-webster.com/dictionary/barnstorm.
2. "Daredevil Lindbergh and his barnstorming day," retrieved from http://www.pbs.org/wgbh/amex/lindbergh/sfeature/daredevil.html.
3. Personal remembrance of the author.
4. Thomas Barthel, *Barnstorming and Exhibition Games 1900–1962: A History of Off-season Major League Play.* (Jefferson, NC: McFarland, 2007), 7–8.
5. *Ibid.*, 5.
6. William C. Kashatus, *Lou Gehrig: A Biography* (Westport, CT: Greenwood, 2004), 53.
7. Barthel, 5.
8. "Trout Recruits Barnstormers," *The Sporting News*, 7 September 1949, 29.
9. Barthel, 226–229.
10. Hal Hedwick, "Mexicans warmed by movie," *Miami News*, 12 October 1958, 112.
11. "Sophomore slump," retrieved from http://www.urbandictionary.com/define.php?term=sophomore slump.
12. "Sophomore slump: What is it? How do I deal with it?" retrieved from www.muhlenberg.edu/pdf/main/aboutus/counseling/sophomore_slump.pdf.
13. "Walt Dropo," retrieved from http://www.baseball-reference.com/players/d/dropowa01.shtml.
14. "Rick Sutcliffe," retrieved from http://www.baseball-reference.com/players/s/sutclri01.shtml.
15. "Joe Charbonneau," retrieved from http://www.baseball-reference.com/players/c/charbjo01.shtml.
16. Bob Broeg, "Eager-Beaver Sievers Gets Set for Comeback as Brownies Star," *The Sporting News*, 21 February 1951, 19.
17. "Brownie Brevities," *The Sporting News*, 31 May 1950, 10.
18. "Zack Taylor Works Hard to Improve

Sievers' Hitting," *The Sporting News*, 28 June 1950, 18.

19. "Brownies Won't Sell any 'Name' Players Says Chas. DeWitt," *The Sporting News*, 14 June 1950, 18.

20. "Brownies Foil Hoax to Get Sievers Away," *The Sporting News*, 19 July 1950, 12, and Roy Sievers interview.

21. "A Demented Fan and the Natural," retrieved from http://phillysportshistory.com/2011/06/14/this-day-in-philly-sports-history-a-demented-fan-and-the-natural/. And "Ruth Ann Steinhagen Is Dead at 83." Retrieved from http://www.nytimes.com/2013/03/24/sports/baseball/ruth-ann-steinhagen-83-troubled-shooter-of-the-phillies-eddie-waitkus.html.

22. . Bruce Nash and Allan Zullo. *The baseball hall of shame. The bottom of the barrel: The St. Louis Browns, 1902–1953* (New York: Pocket Books, 1990).

23. Bill James, "The Four Sluggers," 24 March 2014, retrieved from http://www.billjamesonline.com/four_sluggers/?Month=3&Year=2014.

24. "Sisler's Bat Tips Help Brownies Polish Edges," *The Sporting News*, 14 March 1951, 17.

25. "Eager-Beaver Sievers Gets Set for Comeback as Brownies Star," *The Sporting News*, 21 February 1951, 19.

26. "Zack Pulls Sievers Off Third; Browns Defense Too Sieve-Like," *The Sporting News*, 11 April 1951, 6.

27. "Roy Sievers Injured, Lost to Missions Rest of Season," *The Sporting News*, 15 August 1951, 29.

28. Wheatley, Tom, "HR Champ Roomed with Paige, Herzog," *St. Louis Post Dispatch*, 31 May 1991, 30.

29. *Ibid.*

Chapter 5

1. Bill James, "The Four Sluggers," 24 March 2014, retrieved from http://www.billjameson line.com/four_sluggers/?Month=3&Year=2014.

2. "Bill Veeck," retrieved from http://sabr.org/bioproj/person/7b0b5f10.

3. Bill James, "The Four Sluggers."

4. "Bill Veeck," retrieved from http://www.baseballreference.com/bullpen/Bill_Veeck.

5. "Eddie Gaedel," retrieved from http://www.sabr.org/bioproj/person/fa5574c8.

6. Bill Veeck and Ed Linn, *Veeck—As in Wreck: The autobiography of Bill Veeck* (Chicago: University of Chicago Press, 1963).

7. "Bill's Zany Promotions at Zenith in Midget Stunt," *The Sporting News*, 4 March 1959, 4.

8. Taped phone interview with Ned Garver, 4 October 2016.

9. David Nemec, *Great Baseball Feats & Facts* (New York: Penguin Books, 1989).

10. Bill James, "The Four Sluggers."

11. "One Platoon, Strong Against All Pitching, Demanded by Rajah," *The Sporting News*, 5 March 1952, 17.

12. "Biographical Sketch: George E. Bennett, MD (1885–1962)," retrieved from https://www.ncbi.nlm.nih.gov/pmc/articles/PMC3348291/.

13. "Obituary: Dr. George Eli Bennett," *The Sporting News*, 28 July 1962, 48.

14. "Noted Surgeon George Bennett Dies," *Baltimore Sun*, 18 July 1962, C8.

15. Personal letter from George Weiss to Dr. Bennett, 14 January 1958. Johns Hopkins University Archives.

16. "Medico Defers Operation on Roy Sievers' Shoulder," *The Sporting News*, 12 March 1952, 9.

17. Email correspondence from Dr. Brand to author.

18. "Sievers Could Be Nats' First HR Champ," *The Sporting News*, 21 August 1957, 3.

19. Taped interview with Dr. Michael Jacobs, 11 May 2016.

20. Bill James, "The Four Sluggers."

21. "Browns Counting on Confident Clint to Lick Soph Jinx," *The Sporting News*, 7 January 1953, 19.

22. *Ibid.*

23. "Veeck Serves Contracts at Lunch; Seven Wield Pen at Mass Signing," *The Sporting News*, 14 January 1953, 9.

24. "140 Games? Old Warhorse Enos Aiming at More," *The Sporting News*, 28 January 1953, 13.

25. "Marion Saves His Oratory Till He Gets a Bigger Crowd," *The Sporting News*, 18 February 1953, 15.

26. "Sievers' Batting Average Booms on Shift to Schoendienst Stick," *The Sporting News*, 29 January 1953, 14–15.

27. *Ibid.*

28. Paul Dickson, *The Dickson Baseball Dictionary*, 3d ed. (New York: W. W. Norton, 2009).

29. "Clint Courtney," retrieved from http://www.sabr.org/bioproj/person/7b7bd803.

30. "Martin Wins Second Scrap by Decision over Courtney," *The Sporting News*, 23 July 1952, 7.

31. Personal communication with the author.

32. "Round Two, Same Opponents—and Clint Again Loses Specs," *The Sporting News*, 6 May 1953, 5–6.

33. Taped phone interview with Don Larsen, 26 May 2015.

34. "Harridge Sets Mass Records for Brawl Fines," *The Sporting News*, 6 May 1953, 5.

35. David Alan Heller, *As Good As it Got: The 1944 St. Louis Browns* (Charleston, SC: Arcadia, 2003).

Chapter 6

1. Warren Corbett, "Bill Veeck," SABR Bio Project. Retrieved from www.sabr.org/bioproj/ person/ 7b0b5f10.

2. Hal Lebovitz, "Roller Coaster Veeck Off on Another Ride," *The Sporting News*, 4 March 1959, 3–4.

3. Warren Corbett, "Bill Veeck," and Nick Acocella, "Baseball's Showman," retrieved from http://www.espn.com/classic/veeckbill000816.html.

4. Corbett, "Bill Veeck."

5. Shirley Povich, "Change of Suits May Change Luck." This Morning with Shirley Povich, *The Sporting News*, 3 March 1954, 9.

6. Shirley Povich, "Sievers Paying Off Patient Bucky with His Power-Socking for Nats," *The Sporting News*, 18 August 1954, 6.

7. "Sievers Off Outfield List; He Can't Throw Overhand," *The Sporting News*, 24 March 1954, 8.

8. Shirley Povich, "Bucky Takes Nats' Grapefruit Losses with Grain of Salt." *The Sporting News*, 31 March 1954, 8.

9. Retrieved from www.baseball-almanac.com/stadium/st-griff.shtml.

10. Bob Burnes, "Highlights and Low Spots of '54 Season." *The Sporting News*, 6 October 1954, 12.

11. Dan Daniel, "Over the Fence." *The Sporting News*, 13 March 1955, 12.

12. Retrieved from www.baseballreference.com/teams/WSH/1955.html.

13. Shirley Povich, "Hard for Chuck to Believe—Need for Benching Sievers." *The Sporting News*, 25 May 1955, 10.

14. Shirley Povich, "Chuck Wanted Lefty Hitter, So Nats Sent Busby to White Sox." *The Sporting News*, 15 June 1955, 9.

15. Shirley Povich, "Nats Show New One-Two Punch, Jar Contenders." *The Sporting News*, 7 September 1955, 7.

16. Retrieved from http://www.baseball-reference.com/players/s/sievero01.shtml.

17. Shirley Povich, "Nats Near Bottom After Dive of Chuck's Hurling." *The Sporting News*, 29 June 1955, 11.

18. Michael Lenchan, "The Last of the Pure Baseball Men," *The Atlantic*, August 1981, retrieved from http://www.theatlantic.com/magazine/archive/1981/08/the-last-of-the-pure-baseball-men/305825/); Kevin Hennessy, "Calvin Griffith," retrieved from http://sabr.org/bioproj/person/5c118751.

19. Mark Stang and Phil Wood, *Nationals On Parade: 70 Years of Washington Nationals Photos* (Wilmington, OH: Orange Frasier Press, 2005); David Krell, "Kings of the World," *Memories and Dreams* 37, no.3, National Baseball Hall Of Fame publications (Summer 2015).

20. "The History of Latinos in Major League Baseball: The Early Years," retrieved from http://www.umich.edu/~ac213/student_projects06/witaw/early%20years.html.

21. Brian McKenna, "Joe Cambria," retrieved from http://sabr.org/bioproj/person/4e7d25a0.

22. Retrieved from http://twinstrivia.com/interview-archives/julio-becquer-interview/.

23. Shirley Povich, "Wiesler-Berberet Battery Long Coveted by Senators," *The Sporting News*, 15 February 1956, 19.

24. Shirley Povich, "Valdy, Nats' .221 Hitter, 'Too Valuable To Trade'," *The Sporting News*, 1 February 1956, 10; "Free-for-All for All of Nat Garden Jobs," 8 February 1956, 21; "Dressen Puts Choker on Valdivielso's Bat," 1 March 1956.

25. Telephone interview with Whitey Herzog, 7 July 2016.

26. "Sievers Stages Hit Show After Pay Hike," *The Sporting News*, 28 March 1956, 38.

27. "Infielders Lead as 'Hot Prospects,'" *The Sporting News*, 18 April 1956, 21.

28. Shirley Povich, "Ike Likes Yankees-Nats Homer Festival and Joins the Shelling—With Peanuts," *The Sporting News*, 25 April 1956, 7.

29. "Tettelbach Raps Home Run for First Major League Hit," *The Sporting News*, 25 April 1956, 7.

30. Povich, "Wiesler-Berberet Battery."

31. Shirley Povich, "Cuban Mound Pair Pegged as Nat Nifties," *The Sporting News*, 9 May 1956, 6.

32. "Sluggers Set One Day Mark by Walloping 39 Home Runs," *The Sporting News*, 9 May 1956, 20.

33. Gregory Wolf, "Roy Sievers," retrieved from http://sabr.org/bioproj/person/c8add426. Statistics retrieved from www.baseball-reference.com/home-runs.

34. Shirley Povich, "Old Fox Would Fume at Nats' Homer Fences," *The Sporting News*, 22 February 1956, 14.

35. Telephone interview with Whitey Herzog, 7 July 2016.

36. Information retrieved from www.baseballreference.com/Sievers/salaries.

Chapter 7

1. Oscar Ruhl, "Sievers Could Be Nats' First HR Champ," *The Sporting News*, 21 August 1957, 3–4.
2. Shirley Povich, "Sievers' Weighty Hitting Lightens Senators' Woes," *The Sporting News*, 1 May 1957, 10.
3. *Ibid.*
4. "Capital Close-ups," *The Sporting News*, 17 April 1957, 14.
5. Povich, "Sievers' Weighty Hitting."
6. Matt Sisson, "Cookie Lavagetto," retrieved from http://www.sabr.org/bioproj/person/fe135be8.
7. *Ibid.*
8. Shirley Povich, "Ousted Dressen Cast Vote for His Successor," *The Sporting News*, 15 May 1957, 9.
9. "Nats Deny 'Rebellion,' Label Chuck 'Fair and Not Tough,'" *The Sporting News*, 15 May 1957, 9.
10. Sisson, "Cookie Lavagetto."
11. Author's telephone interview with Bob Wolff, 5 December 2015.
12. Author's telephone interview with Maury Povich, 12 January 2016.
13. Sievers' home run log on www.baseball-reference.com.
14. Author's telephone interview with Shawn Sievers, October 2014.
15. "Stuffing the Box: The Redlegs and the 1957 All Star Game," retrieved from http://www.redszone.com/forums/showthread.php?60255-Stuffing-the-Box-The-Redlegs-and-the-1957-All-Star-Game.
16. "A Revision of All Star Voting Essential," *The Sporting News*, 10 July 1957, 12.
17. "Disappointed Over His Snub, But Roy's Happy A.L. Won," *The Sporting News*, 17 July 1957, 10.
18. "1957 All Star Game," retrieved from http://www.baseball-almanac.com/asgbox/yr1957as.shtml.
19. Ruhl, "Sievers Could Be Nats' First HR Champ."
20. "Sievers Belts Homer in Six Straight Tilts to Tie Mark," *The Sporting News*, 14 August 1957, 25.
21. Retrieved from http://www.baseball-reference.com/players/a/abernte02.shtml.
22. Game recreation developed from http://www.baseball-reference.com/boxes/WS1/WS1195708030.shtml.
23. Author telephone interview with Brooks Robinson, 9 April 2015.
24. Statistics retrieved from www.baseball-reference.com
25. Joe King, "Sore Shin Slows Mantle, Threatens Triple Crown," *The Sporting News*, 11 September 1957, 10.
26. James Lincoln Ray, "Mickey Mantle," retrieved from http://www.sabr.org/bioproj/person/61e4590a.
27. Hy Hurwitz, "Jensen Swings Into Stretch Run as Surprise Bidder for RBI Title," *The Sporting News*, 18 September 1957, 7.
28. "Nixon, Fans Honor Roy Sievers Tonight," *Washington Post*, 23 September 1957, A20.
29. Bill James, *The Bill James Gold Mine 2008*. Skokie, IL: ACTA Publications, 2008, 123.
30. "Nixon, Fans Honor Roy Sievers Tonight, " *Washington Post*, 23 September 1957, A20.
31. Author telephone interview with Shawn Sievers, 13 September 2014.
32. "Nats Lose on Sievers Night, 9–4," *Washington Post*, 23 September 1957, A17.
33. Author telephone interview with Charlie Brotman, 10 June 2015.
34. "Nixon Joins Washington Fans in Tribute to Slugger Sievers," *The Sporting News*, 25 September 1957, 31.
35. Bob Addie, "MVP Diadem for Sievers? Not in the Cards," *The Sporting News*, 2 October 1957, 12.

Chapter 8

1. "Mays' Stars Add Mexico to Latin Tour," *The Sporting News*, 2 October 1957, 60.
2. "Sievers-to-White Sox Only Deal Vetoed," *The Sporting News*, 6 November 1957, 15.
3. "Groat, Malzone To Be at Show," *The Sporting News*, 13 November 1957, 26.
4. "Sievers Chosen As Leading Sports Figure in St. Louis," *The Sporting News*, 20 November 1957, 25.
5. "Knife & Fork League" column, *The Sporting News*, 11 December 1957, 31; program from the M Club Banquet.
6. Jack Walsh, "Nixon at Capital Salute to Sievers," *The Sporting News*, 22 January 1958, 20.
7. Jesse Linthicum, "Ted, Stan, Lew Get Awards at Maryland Feed," *The Sporting News*, 22 January 1958, 20.
8. *Ibid.*
9. "2,100 to Salute Cobb, Musial, Other Greats at Manchester," *The Sporting News*, 15 January 1958, 23.
10. "Record Turnout of 2,260 Hails Stars at Manchester," *The Sporting News*, 22 January 1958, 21; "Recording Confirms Remark by Sievers

on Bosox Trade," *The Sporting News*, 29 January 1958, 22.

11. Ray Gillespie, "1,000 Salute St. Louis' All-Time Team," *The Sporting News*, 29 January 1958, 19.

12. Shirley Povich, "Royal Roy's Double Crown Adds Glitter to Cellar Nats," *The Sporting News*, 9 October 1957, 17.

13. Shirley Povich, "Senators Ready to Listen in Lane Plans to Talk Deals," *The Sporting News*, 20 November 1957, 17.

14. Shirley Povich, "Sievers Inks $36,000 Pact with Nats," *The Sporting News*, 5 March 1958, 4.

15. "Tighe Raps Field at Orlando, Excuses Six Tiger Regulars," *The Sporting News*, 26 March 1958, 27.

16. This famous phrase was penned in 1904 by Charles Dryden (1860–1931), writing for the *Philadelphia North American*, which later became the *Philadelphia Inquirer.*

17. Sievers' home run stats retrieved from www.baseball-reference.com.

18. Shirley Povich, "Hats Off! Roy Sievers," *The Sporting News*, 30 April 1958, 23.

19. Author's telephone interview with Bill Turner, 13 October 2016.

20. Lee Kavetski, "Sievers and Pearson Thrill Japan With Trans-Ocean Air Interview," *The Sporting News*, 7 May 1958, 26.

21. Shirley Povich, "Nats Step Up Pitch for Three-Way Help," *The Sporting News*, 28 May 1958, 16.

22. Shirley Povich, "Little Albie Swings Busy Bat with Nats," *The Sporting News*, 2 July 1958, 8.

23. Shirley Povich, "Punch and Pitching Perking Up Senators," *The Sporting News*, 11 June 1958, 16.

24. Author's telephone interview with Bill Turner.

25. "Versatile Rookie Pearson Joins 'Singing Senators', " *The Sporting News*, 11 June 1958, 44.

26. Author telephone interview with Bob Wolff, 5 December 2015.

27. Herb Heft, "Singing Nats Big Hits on Network TV," *The Sporting News*, 18 June 1958, 25.

28. Author telephone interview with Bob Wolff, 5 December 2015.

29. "Damn Yankees," retrieved from http://www.theatrehistory.com/american/musical017.html, and "Damn Yankees," retrieved from http://www.baseball-reference.com/bullpen/Damn_Yankees.

30. "History of the Congressional Baseball Game," retrieved from https://www.congressionalbaseball.org/history/; author's interview with Charlie Brotman.

31. Author's telephone interview with Bill Turner, 13 October 2016.

32. Mike Grahek, "Clark Griffith," retrieved from http://www.sabr.org/bioproj/person/96624988; "Players Protective Association," retrieved from http://www.baseball-reference.com/bullpen/Players_Protective_Association.

33. Grahek, "Clark Griffith."

34. Author's telephone interview with Bob Wolff, 5 December 2015.

35. "Reserve Clause," retrieved from http://www.baseball-reference.com/bullpen/Reserve_clause.

36. Fredrick Turner, *When the Boys Came Back: Baseball and 1946* (New York: Henry Holt, 1996); David Voigt, "The Owner-Player Conflict," retrieved from http://research.sabr.org/journals/owner-player-conflict.

37. Author's telephone interview with Robin Sievers, 8 October 2015.

Chapter 9

1. Hal Lebovitz, "Mays and Avila Squads to Play Mexico Series," *The Sporting News*, 10 September 1958, 1.

2. Larry Rohter, "Marcos Pérez Jiménez, Venezuela Ruler," *New York Times*, 22 September 2001, retrieved from http://www.nytimes.com/2001/09/22/world/marcos-perez-jimenez-87-venezuela-ruler.html.

3. "Nixon Attacked By Angry Venezuelans," retrieved from http://www.history.com/this-day-in-history/nixon-attacked-by-angry-venezuelans.

4. "Events and Discoveries: Without Portfolio," *Sports Illustrated*, 3 November 1958, 23–24.

5. "YMCA Award for Roy Sievers," *The Sporting News*, 12 November 1958, 20.

6. Author's telephone interview with Bill Turner, 13 October 2016.

7. Author's telephone interview with Phil Wood, 10 September 2015.

8. "The Scouting Report: What Are the Senators' Chances?" *Sports Illustrated*, 13 April 1959, 70–71.

9. Shirley Povich, "Cookie Collars Roy for Return to First Base," *The Sporting News*, 29 October 1958, 21; Shirley Povich, "Nats High on Kid Flash—Shift Roy to Gateway Duty," *The Sporting News*, 25 February 1959, 18.

10. Shirley Povich, "Nats High on Kid Flash," and "'Nat Defense Tighter' Cal Tells Critics," *The Sporting News*, 15 April 1959, 22.

11. Shirley Povich, "Cookie Sees Bright Spots

in Nat Scene" and "Regular Jobs Up for Grabs When Senators Open Camp," *The Sporting News*, 18 February 1959, 16.

12. "Major Flashes," *The Sporting News*, 15 April 1959, 29.

13. Shirley Povich, "Capital People, Capital Hurling, Capital Victory," *The Sporting News*, 15 April 1959, 23.

14. *Ibid.*

15. Shirley Povich, "Senators Flexing Strong Muscle in Bid for A.L. Power Leadership," *The Sporting News*, 20 May 1959, 24.

16. Bob Addie, "Bob Addie's Atoms," *The Sporting News*, 29 July 1959, 12.

17. All statistics retrieved from team pages at www.baseball-reference.com.

18. "Nixon and Khrushchev have a 'kitchen debate'," retrieved from http://www.history.com/this-day-in-history/nixon-and-khrushchev-have-a-kitchen-debate.

19. Shirley Povich, "Sievers Sees Bright Future Despite Slump," *The Sporting News*, 2 August 1959, 10.

20. *Ibid.*

21. Edgar Munzel, "'Want Sievers? Give Us Landis' Cal Tells Chisox," The *Sporting News*, 25 March 1959, 22.

22. Edgar Munzel, "Veeck's 400 Gs Package Bid for Sievers Refused," *The Sporting News*, 24 June 1959, 4.

23. Shirley Povich, "Nats Eager to Swap," *The Sporting News*, 18 November 1959, 6.

24. Bob Hunter, "Buzzie Chills Sievers Swap When Nats Get Hot on Lillis," *The Sporting News*, 16 December 1959, 8.

25. "Stengel Offers Carey in Trade for Sievers," *New York World-Telegram and Sun*, 5 December 1959.

26. "Three Senators Balk at Signing, Two Seeking Raise," *New York World-Telegram and Sun*, 18 February 1960.

27. "Sievers at the Mike," *New York World-Telegram and Sun*, 4 March 1960.

28. Robert L. Burnes, "Griffith Sits Back, Awaits Sign on Minneapolis Move," *The Sporting News*, 14 October 1959, 8.

29. Shirley Povich, "Cal and Frick Tangle Over Move," *The Sporting News*, 14 October 1959, 4.

30. Oscar Kahan, "Nats Puzzled by Obstacles in Shift Path," *The Sporting News*, 21 October 1959, 4; Dave Brady, "Justice Warren Asked to Block Senators' Move," *The Sporting News*, 21 October 1959, 8.

31. Ed Edmonds, "Over Forty Years in the On-Deck Circle: Congress and the Baseball Antitrust Exemption," retrieved from http://scholarship.law.nd.edu/law_faculty_scholarship/470/.

32. Dave Brady, "Report of Nats' New Shift Bid Stirs Loud Rumble in Congress," *The Sporting News*, 14 October 1959, 8.

33. Dave Brady, "Justice Warren Asked to Block Senators' Move," *The Sporting News*, 21 October 1959, 8.

34. "The Senators Move to Minnesota: The League Meeting," retrieved from https://clarkgriffithblog.com/2013/12/01/the-senators-move-to-minnesota-the-league-meeting-2/.

35. Dave Brady, "Ex-Sen. Bender Makes Offer to Buy Club From Griffith," *The Sporting News*, 14 October 1959, 6.

36. Jerry Holtzman, "Big Timers Clearing Decks for Expansion," *The Sporting News*, 10 August 1960, 3.

37. Tom Deveaux, *The Washington Senators, 1901–1971* (Jefferson, NC: McFarland, 2001), 202.

38. Author telephone interview with Sam Mele, 10 January 2016.

39. Herb Heft, "Strong-Boy Allison Kayoed Forecasters," *The Sporting News*, 25 November 1959, 3–4.

40. Shirley Povich, "Worried Nats Offer Sievers as Bait for Backstop, Infielder," *The Sporting News*, 6 April 1960, 16.

41. Statistics retrieved from www.baseball-reference.com/1959whitesox.

42. Shirley Povich, "Nats Plug 2 Holes with Pair of Swaps," *The Sporting News*, 13 April 1960, 10.

43. "Bombers Blocked by Sievers Swap," *The Sporting News*, 14 September 1960, 2; Herb Heft, Letter to the editor in "The Beef Box," *The Sporting News*, 21 September 1960, 10.

44. Author telephone interview with Maury Povich, 12 January 2016.

45. "Slugger Destined for Utility Roll," *New York Times*, 5 April 1960.

46. Jerry Holtzman, "Al Smith's Steady Swatting Perks Up Sox' Puny Attack," *The Sporting News*, 22 June 1960, 9.

47. Statistics retrieved from www.baseball-reference.com/roysievers/stats.

48. "Diamond Facts and Facets," *The Sporting News*, 27 July 1960, 16.

49. Bob Addie, "Faith, Sweat Restored Sock to Roy's Bat," *The Sporting News*, 7 September 1960, 3.

50. *Ibid.*

51. "Sievers and Ford Top Performers Against Birds," *The Sporting News*, 11 January 1961, 7.

52. Howard Roberts, "Runs-Scored Column Pinpoints Roy's Value," *The Sporting News*, 14 September 1960, 2.

53. Statistics retrieved from www.baseball-reference.com/teams/chw/1960.

54. Edgar Munzel, "Roy Stops Show with Quick Okay of Veeck's Offer," *The Sporting News*, 1 February 1961, 9.

Chapter 10

1. Author telephone interview with Shawn Sievers, 13 October 2016.

2. Edgar Munzel, "Senor Kayoes Rumor, Signs '61 Chisox Pact," *The Sporting News*, 5 October 1960, 46.

3. Edgar Munzel, "'Best Club Blew Flag,' Saddened Burrhead Wails," *The Sporting News*, 5 October 1960, 42, 46.

4. "Breeding Unsung Hero of Orioles Surge," *The Sporting News*, 12 October 1960, 14.

5. Statistics retrieved from www.baseball-reference.com/1960leagueleaders.

6. Clark Nealon, "Hemus All-Stars Top A.L. Crew in Charity Game," *The Sporting News*, 2 November 1960, 2.

7. "Diamond Facts and Facets," *The Sporting News*, 25 January 1961, 12.

8. Edgar Munzel, "Roy Stops Show With Quick Okay of Veeck's Offer," *The Sporting News*, 1 February 1961, 9, 14.

9. Edgar Munzel, "Sportshirt Says 'Nix' to Soriano Proposal," *The Sporting News*, 8 February 1961, 2.

10. "Roy Down to Playing Weight," *The Sporting News*, 1 February 1961, 14.

11. Frederic J. Frommer, *The Washington Nationals 1859 to Today* (Lanham, MD: Taylor, 2006), 87.

12. Game re-creation taken from www.baseballreference.com/boxes/WS2/WS196104100.

13. Data taken from www.baseballreference.com/sievers/hrlog and player stats.

14. Box score of 6/28/61, *The Sporting News*, 5 July 1961, 5; and baseballreference.com/boxes/CHA/CHA1961.

15. Information retrieved from www.baseballreference.com/ teams/CHW/1961.

16. Hy Hurwitz, "Sievers No. 1 Target in Bosox Swap Talks," *The Sporting News*, 4 October 1961, p. 40.

17. Corbett, Warren. "Bill Veeck," Retrieved from http://www.sabr.org/bioproj/person/7b0b5f10.

18. Lewis, Allen. "Phils Tab Torre Bargain Buy, Slick Sub for Slugger Sievers," *The Sporting News*, 13 December 1961, 22.

19. Data retrieved from www.baseballreference.com/genemauch.

20. Mel Marmer and Bill Nowlin, *The Year of the Blue Snow: The 1964 Philadelphia Phillies* (Phoenix, AZ: SABR, 2013), 248–249.

21. Allen Lewis, "Don't Try Tripping Mauch on Rulebook," *The Sporting News*, 23 July 1966, 13.

22. Ed Richter, (2013). *A View from the Dugout: A Season with Baseball's Amazing Gene Mauch* (Philadelphia, PA: Chilton Books, 2013), xii.

23. Stan Hochman, "'Remembering 1961 Phillies' 23-Game Losing Streak." Retrieved from http://www.philly.com/philly/columnists/stan_hochman/20110805_Stan_Hochman_.htm.

24. Marmer and Nowlin, 249.

25. Sandy Grady, "Sievers Is Solo Artist in Batting Cage," *Philadelphia Evening Bulletin*, 9 March 1962.

26. Stats retrieved from www.baseballreference.com/sievers/stats.

27. Allen Lewis, "Phil Fans Give Cold Shoulder to Reports of Mahaffey Trade," *The Sporting News*, 27 October 1962, 30.

28. Allen Lewis, "Lady Luck Frowns on Phils—Sievers Goes to Sidelines," *The Sporting News*, 6 April 1963, 32.

29. Allen Lewis, "Hats Off: Roy Sievers." *The Sporting News*, 3 August 1963, 23.

30. "Sievers Breaks Craig's Heart...'A Bad Pitch'," *Philadelphia Evening Bulletin*, 20 July 1963.

31. Mickey Herskowitz, "Burned to Crisp, Mauch Splatters Walls with Food," *The Sporting News*, 5 October 1963, 39–40.

Chapter 11

1. "Phillies Not Coming Club, They're Here, Says Podres," *The Sporting News*, 12 October 1963, 11.

2. "Scouting Report: Philadelphia Phillies," *Sports Illustrated*, 13 April 1964, 40.

3. Neal Russo, "Tribute to the Man Who Came to Dinner," *The Sporting News*, 2 November 1963, 5–6.

4. *Ibid.*

5. Ralph Horton, "With Stan Retired, Six Players Inherit His Batting Laurels," *The Sporting News*, 18 April 1964, 40.

6. Neal Russo, "Redbirds to Hop at Lively Tempo Under Eberhardt," *The Sporting News*, 15 February 1964, 25.

7. *Ibid.*

8. www.baseball-reference.com/teams/PHI/1964.

9. "Sievers Eyes First Pennant," *Philadelphia Evening Bulletin*, 11 March 1964, 51.

10. Bob Smith, "Big Time Stars Will Test TenpinSkills in 'Showdown' TV Match," *The Sporting News*, 28 March 1964, 24.

11. Allen Lewis, "Magic Number for Phils—'95 Wins,' Claims Mauch," *The Sporting News*, 8 February 1964, 14.

12. "N.L. Writers Make Their Picks," *The Sporting News*, 25 April 1964, 12.

13. www.baseball-reference.com/boxes/PHI/PHI196404140.

14. "Phils and Cubs Belt Five Home runs in One Inning," *The Sporting News*, 2 May 1964, 28.

15. "Spouse Wants Sievers to Retire from Diamond," *The Sporting News*, 11 April 1964, 16.

16. "Robby Searches Frantically In Game of 'Hide the Ball'," *The Sporting News*, 23 May 1964, 12.

17. "Phils Sell Sievers to Nats; Seek Waivers on McLish," *The Sporting News*, 25 July 1964, 6.

18. "Sievers' Wife Had Dream—That Roy Would Rejoin Nats," *The Sporting News*, 1 August 1964, 18.

19. "Phil Taking Strange Pennant Path," *The Sporting News*, 8 August 1964, 22.

20. Mel Marmer and Bill Nowlin, eds., *The Year of the Blue Snow: The 1964 Phillies*. (Phoenix, AZ: SABR, 2013).

21. Author interview with Frank Thomas at 2015 Phillies Fest.

22. Bob Addie, "Log-Jam Develops As Senators Corral Three First Sackers," *The Sporting News*, 1 August 1964, 18.

23. Bob Addie, "Limping Senators Resemble Cast for TV Hospital Drama," *The Sporting News*, 8 August 1964, 18.

24. "Stan No. 1 Diamond Hero Since Ruth Heyday," *The Sporting News*, 15 August 1964, 20.

25. Neal Russo, "Redbirds Boast Best Team Balance, Says Vet Slugger Sievers," *The Sporting News*, 6 March 1965, 10.

26. Author's telephone interview with Frank Howard, 29 September 2014.

27. Ron Young, "Big League Bowling Championship Won by Frank Robinson," *The Sporting News*, 10 April 1965, 29.

28. Earl Lawson, "Reds Blend Age and Youth on Nearly-New Coach Corps," *The Sporting News*, 13 November 1965, 17; Earl Lawson, "Jay Ready to Just All Comers for Job," *The Sporting News*, 12 March 1966, 8, 10.

29. Statistics from www.baseball-reference.com/players/s/swoboda01.

30. Maury Allen, *The Incredible Mets*. (New York: Hachette Books, 1969).

31. Jack Lang, "Mets Look to 'Prof' Sievers for Answer on Swoboda Puzzle," *The Sporting News*, 25 March 1967, 28.

32. "Fence Looks Different to Sievers as Manager," *The Sporting News*, 6 May 1967, 35.

33. "Sievers Proves Patient," *The Sporting News*, 20 May 1967, 39.

34. "Met Rookie Club Based at St. Pete," *The Sporting News*, 16 September 1967, 18.

35. Retrieved from http://www.recording-history.org/HTML/answertech9.php.

36. Author telephone interview with Whitey Herzog, 7 July 2016.

37. Author interview with Robin Sievers, 12 February 2016.

38. Bill Madden, "Sievers Spurns Bids for Brownie Uniform," *The Sporting News*, 12 August 1978, 46.

39. Personal remembrance of the author.

40. Author interview with Bob Wolff, 15 December 2015.

41. Author interview with Robin Sievers, 8 October 2015.

Bibliography

Personal Interviews

Vince Bagli
Charlie Brotman
Jim Bunning
Allan Feinberg
Joe Garagiola
Ned Garver
Phil Hockberg
Frank Howard
Dick Hyde
Bill James
Russ Kemmerer
Don Larsen
Juan Marichal
Sam Mele
Albie Pearson
Herb Plews
J. W. Porter
Maury Povich
Boog Powell
Brooks Robinson
Bobby Shantz
Roy Sievers
Shawn and Robin Sievers
William Sievers
Mark Stang
Rod Swoboda
Steve Terman
Frank Thomas
Fred Valentine
Bob Wolff
Phil Wood

Libraries and Archives

Johns Hopkins University
The National Archives, Washington, D.C., and College Park, Maryland
The National Baseball Hall of Fame
Southern Methodist University
The University of Maryland

Periodicals

Atlantic Monthly
Chicago Sun-Times
Miami News
The National Pastime (SABR)
New York World Telegram and Sun
Orlando Sentinel
Philadelphia Evening Bulletin
St. Louis Post-Dispatch
The Sporting News
The Sunday Grit
Washington Post
Washington Star

Books and Articles

Allen, Maury. *The Incredible Mets.* New York: Paperback Library, 1969.

Barthel, Thomas. *Barnstorming and Exhibition Games, 1900–1962.* Jefferson, NC: McFarland, 2007.

Cramer, Richard Ben. *Joe DiMaggio: The Hero's Life.* New York: Simon & Schuster, 2013.

Deveaux, Tom. *The Washington Senators, 1901–1971.* Jefferson, NC: McFarland, 2001.

Dickson, Paul. *The Dickson Baseball Dictionary (3rd ed.).* New York: W. W. Norton, 2011.

Frommer, Frederic J. *The Washington Nationals, 1859 to Today.* Boulder, CO: Taylor Trade Publishing, 2006.

James, Bill. *The New Bill James Historical Baseball Abstract.* New York: The Free Press, 2010.

Kashatus, William C. *Lou Gehrig: A Biography.* Portsmouth, NH: Greenwood, 2004.

Krell, David. "Kings of the World." *Memories and Dreams Magazine,* 37 (3), 2015.

Marmer, Mel, and Bill Nowlin, eds. *The Year of the Blue Snow: The 1964 Phillies.* Phoenix, AZ: SABR Books, 2013.

Nash, Bruce, and Allan Zullo. *Baseball Hall of Shame IV.* New York: Pocket Books, 1990.

Nemec, David. *Great Baseball Feats and Facts.* New York: Penguin Books, 1989.

Richter, Ed. *A View from the Dugout: A Season with Baseball's Amazing Gene Mauch.* Philadelphia, PA: Chilton Books, 1964.

Veeck, Bill, with Ed Linn. *Veeck—As In Wreck: The Autobiography of Bill Veeck.* Chicago: University of Chicago Press, 1962.

Wolff, Bob. *It's Not Who Won or Lost the Game—It's How You Sold the Beer.* South Bend, IN: Diamond Communications, 1996.

Wood, Phil, and Stang, Mark. *Nationals on Parade: 70 Years of Washington Nationals Photos.* Wilmington, OH: Orange Frazer Press, 2005.

Internet Sources

AmericanLegion.com

Baseball-Reference.com

baseballalmanac.com

history.com

sabr.org. (Bio Project, Paper of Record)

St.Louis-Mo.gov/archives/historyofstlouisneighborhoods

SportsIllustrated.com

WBEZ.com

www.history.com/thisdayinhistory/VicePresidentNixonisattacked

www.ncbi.nih.gov, Biographical Sketch; George E. Bennett (1885–1962)

www.philly.com

www.twinstrivia.com/interview-archives/julio-becquer-interview

www.umich.edu/ThehistoryofLatinosinMajorLeagueBaseball

Index

Numbers in ***bold italics*** indicate pages with illustrations.
Roy Sievers is indicated by RS.

Aaron, Hank 4–5, 9, 58, 81, 97
Abbott, George 110
Abernathy, Ted 70, 75, 76, 84, 123
Abner, Al 83, 84
Abrams, Cal 173
Adcock, Joe 43, 176
Addie, Bob 78, 84, 89, 92–93, 167
Adler, Richard 110
Alex Kellner 35
Alexander, Grover Cleveland 20
All-Star Game 72, 80–82, 166
Allen, Richie 161, 164, 166
Allen, Woody 5
Allison, Bob: mentored by RS 135; 1959 season 11, 123, 125–128, 130, 169; 1960 season 130, 135; and Nixon 28
Allyn, Arthur 149
Allyn, John 149
Almeida, Raphael 67
Altrock, Nick 87–88
Amaro, Ruben, Sr. 152, 154, 159, 162, 166
American Association 114, 115
American Baseball Guild 116
American League: All-Star Games 72, 80–82; American Legion league sponsorship 27; establishment 114; expansion 133–134; Most Outstanding Player 94; Most Valuable Player 67, 86, 91–93, 102; Rookie of the Year 35, 40, 67, 127
American Legion league 27–29
American National Exhibition 128
Anderson, Sparky 27
Anson, Cap 114
Antonelli, Johnny 147
Aparicio, Luis 136, 141, 143, 144, 148
Arcaro, Eddie 52
Arends, Leslie ***92***
Arlin, Harold W. 21
"The Art of Hitting" (Creamer) 103–104
Ashburn, Richie 103
Aspromonte, Bob 157
Aspromonte, Ken 90, 100, 104, 122, 127
Averill, Earl 154
Avila, Bobby 119–120
Bagwell, Jeff 27
Baker, Dusty 27
Baker, Gene 119
Baldschun, Jack 153, 161
Baltimore Orioles: front office staff 25; move from St. Louis 57, 61–62, 131; 1955 season 64; 1957 season 75–76, 84; 1958 season 101, 102, 105; 1959 season 123–124, 126; 1960 season 140, 143; orthopedic surgeon 52, 53–54; trading RS to Senators 62, 89
Banks, Ernie 39, 82, 119, 160, 178
Barber, Red 96
Barnard, E.S. 27
Barnes, Frank 119
barnstorming 37–39, 94, 98, 119–120
Barth, Gene 25
baseball: history 20–21; variations 17–20
Baseball Writers' Association of America (BBWAA) 35, 91, 97–98
basketball ***26***, 26–27
Bateman, John 157
Battey, Earl 129, 137
Bauer, Hank 58
Bauman, Bob: Joan Sievers heart attack hoax 41–42; 1951 season 45; 1952 season 50; 1953 season 54, 59; RS training with 145; scouting RS 29
Bauman, Frank (trainer) 50, 130
Baumann, Frank (player) 143
Bavasi, Buzzie 130
Baxter, Freddie 106, 113
BBWAA *see* Baseball Writers' Association of America
Beaumont, William 24
Beaumont High School, St. Louis 24–26, ***25***, ***26***, ***28***, 29, ***29***
Becquer, Julio: 1956 season 68, 71; 1957 season 83; 1958 season 104; 1959 season 122; 1960 season 136; scouted by Cambria 67, 68
Bell, "Cool Papa" 39
Bell, Gus 81–82
Bench, Johnny 27
Bender, George E. 134
Bennett, Dennis 154, 162
Bennett, George 52–54, 62, 82, 96–97, 179

Bennett, Tony 110
Berardino, Johnny 45
Berberet, Lou: 1956 season 68, 70; 1957 season 74, 83, 87; 1958 season 99; Roy Sievers Night 89
Berger, Bozie 94
Bergman, Arthur "Dutch" 96
Bergman, Hugh "Skip" 181
Bergman, William "Skip" 4
Berle, Milton 111
Berra, Lawrence 179
Berra, Yogi: American Legion league 28; Musial's retirement dinner 160; 1951 season 57; 1952 season 57; 1953 season 58; 1956 season 70; 1957 season 81, 87
Bertoia, Reno 122, 123, 124, 130, 136
Better Sports Club banquet (1957) 95
Bevins, Bill 78
"Big League Secrets" *(Sports Illustrated)* 103–104
Birdie Tebbetts All Stars 38–39
Bishop, Max 97
Blasingame, Don 161
Blatner, Bud 25
Bluege, Ossie 94
Boak, Chester 146
Bobby Avila All Stars 119–120
Bolling, Frank 39, 83, 94, 98, 119
Bolling, Milt 8, 39, 83, 94, 98
Bonura, Zeke 64
Boone, Ray 83
Boozer, John 165
Boros, Steve 83
Bosqui, Frank 173
Boston Braves 35, 131
Boston Celtics 26
Boston Red Sox: front office staff 25; 1947 season 135; 1949 season 33; 1957 season 86, 90; 1958 season 101, 105; president 114; Red Cross benefit game 66; trades 68, 148
Boston Red Stockings 131
Boston Reds 114
Boyd, Bob 124
Boyer, Ken 161
Brady, Dave 133
Brand, Richard 53
brawls 56–60
Brecheen, Harry 56
Brewer, Tom 105
Brickell, Fritzie 130
Bridges, Rocky: with Jerry Lewis and RS ***95***; 1957 season 76, 83; 1958 season 99, 100, 101, 104, 105; traded to Tigers 123
Brinkman, Ed 167
Bristol, Dave 170
Brock, Lou 164
Brodowski, Dick 68, 75
Broeg, Bob 40
Brooklyn Dodgers 78, 85, 116, 131, 133
Brotman, Charlie 90, 111
Brown, Hal 156
Brown, Johnny 98
Browne, Leo 27
Buckholtz, Bob 50
Bunker Hill (aircraft carrier) 17
Bunning, Jim: barnstorming 39, 94, 119; Major League Baseball Bowling Tournament 162; 1964 season 161, 166; perfect game 166
Burdette, Lew 96, 97
Burger Beer 80
Burlington Bees 171–172
Burnes, Bob 144
Busby, Jim 65, 70
Busch, August A., Jr. 61
Busch Stadium, Houston 144
Busch Stadium, St. Louis 57–58, 80–82; *see also* Sportsman's Park
Bustin' Babes 38
Buzhardt, Johnny 149, ***150***
Byerly, Bud: 1957 season 74, 75, 78, 83; 1958 season 99, 105
Byrd, Harry 83
Byrd, H.C. "Curley" 95
Byrne, Tommy 34

Cain, Bob 49, 58
California Angels 145–146
Callison, Johnny: 1962 season 152; 1963 season 154, 155, 158; 1964 season 161, 164, 166
Cambria, Joe 8, 67–68, 76, 131
Camden Yards, Baltimore 85
Camilli, Dolph 97
Cantwell, Ben 94
Carey, Andy 130
Carmichael, John P. 61
Carr, Edward R. 87, 91
Case, George 67–68
Castiglia, Jim 94
Cater, Danny 161, 162, 165
Cedar Rapids Cardinals 172
Celler, Emanuel 133
Central Association 31–32
Cepeda, Orlando 147–148
Cerv, Bob 59
Chakales, Bob 65, 76
Charbonneau, Joe 40
Chattanooga Lookouts 62
Chicago Cubs 48, 126, 164
Chicago Daily News 61
Chicago Tribune 146
Chicago White Sox: 1901 season 114; 1949 season 33, 34; 1950 season 41; 1955 season 65, 70; 1957 season 73, 79–80; 1959 season 129, 136; 1960 season 137–143; 1961 season 145–148; promotions and gimmicks 148–149; trades 5, 70, 73, 129, 148–150, ***150***
Chicago White Stockings 114
Chrisley, Neil 68, 75, 104
Cicotte, Al 105
Cincinnati Reds: All-Star Games 80–81; 1909–1911 seasons 67, 114; 1956 season 69,

80; 1957 season 74, 80–81; 1963 season 154; 1964 season 164–165; RS as batting coach 170
Cincinnati Times-Star 80
Clark, Tom 96
Clark Griffith blog 134
Clark Griffith Memorial Trophy 96
Cleveland Indians: Minneapolis's courting of 31–132; 1949 season 33–34; 1953 season 55; 1954 season 64, 66; 1955 season 66; 1959 season 126; 1961 season 147; ownership 48
Clevenger, Truman "Tex": 1957 season 75, 78, 83; 1958 season 105; 1959 season 122; "The Singing Senators" 8, 107, ***108***, 109; traded to Washington Senators 68
Close, Glenn 42
Coan, Gil 62
Cobb, Ty 20, 97
Cobey, William 95
Colavito, Rocky 13, 105, 126
Colburn, Joan *see* Sievers, Joan
Coleman, Jerry 35
Coleman, Joe 39
Coleman, Ray 40
Collins, Joe 58
Collins, Moss 106
Comiskey, Charles 73, 114
Comiskey Park 139, 149, 178
Condon, David 146
Congress, U.S. 111, 133
Connie Mack Stadium 149–151, 155, 164, 178
Continental League 133–134
"Cool Papa" Bell All Stars 39
Coombs, Jack 108
Corbett, Warren 61, 148–149
cork ball 17–18
County Stadium, Milwaukee 153
Courtney, Clint "Scrap Iron": barnstorming 39; competitiveness 56–59, 70; home run contest 7; as injury-prone 136; 1953 season 58–59; 1955 season 65; 1956 season 68, 70; 1957 season 73, 74, 76, 87–89; 1958 season 11, 99, 100, 101; 1959 season 22, 123, 127; Roy Sievers Night 88–89; trade rumors 73; trade to White Sox 65
Covington, Wes 119, 157, 161
Coyle, Joseph 147
Craft, Harry 156–157
Craig, Roger 155–156
Cramer, Richard Ben 179
Crandell, Del 103
Creamer, Robert 103–104
Cronin, Joe 98, 160
Crosetti, Frankie 52, 97
Crow, John 96
Crowe, George 80, 119
Cuban ballplayers 8, 67–68; *see also specific players*
Culp, Ray 154
Cunningham, Joe 160, 161, 167
Curtis, Al 68
Dailey, Pete 146
Dalrymple, Clay 154, 157
Damn Yankees (play and film) 66, 110–111, ***112***
Dark, Alvin 35
"Dave Garroway Show" 87
Dawson, Andre 178
Dean, Dizzy 48, 52, 97, 98
The Defiant Ones (film) 120
Delsing, Jim 39, 49, 55, 122
Demeter, Don 152, 153, 154, 155, 158
Depression *see* Great Depression
designated hitter, precursor to 145
Detroit Tigers: 1934 World Series 21; 1937 season 126; 1944 season 60; 1949 season 33, 155; 1951 season 49; 1956 season 71; 1957 season 82–84; 1958 season 109; 1959 season 123, 124; 1960 season 134; 1961 season 147; trades 123; Walter Sievers's tryout 16–17
Devine, Bing 173
Devron, Howard 8, 107, ***108***
DeWitt, Bill: contract negotiations 113; Joan Sievers heart attack hoax 42; Philadelphia Athletics' offer for RS 36; recognizing RS's greatness 29, 179; RS as batting coach for Cincinnati Reds 170; RS's contract 45
DeWitt, Charles 29, 41
Diering, Chuck 25
Dillon, Steve 162
DiMaggio, Dominic 27, 38–39, 60
DiMaggio, Joe: autograph shows 174; Bennett as orthopedic surgeon for 52, 97; "Ed Sullivan Show" appearance 94; hitting skills 85, 179; personality 4–5; RS compared to 35; World War II service 60, 135
Ditmar, Art 84, 147
Dixon, Rand 133
Dizzy Trout All Stars 38
Dobbek, Dan 123
Doby, Larry 47, 64
Donen, Stanley 110
Donovan, Dick 146
Dorsey, Tommy 111
Dotterer, Dutch 146
Douglass, Stephen 110
Draudt, Jay 32
Dressen, Charlie: fired as Washington Senators' manager 78; friendship with Lavagetto 78; 1955 season 64, 65; 1956 season 68, 70, 71–72; 1957 season 75, 76, 78, 123; on RS's respectfulness 180
Dropo, Walt "Moose" 40
Dryden, Charles 109–110
Drysdale, Don 136
Duckworth, Jim 167
Duke University 108
Dunn, Jack 89
Duren, Ryne 154, 164
Durney, Bill 42, 56
Dyck, Jim 58
Dyer, Duffy 171
Dykes, Jimmy 62

Easter, Luke 47
Eastern League (Class A) 32, 171
Eberhardt, Walter 160–161
"Ed Sullivan Show" 94
Edwards, Bruce 65
Edwards, Hank 58
Edwards, John 165
Eisenhower, Dwight: foreign relations 119–120, 128; Jim Lemon as favorite player of 91; Opening Day pitch 64, 69, 75–76, 101, 102
Elkins, Wilson 95
Elks Lodge No. 9's Outstanding Sportsman of the Year award 95
Elliott, Bob 58
Elliott, Ray 25
Elmira Pioneers 32, 170, 171
Esposito, Sammy 137

Fairly, Ron 130
Falstaff Brewing Company 49
Farmer, Bob ***107***
Farrell, Turk 156–157
Feller, Bob: American Legion league 28; childhood skills development 20; Musial's retirement dinner 160; 1954 season 64; 1955 season 66; RS's opinion of 175; World War II service 60
Fenway Park 105, 178
Fischer, Bill 123
Fisher, Eddie 111
Fitz Gerald, Ed: 1955 season 65; 1956 season 68; 1957 season 74, 83; 1958 season 99, 101; 1959 season 123
Florida International Gulf Coast League 172
Florida International League 67
Foiles, Hank 81–82
Forbes Field, Pittsburgh 151
Ford, Whitey 64, 74, 84
Fornieles, Mike 76, 101
Fort Knox, Kentucky 31
"Four Sluggers" (online magazine) 43–44
Fournier, Jacques "Jack" 29, 30, 32, 179
Fox, Nellie 9, 136, 140, 141, 144, 148
Foxx, Jimmie 21, 38, 160
Foytack, Paul 82, 119
Francona, Tito 144
Freese, Gene 129, 139, 141
Frick, Ford 81, 132, 160
Friend, Owen 43, 44
Frisch, Frankie 97
fuzz ball 19

Gaedel, Eddie 49–50
Garagiola, Joe: American Legion league 28; Major League Baseball Bowling Championship 169; March of Dimes benefit game 55; Musial's retirement dinner 60; "Tops in Sports" banquet 97; Touchdown Club awards banquet 96; Union Leader Charity Fund baseball dinner 97
Garcia, Mike 35, 64, 146
Gardella, Danny 116
Gardner, Billy 96
Garland, Judy 16
Garraway, Dave 108, 109
Garver, Ned: barnstorming 39; 1949 season 34, 35; 1951 season 49; 1957 season 84; on RS 5, 35; as St. Louis Browns MVP ***51***
Gates, Jim 3
Gehrig, Lou: barnstorming 38; home runs 13, 21, 82; as RS's boyhood favorite 22; streak of straight games played 85
Gentile, Jim 148
Gerdeman, Evelyn 157
Gerdeman, Norm 157
Gernert, Dick 89, 90
Gibson, Josh 8, 63
Giles, Warren 160
Gillespie, Ray 56
Gold Glove Award 166
Gomez, Lefty 52, 97
Gonzalez, Tony 152, 154, 155, 157, 161
Goodman, Billy 129, 148
Goodwin, Jim 25
Gordon, Joe 60
Goslin, Goose 13, 105
Grady, Sandy 152–153
Gray, Pete 32, 60
Great Depression 22–23, 27
Greenberg, Hank 60
Griffith, Calvin: background 66; and Cambria 67–68; Griffith Stadium size and shape 71; integrating Washington Senators 67; as miserly 14, 68, 73, 112–113, 115, 180; move of Senators to Minneapolis 99, 131–133, 134; 1955 season 65; 1956 season 70, 71; 1957 season 73–74, 78; 1959 season 11, 122; Roy Sievers Night 9; salary negotiations 98–99, 130; taking over as Washington Senators owner 66; trades and trade rumors 11, 65, 68, 97, 98, 129–131, 135–137
Griffith, Clark 62, 66, 67, 114–115, 179
Griffith, John L. 27
Griffith, Mildred 98
Griffith, Thelma 66
Griffith Stadium ***2***; *Damn Yankees,* filming of 110; Homestead Grays rental of 8, 14; Opening Day 101; Picture Day 1, ***2***; size and shape 7, 63, 71, 178
Griggs, Hal 105, 123
Grim, Bob 81, 82
Groat, Dick 95
Grote, Jerry 152
Groth, Johnny 35, 58, 65, 70, 83

Hacker, Warren 74, 148
Hagan, Vernon 154
Hall, Irv 32
Hall of Fame *see* National Baseball Hall of Fame
hand-eye skills 19–20
Hannibal (Missouri) Pilots 31–32

Harder, Mel 170
Harridge, Will 50
Harris, Bucky 63, 78, 79, 179
Harris, Lum 89
Harshman, Jack 79, 105, 124
Havana Cubans 67
Haynes, Joe 66
Hayworth, Rita 111
Heffner, Don 170
Heft, Herb 86–87, 135, 137
Hemus, Solly 144
Henrich, Tommy 52, 97
Henry, Bill 158
Herrera, Pancho 149
Herrnstein, John 159, 161, 162, 165
Herzog, Whitey: hiring RS to manage Burlington Bees 171–172; as New York Mets Director of Player Development 171–172; 1956 season 68–69, 70, 72; 1957 season 76; 1958 season 101; on RS's skills 180
Heydler, John 27
Hicks, Joe 146
Higgins, Mike 148
Hill, Robert C. 120
Hirt, Anna *see* Sievers, Anna
Hoak, Don 154, 157
Hodges, Gil 60, 82, 168
Hoeft, Billy 83
Hofman, Bobby 25, 28
Holmes, Tommy 173
Home Plate Club, Washington, D.C. 94
Homestead Grays 8, 14
Hope, Bob 55, 111
Hopp, Johnny 29
Hornsby, Rogers: batting stance 33; mentioned 21; on St. Louis all-time team 97; as St. Louis Browns manager 46, 48, 50–51, 57
Houston, Texas 132
Houston Colt .45s 156–157
Houston Professional Baseball Players Association 144
Houtteman, Art 39
Howard, Elston 119
Howard, Frank 14, 169, 173, 180
Howell, Dixie 80
Hunter, Billy 58
Hunter, Tab 110, 112
Hurley, Ed 49
Hutchinson, Fred 33, 155
Hyde, Dick: 1957 season 75, 78, 83; 1958 season 105; 1959 season 122, 123, 130

Illinois-Indiana-Iowa League 32
Iman, Ken 25
Indian ball 19
International Film Festival (Mexico City) 120
International League 161

Jackson, Al 164
Jackson, Michael 178–179
Jacobs, Michael 52, 53–54
James, Bill 13, 43–44, 54, 176, 180
James, Charlie 161
Japan: radio interviews 103
Jennings, Bill 55
Jensen, Jackie 13, 89, 90, 98, 100
Jiménez, Marcos Pérez 119
Jimmy Fund for Cancer 89
Johnson, Alex 162
Johnson, Ban 114
Johnson, Connie 119
Johnson, Deron 165
Johnson, Jerry 171
Johnson, Walter 20, 38, 66
Judge, Joe 38, 94
Jurges, Bill 94

Kaat, Jim 138
Kaline, Al: American Legion league 27; 1957 season 81, 83, 84; 1959 season 124; Union Leader Charity Fund baseball dinner 97
Kansas City Athletics: 1955 season 65–66, 131; 1956 season 69, 71; 1957 season 82, 84; 1959 season 124, ***125***
Kansas City stadium 178
Kefauver, Estes 133, 134
Kell, George 96
Keller, Charlie 52, 97
Kemmerer, Russ: 1957 season 76, 83, 90; 1958 season 99, 105; 1959 season 122, 123, 130; 1960 season 138; "The Singing Senators" 8, 107, ***108***, 109
Kennedy, John F. 146
Keough, Marty 146
Khrushchev, Nikita 128
Killebrew, Harmon: 1956 season 68; 1957 season 89, 90; 1958 season 100; 1959 season 11, 123–128, 130, 169; 1960 season 130, 144; 1961 season 147–148; and Nixon 128; Roy Sievers Night 89; RS as mentor to 135, 169
Kiner, Ralph 116
King, Jim 167
Klaus, Billy 154
Kline, Bobby 65
Kline, Ron 68
Kling, Johnny 40
Klippstein, Johnny 154, 157, 161, 162
Kluszewski, Ted 43, 136, 137–139, 145–146, 176
KMOX (St. Louis radio station) 21–22
"Knife and Fork League" 94
Kokos, Dick 36
Koosman, Jerry 171
Korcheck, Steve 100, 123, 136
Koufax, Sandy 136
Kreiger, Kurt 55
Kryhoski, Dick 56, 58
Kucks, Johnny 74
Kuenn, Harvey: 1957 season 83
Kuzava, Bob 35, 38

Labine, Clem 82
Landis, Jim 136, 139, 141, 144

Landis, Kenesaw Mountain 27, 114
Lane, Frank 65, 105
Lang, Jack 170
Lang Field, Sarasota 172
Lanier, Max: Mexican Baseball League 116
Larrupin' Lous 38
Larsen, Don 59, 70, 166
Lary, Frank 130, 134
Lasorda, Tommy 173
Laux, France 22
Lavagetto, Cookie: Bennett as orthopedic surgeon for 97; friendship with Dressen 78; 1956 season 69; 1957 season 78–79, 83–84, 98; 1958 season 9–100, 104–105; 1959 season 122–123, 124; 1960 season 135; recognizing RS's greatness 179; RS's batting stance 150, 153
Lawrence, Brooks 119
LeMay, Curtis 95–96
Lemon, Bob 33–34, 64, 66
Lemon, Jim: barnstorming 39, 94, 119; discussing hitting with RS 104; as Eisenhower's favorite player 91; fielding abilities 75; home run contest 87; mentoring younger players 169; 1956 season 68, 69, 71; 1957 season 11, 74–76, 83, 84, 87; 1958 season 11, 99–101, 104, 105; 1959 season 11, 122–123, 125–128, 130, 169; 1960 season 130, 135, 144; 1963 season 154; and Nixon 28; off-season jobs 37; salary 130; Senators-Dodgers reunion 173; "The Singing Senators" 8, 107, ***108***, 109
Lenhardt, Don 32, 55
Lent, Cassidy 3
Lerner, Alden 106
Leukemia and Lymphoma Society of America 1, 173
Levinson, Barry 42–43
Lewis, Allen 149–150, 154, 155
Lewis, Jerry ***95***
Lewiston Broncs 172
Lillis, Bob 130
Lindbergh, Charles 37
Lindblad, Paul 171
Liscio, Joe 154
Lockman, Whitey 97
Loes, Billy 76
Lollar, Sherman 34, 38, 136, 141, 148
Long, Dale 146
Lopat, Eddie 34
Lopata, Stan 97
Lopez, Al 137–140, 142, 143, 148, 179
Los Angeles Dodgers 130, 136, 173
Louisiana Purchase Exposition 16
Lown, Turk 148
Lumenti, Ralph 90, 100
Lumpe, Jerry 124, ***125***
Luque, Adolfo "Dolf" 67
Luttrell, Lyle 75, 76

Macauley, Ed 26
MacDonald, Arch 109
Mack, Connie 35–36, 73, 113
Madden, Bill 173
Maddux, Greg 27
Maglie, Sal 96, 103, 116
Magoula, Lou 29, 179
Mahaffey, Art 154, 161, 162, 164
Major League Baseball (MLB): American Legion league sponsorship 27; Bowling Tournaments 162, 169–170; home run record for ten games in one day 71; reserve clause 116
Malamud, Barnard 42
Malkmus, Bob 100
Maloney, Jim 154
Malzone, Frank 82, 90, 95, 98
Manchester Union Leader 97
Mantle, Mickey: All-Star Games 81; and Comiskey Park's exploding scoreboard 149; on Early Wynn 64; "Ed Sullivan Show" appearance 94; as fastball hitter 58; Griffith Stadium, success at 63; home run contests 87, 111; home runs 9; "Kefauver Hearings" 133; leg problems 85–86; Musial's retirement dinner 160; MVP crown (1957) 91, 93; 1953 season 58; 1956 season 69–70; 1957 season 13, 81, 85–87, 91, 93; 1958 season 13, 98, 111; 1960 season 144; 1961 season 147; personality 5; Ramos's sprint race challenge 88; respect for RS 175; salary 98
March of Dimes benefit game 55
Marciano, Rocky ***77***
Marion, Marty 48, 55–56, 58, 97
Maris, Roger 144, 147
Markwort Sporting Goods 19
Marrero, Connie 148
Marsans, Armando 67
Martin, Billy 57, 58, 59
Martin, Freddie 116
Maryland Professional Baseball Players' Association 96–97
Mathews, Eddie 82
Mathewson, Christy 20
Mauch, Gene: 1962 season 152, 153; 1963 season 154, 155, 156–157; 1964 season 161, 163–164, 166; as Philadelphia Phillies manager 151–152; recognizing RS's greatness 179; temper 151–152, 157
Maxwell, Charlie 83
Mays, Willie: All-Star Game 81; barnstorming 39, 119–120; "Ed Sullivan Show" appearance 94; Musial's retirement dinner 160; personality 4–5; World Series 151
McAleer, Jim 114
McCarthy, Ralph 86
McCormack, John 111
McCullough, Clyde 171
McDermott, Mickey 66, 68
McDevitt, Danny 130
McDougald, Gil: All-Star Game 81; "Big League Secrets" *(Sports Illustrated)* 103; 1953 season 58; 1956 season 69; 1957 season 81; "Tops in Sports" banquet 96; trade talks 130

McGhee, Ed 65
McGuire, Jack 25
McGwire, Mark, Sr. 14, 169
McKenna, Brian 67–68
McLish, Cal: barnstorming 119; Major League Baseball Bowling Tournament 162; 1961 season 141, 148; 1963 season 154; 1964 season 161–162, 165, 166; Senators-Dodgers reunion 173
McMillan, Roy 172
McQuinn, George 94
Medwick, Joe 'Ducky' 22, 172
"Meet Me in St. Louie, Louie" (song) 16
Mele, Sam 135
Memorial Stadium, Baltimore 57, 105, 178
Memphis Blues 171
Merritt, Lloyd 25
Mexican Baseball League 116
Miami Marlins 76
Michaels, Cass 38, 39
Michaels, Lou 96
Midwest League 171–172
Miller, Bob 25
Miller, Julius 116
Mills, Kerry 16
Milwaukee Braves 131, 136, 153
Milwaukee Brewers (American Association) 48
Mincher, Don 137
Minneapolis Millers 131, 151
Minnesota Twins 87, 115, 131–133, 134, 135
Miñoso, Minnie: All-Star Game 81–82; 1957 season 73, 81–82; 1960 season 137–138, 139, 141, 143, 144; 1961 season 146, 148; trade 73, 129
Mize, Johnny "The Big Cat" 60
MLB *see* Major League Baseball
Moon, Wally 160
Moore, Ray 84–85, 129
Moore, Terry 97
Morgan, Bobby 173
Morgan, Joe 157
Mossi, Don 81–82, 147
Most Valuable Player voting 177–178
Muhlenberg College 39
Municipal Stadium 178
Munzel, Edgar 129
Murphy, H. Gabriel 132
Murphy, Robert 116
Musial, Stan: All-Star Game 81; batting stance 168; debut 21; National League dominance 21; off-season training 130, 161; as President's Council on Physical Fitness consultant 168; retirement dinner 159–160; on St. Louis all-time team 98; in St. Louis Cardinals outfield 29; "Tops in Sports" banquet 96; Union Leader Charity Fund baseball dinner 97

Naragon, Hal 136
National Association of Baseball Players (NABBP) 20
National Baseball Hall of Fame 3, 175, 176–177
National Congressional Baseball Game 111
National League: All-Star Games 80–82; American Legion league sponsorship 27; expansion 133–134; history 114; Most Valuable Player award 92; reserve clause 115; Rookie of the Year 35, 40
Nats Talk Live 121
"The Natural" (film) 42–43
NBC "Sports in Action" 169–170
NBC Sports Special 162
Negro Leagues 14, 47, 88
The New Bill James Historical Baseball Abstract (James) 13
New York City, stickball 18
New York Giants: American Legion league alumni 28; and Mexican Baseball League 116; move to San Francisco 131, 133; 1957 season 85; World Series 66, 86
New York Highlanders 114
New York Knickerbockers Social Club 20
New York Mets 87, 155–156, 162, 164, 170
New York Yankees: arrogance 57; Bennett as orthopedic surgeon for 52; and Mexican Baseball League 116; 1919 season 21; 1927 season 125–126; 1949 season 34; 1950 season 43; 1951 season 86; 1952 season 57; 1953 season 57–60; 1955 season 64–65, 68; 1956 season 68, 69–70, 126; 1957 season 74, 84, 87; 1958 season 102; 1959 season 130; 1961 season 147; 1964 season 166; trades 68, 130; World Series 86, 166
Newcombe, Don 35
Newhouser, Hal 64, 175
NHK (national radio station of Japan) 103
Nicola, Toufick 53
Nieman, Bob 57
Nixon, Richard: foreign relations 119–120, 128; Roy Sievers Night 9, ***88***, 89, 91; RS as favorite player of 91, ***92***, 128; throwing out first pitch 123; Touchdown Club awards banquet 96
Nixon, Tricia 91
Nixon, Willard 39
Norman, Bill 54–55
Northwest League 172
Nortrup, Henry 16
Novosel, John 32
Nuxhall, Joe 164

Oakland Oaks 78
OB *see* Organized Baseball
O'Connell, Dick 148
O'Dell, Billy 119
Old Timers Games 173
Oldis, Bob 154
Oliva, Tony 67
Olson, Karl 68, 70
Olympic Games (1904) 16
O'Malley, Walter 133
Orangeburg Cardinals 172

Organized Baseball (OB): American Legion league sponsorship 27; antitrust laws 133–134
Owen, Mickey 116

Pacific Coast League 145
Page, Joe 34
Paige, Satchel 39, 46–47
Papai, Al 34
Parnell, Mel 39
Pascual, Camilo: curve ball 64, 76; 1956 season 69–70; 1957 season 75, 76; 1958 season 99, 105; 1959 season 122, 123, 127, 130; 1964 season 168; RS's opinion of 175; scouted by Cambria 67; trade rumors 130, 137
Pasquel, Jorge 116
Paul, Gabe 137
Paula, Carlos: integrating Washington Senators 67; 1955 season 65, 66; 1956 season 68, 69, 70; 1957 season 75
Pavlick, Pete 171
Pearson, Albie: 1958 season 11, 100, 101, 103–105; 1959 season 122, 123, 127; "The Singing Senators" 8, 107, ***108***, 109
Peckinpaugh, Roger 20–21
Pendleton, Jim 119
Pérez Jiménez, Marcos 119
Pesky, Johnny 39
Philadelphia Athletics 33, 34, 35–36, 131
Philadelphia Evening Bulletin 152–153, 162
Philadelphia Inquirer 149–150
Philadelphia Phillies: celebrity stalking 42; general manager 25; 1960 season 152; 1961 season 152; 1962 season 152, 153; 1963 season 154–158; 1964 season 159, 161–167; radio broadcasts 21; RS traded to 149–150, ***150***; sale of RS to Washington Senators 165
Philadelphia, stickball 18
Phillips, Bubba 136
Phillips, Dick 167
Philly, Dave 39
Pierce, Billy 79, 81–82, 97
Piersall, Jimmy 90, 149
Pignatano, Joe 173
Pilarcik, Al 76
Pilot Field, Buffalo, NY 173
"pinch hitter" rule 145
Pippin, Roger 96
Pittsburgh Pirates 21
Pizarro, Juan 141
Players Protective Association 114
Plews, Herb: 1956 season 68; 1957 season 75, 76; 1958 season 100, 101, 104; 1959 season 122
Podres, Johnny 136, 159
Polo Grounds, San Francisco 151
Porter, J.W. 57, 123, 129
Porterfield, Bob 62, 65, 68
Post, Wally 71, 81
Povich, Maury 79, 137
Povich, Shirley 79, 84, 128–129, 132
Power, Vic 161
Powis, Carl 76
Priddy, Gerry 40

Quincy Gems 35
Quinn, John 149, 154, 167

Rackley, Howard 17
radio broadcasts 21–22, 61, 103
Ramos, Pedro: 1956 season 69; 1957 season 75, 76, 90; 1958 season 99, 101, 105; 1959 season 122, 123–124, 130; Roy Sievers Night 88–89; scouted by Cambria 67
Raschi, Vic 58, 97
Rawlings Company 144–145
Rayburn, Sam 111
Raymond, Claude 153
Reading Phillies 171
Redford, Robert 42, 43
Reese, Pee Wee 27, 52, 60, 97
Regan, Phil 134
Reiser, Pete 25
reserve clause 14, 115–116, 133, 177
Resta, George 82, 167
Reynolds, Allie 52, 58, 59, 175
Rice, Del 55, 161
Rice, Sam 38, 94
Rickey, Branch 73, 133–134
Ripken, Cal, Jr. 85, 178
Rivera, "Jungle" Jim 73, 129, 146, 148
Rizzuto, Phil: barnstorming 39; Bennett as orthopedic surgeon for 97; 1953 season 58, 59; on RS's 1953 season 56; World War II service 135
Roberts, Robin 95
Robertson, Billy 66
Robertson, Jimmy 67
Robertson, Sherry 66
Robinson, Brooks 3, 84–85, 105
Robinson, Eddie 97
Robinson, Frank 27, 164–165
Robinson, Jackie 35, 47, 133
Rodgers, Packy 32
Rodriguez, Alex 178
Rolfe, Red 52, 97
Roll Call (Capitol Hill newspaper) 111
Rollins, Robert 120
Romano, Johnny 129
Romonosky, John 123
Ross, Jerry 110
Roy Sievers Fund 91
Ruhl, Oscar 53
Ruiz, Chico 166
Runnels, Pete: barnstorming 119; Boys Harbor of La Porte, TX benefit game 144; 1955 season 65; 1956 season 68, 69, 70, 71; 1957 season 74, 75, 76, 78; 1958 season 7–8, 100, 129
Russo, Neal 168
Ruth, George Herman "Babe": American Legion league 27–28; barnstorming 38; Griffith Stadium, success at 63; home runs 9, 21, 147; 1919 season 21

Ryan, Jim 102, 106, ***107***
Ryan, Nolan 171

SABR (Society for American Baseball Research) 67–68
Saigh, Fred 48, 61
St. Louis, Missouri: All-Star Game 80–82; all-time team 97–98; baseball 21; BBWAA gala dinner 97–98; cork ball 17–18; Elks Lodge No. 9 95; history 15–17; Indian ball 19; radio broadcasts 21–22
St. Louis Browns: all-time team 97–98; 1890s 114; farm teams 31–32; Garver as MVP ***51***; move to Baltimore 57, 61, 131; 1944 season 60; 1949 season 13, 32, 33–36; 1950 season 40–44; 1951 season 45, 48–50; 1952 season 50–52, 57; 1953 season 55–60; promotions and gimmicks 34, 48–50; radio broadcasts 22; scouting RS 29–30; Sportsman's Park 22; Veeck's purchase of 48
St. Louis Browns Fan Club 4, 181
St. Louis Cardinals: all-time team 97–98; farm system 54; front office staff 25; "Gashouse Gang" 21; 1934 season 21; 1944 season 60; 1964 season 166; 1965 season 168; off-season training 160–161; ownership 48, 61; radio broadcasts 22; scouting RS 28–29; Sportsman's Park 22; World Series 21, 166
St. Louis Globe-Democrat 144
St. Louis Post Dispatch 130–131
St. Louis World's Fair 16
Saito, Masato 103
Salk, Jonas 125
Samford, Ron 83, 122, 123
San Antonio, Texas 33, 45–46
San Francisco Giants 131
Sandberg, Ryne 27
Sarasota Cardinals 172
Saucier, Frank 49
Sawyer, Eddie 151
Scarborough, Ray 39, 58
Schacht, Al 87–88
Scheffing, Bob 171
Schmitz, Johnny 58, 68
Schoendienst, Red 56, 98, 130, 160
Schoonmaker, Jerry 75, 83
Schult, Art 83, 89
Schwenk, Bud 25
Scimonelli, Glenn 11–13
Scimonelli, Paul 11–13, ***174***
Selkirk, George 168
Severeid, Hank 98
Shadow Ball 88
Shannon, Wally 28–29, 179
Shantz, Bobby 33–34, 97, 146, 155
Shea, Frank 8, 66
Shepard, Jack 71
Sherry, Larry 136
Shocker, Urban 98
Shockley, Costen 161, 162, 165
Shore, Ray 170
Short, Chris 154, 156–157, 161, 166
Siebern, Norm 130, 161
Sievers, Anna (mother) 16, 80, 89
Sievers, Emma (grandmother) 16
Sievers, Joan (wife): accepting awards on RS's behalf 120; All-Star Game 80; death 173; dream about RS returning to Washington 165; family life ***117***, 142; heart attack hoax 41–42; meeting RS 32–33; Roy Sievers Night 89; RS's "Ed Sullivan Show" appearance 94; wanting RS to retire 164; wedding 33
Sievers, Robin (son): All-Star Game 80; birth and childhood 54, ***117***, 117–118; on Mantle 175; minor league career 54, 172–173; Roy Sievers Night 89; RS's death 181
Sievers, Roy: achievements 183; All-Star teams 72, 80–82, 93; American Legion league 27–29; Army service 31; athleticism 169; autograph shows 1, 173–174; awards and honors 35, 64, 87–91, ***88***, 94–98, 120, 164, 183; barnstorming 38–39, 94, 98, 119–120; as batting coach 170; batting skills 9, 14, 19, 64, 84–86, 103–104, 109, 152–153, 169, 179–181; batting stance 33, 35, 44, 150, 153; Beaumont High School 24–27, ***25***, ***26***, ***28***, 29, ***29***; "Big League Secrets" *(Sports Illustrated)* 103–104; bowling tournaments 162, 169–170; Boys Harbor of La Porte, TX benefit game 144; as Burlington Bees manager 171–172; career highlights 183–184; career reflections and testaments 175; childhood 15, 16–17, 19, 22–25; in *Damn Yankees* (film) 110–111, ***112***; death 181; "Ed Sullivan Show" appearance 94; as Elmira Pioneers manager 170, 171; as Elmira Pioneers player 32; endorsements 144–145; family background 16–17; family life 32–33, 41–42, 54, 64, ***117***, 117–118, 142; fans, respect for 5, 121; as first baseman 54–56, 66, 68, 139; "Four Sluggers" (James) 176, 180; at Griffith Stadium ***2***; Hannibal Pilots 31–32; home run contests 87, 111; home runs 147, 155–156; with Jerry Lewis and Rocky Bridges ***95***; "Knife and Fork League" 94; leadership 151; as left fielder 63, ***77***; lifetime statistics 185; March of Dimes benefit game 55; as Memphis Blues manager 171; mentoring younger players 135, 169; as "Mr. Clutch" 71; Musial's retirement dinner 159–160; MVP votes 91–93; 1947 season 31–32; 1948 season 32; 1949 season 13, 32–36, 45; 1950 season 40–41, 43–45; 1951 season 45–46, 50; 1952 season 50–54; 1953 season 55–56, 58–59; 1954 season 13, 62–64, ***63***, 72, 110; 1955 season 64–66, 72; 1956 season 68–72; 1957 season 10, 11, 13, 72–76, 78–93, ***92***; 1958 season 9, 11, 13, 98–105, 112, ***127***; 1959 season 1, 11, 14, ***77***, 112–113, 121–126, ***125***, 128–129, 131, 169; 1960 season 130–131, 134–135, 137–145, ***138***; 1961 season 144–148; 1962 season 152, 153; 1963 season 154–158; 1964 season 159, 160–162, 164–165, 167–168; 1965 season ***163***,

167, 168–169; 1966 season 170; and Nixon 91, ***92***, 128; off-season training 130, 160–161; Old Timers Games 173; with Paul Scimonelli ***174***; on Philadelphia Phillies 34, ***156***; as pitcher 31; post-playing career 4, 170–172, 173; practical jokes 168; reserve clause 116; retirement 169, 173; "Rookie of the Year" ***30***; Roy Sievers Night 9, 87–91, ***88***; St. Louis Browns 29–30, ***30***, 32–35, ***51***; salary (1949) 33, 45; salary (1950) 45; salary (1951) 45, 50; salary (1952) 50; salary (1954) 72; salary (1955) 72; salary (1956) 72; salary (1957) 72, 73; salary (1958) 9, 98–99; salary (1959) 14, 112–113, 131; salary (1960) 130–131, 145; salary (1961) 144–145; salary (1963) 154; San Antonio farm team 45–46; scouted 28–29; Senators-Dodgers reunion 173; shoulder surgery 82, 96–97, 179; "The Singing Senators" 8, 66, 87, 107, ***108***, 109; sold to Senators 165–166; "sophomore jinx" 40–41; sports broadcasting 131; Springfield Browns 32; "Squirrel" nickname 25–27; as team player 140; as third baseman 31, 40, 43–44, 45, 66; as thoughtful and charming 1–3, 34, 35, 109, 120–121, 179, 180; Toledo Mud Hens 32; "Tops in Sports" banquet 96–97; trade talks and rumors 73, 97, 98, 129–130, 135–136, 148; traded to Phillies 149–151, ***150***; traded to Senators 62; traded to White Sox 121, 136–137, ***138***; on waivers 168; Washington Senators ***63***; what ifs? 176–181; Yellow Freight Systems 4, 173
Sievers, Russell (brother) 16
Sievers, Shawn (daughter): birth and childhood 64, 80, ***117***, 118, 142; Roy Sievers Night 89; RS's death 181
Sievers, Walter (father): career 16–17; family life 16, 19, 24; Roy Sievers Night 89; RS's career 28–29, 80
Sievers, Walter, Jr. (brother) 16
Sievers, William (brother): All-Star Game 80; birth and childhood 16, 19, 22–23; on father's baseball career 17; Roy Sievers Night 89; on RS's St. Louis Browns career 30, 35; on RS's "Squirrel" nickname 26
Sievers, William (grandfather) 16–17
Signaigo, Bobby 35
Simpson, Harry "Suitcase" 119
Sinatra, Frank 111
"The Singing Senators" 8, 87, 107–109, ***108***
Singleton, Kenny 171
Sisler, Dick 55
Sisler, George 21, 44, 97
Skowron, Bill "Moose" 39, 81, 87, 167
Slaughter, Enos 29
Smith, Al: barnstorming 119; booed by fans 149; 1956 season 71; 1959 season 129, 136; 1960 season 137, 139, 141, 143; 1961 season 148
Smith, Charlie 149, ***150***
Snyder, Jerry 69, 71, 75, 76
Society for American Baseball Research (SABR) 67–68
softball 22–23
Somers, Bill 43
"sophomore jinx" 39–41
Soriano, Dewey 145
Soviet Union 128
Sowers, Dan 27
Spahn, Warren 27, 60
The Sporting News: Addie interview of Runnels 78; All-Rookie Team 70; Bucky Harris on RS 63; "Comeback Player of the Year" 64; on RS as "Best Bet" for hitting titles 69; RS as "Most Impressive Veteran" 164; RS interview 56; on RS's 1951 contract 45; on RS's shoulder surgery 53, 82; on RS's sophomore year 40; on RS's trade to Chicago White Sox 137; "Tops in Sports" banquet 96; on Washington Senators 100
Sports Illustrated: "Big League Secrets" 103–104; Corbett's description of Veeck 148–149; on International Film Festival 120; on Philadelphia Phillies 159; on Washington Senators 74–75, 99–100, 121–122
Sportsman's Park, St. Louis 22–23, 35, 48, 60; *see also* Busch Stadium
Springfield (Illinois) Browns 32
Staley, Gerry 148
Stallard, Tracy 155, 156
Staub, Rusty 157
Steger, Russ 28
Steinhagan, Ruth Ann 42
Stengel, Casey: All-Star Game 81; and Berra 57; and Comiskey Park's exploding scoreboard 149; concern about Mantle's legs 86; "Kefauver Hearings" 133; Musial's retirement dinner 160; 1953 season 58; 1957 season 81, 86; as Oakland Oaks manager 78; on Swoboda 170; trade talks 130
Sterling, Andrew B. 16
Stevens, John 59
stickball 18–19
Stobbs, Chuck: 1956 season 69; 1957 season 74, 75, 76, 78; 1958 season 99; 1959 season 123
Stone, Dean 69
Stoneham, Horace 133
Stuart, Dick 14, 169
Suder, Pete 38
Sullivan, Ed 94
Sullivan, Frank 105
Sutcliffe, Rick 40
Suzuki, Sotaro 103
Swoboda, Ron 170
Symington, Stuart 160

Taylor, Tony 154, 159
Taylor, Zack 33, 34, 41–45, 49–50
Tebbetts, Birdie 38–39, 74, 160
Teixeira, Mark 27
televised baseball 38, 61

Temple, Johnny 157
Tener, John 111
Tettelbach, Dick 68, 70, 75, 76
Texas League 45–46, 171
Thomas, Frank 14, 167
Thomas, Lee 25
Thompson, Chuck 11, 96
Three-I League 35
Throneberry, Faye 84, 89, 100, 104, 122
Tick-Tock Liquor Store, Takoma Park, Maryland 37
Tiger Stadium, Detroit 110, 124, 174, 178
Tighe, Jack 83
Timko, David 1
Today (television show) 109
Tokyo Giants 103
Toledo Mud Hens 32
Torgeson, Earl "Torgy" 129, 139, 148
Torre, Frank 155
Touchdown Club 96
Tracy, David 43
Triandos, Gus 94, 119, 124, 161
triple plays 105
Trout, Dizzy 64, 175
Trucks, Virgil 38
Tucker, Raymond 160
Tunney, Gene 151
Turley, "Bullet" Bob 39, 97
Turner, Bill 102, ***107***, 113, 121
Tuttle, Bill 39, 82, 94
Tuttle, Tommy 162
Twinstrivia blogsite 68

Umphlett, Tom 65, 68
Union Leader Charity Fund 97
unionization of players 115–116
U.S. Information Agency 103
University of Maryland M Club 95–96
Upright, Dixie 58
Usher, Bob 8, 83

Valdivielso, Jose: 1956 season 68, 70, 71; 1957 season 75; 1959 season 122, 123; scouted by Cambria 67
Valentinetti, Vito 105
Valo, Elmer 38
Vander Meer, Johnny 60
Veal, Coot 146
Veeck, Bill: background 48; ballpark promotions and gimmicks 48–50, 61, 148–149; as Chicago White Sox owner 129; hiring hypnotist for St. Louis Browns 42–43; 1950 season 42–43; 1960 season 142–143; recognizing RS's greatness 140, 179; retirement 149; as St. Louis Browns owner 46, ***51***, 61; salary negotiations 144–145; trades 129, 136–137; treating players with dignity and respect 50, 54, 55, 148–149
Veeck, Eleanor 48
Vernon, Mickey: barnstorming 39; 1953 season 62; 1955 season 64, 65; 1956 season 68; Roy Sievers Night 89; on RS's 1953 season 56; scouted by Cambria 67–68; Senators-Dodgers reunion 173; traded to Red Sox 68; as Washington Senators' first baseman 62; as Washington Senators' manager 146
Versalles, Zoilo "Zorro" 67, 136
Virdon, Bill 171

Wagner, Honus 21
Waitkus, Eddie 42
Walker, Harry 29
Wall, Murray 101
Wallop, John Douglass 110
Walnut Park Elementary School, St. Louis 24
Waner brothers 38
Warren, Earl 132
Warwick, Carl 157
Washington Evening Star 85
Washington Nationals 90, 180
Washington Post 84, 85, 92–93, 102
Washington Redskins 8
Washington Senators: batboys 66, 79, 102, 106, ***107***, 113, 121; Cuban players 67–68; franchise records 13, 64, 71, 105, 110; integration 67; move to Minneapolis 99, 115, 131–133, 134; as "Nation's Team" 101; 1924 season 66; 1949 season 33; 1950 season 43–44; 1954 season 62–64, ***63***; 1955 season 64–66; 1956 season 68–72; 1957 season 11, 13, 73–76, 78–80, 82–90; 1958 season 11, 13, 99–102, 104–105, 109, ***127***; 1959 season 11, ***77***, 121–129, 169; 1960 season 79, 134–135, 138; 1961 season 146; 1965 season 168–169, 180; ownership 66, 114–115; promotions and gimmicks 86–87; Red Cross benefit game 66; RS sold to (1964) 165; RS traded to (1954) 62; scouts 67–68; Senators-Dodgers reunion 173; "The Singing Senators" 107–109, ***108***; trades 62, 68, 123, 129–130
Washington Star 84
Weaver, Earl 25
Weber, Dick 162
Weekly, John 157
Weiss, George 52, 130
Wertz, Vic 39, 43, 58, 71, 96, 176
Western Carolina League 172
Westrum, Wes 170
White, Bill 161
White, Hal 58
White, Jo-Jo 45–46
White, Sammy 90
Wiesler, Bob 25, 68, 69, 71, 75
Wietelmann, Whitey 170
Wilber, Del 55
Williams, Billy 164
Williams, Dick 25, 76
Williams, Ken 13, 82, 97
Williams, Ted: All-Star Game 81; American Legion league 27; autograph shows 174; batting skills 179; Bennett as orthopedic surgeon for 97; Clark Griffith Memorial Tro-

phy 96; discussing hitting 104; friendship with RS 99; MVP voting 91, 93; 1947 season 135; 1957 season 13, 81, 85–86; personality 4; Roy Sievers Night 89; as RS's mentor 168; on RS's swing 14, 169, 180–181; "Tops in Sports" banquet 96; World War II service 60
Wilson, Red 83
Wine, Bobby 154, 166
Wise, Rick 161
WLOF-AM radio 131
Wolff, Bob: broadcasting career 10, 11, 108–109; on camaraderie of players 175; foreword 7–10; on Griffiths 115; on Lavagetto 79; "The Singing Senators" 8, 87, 107–109, ***108***
Wood, Phil 121
Woodling, Gene 58, 146
World Series: (1924) 66, 115; (1925) 115; (1933) 115; (1934) 21; (1944) 60; (1947) 78; (1951) 86; (1954) 151; (1956) 166; (1959) 136; (1964) 166; (1965) 135
World War II 17, 31, 60
World's Fair, St. Louis 16
WRC Channel 4 109
WTTG television 108
Wyatt, Whit 97
Wynn, Early 64, 146, 148
Wynn, Jim 157

Yankee Stadium 178
Yastrzemski, Carl 27
The Year the Yankees Lost the Pennant (Wallop) 110
Yellow Freight Systems 4, 173
YMCA Industrial Athletic Association, St. Louis 120
Yost, Ed "The Walking Man": 1955 season 65; 1956 season 68, 70; 1957 season 74, 75, 76, 78, 83; 1958 season 11, 99, 100, 101, 104–105; 1959 season 123; Senators-Dodgers reunion 173
"You Gotta Have Heart" (song) 66
Young, Bobby 58
Young, Cy 20

Z-Bar, Cincinnati, Ohio 80
Zauchin, Norm: 1958 season 100, 101, 104; 1959 season 122, 124, 127
Zimmer, Don 130, 167, 169